SCIENCE
EXPERIENCES

Cooperative Learning and the Teaching of Science

JACK HASSARD

Georgia State University

▲ Addison-Wesley Publishing Company
Menlo Park, California • Reading, Massachusetts • New York
Don Mills, Ontario • Wokingham, England • Amsterdam • Bonn
Sydney • Singapore • Tokyo • Madrid • San Juan

Photo Acknowledgments

Page	Credit
003	Elliott Smith*
029	Elliott Smith*
051	Elliott Smith*
091	NASA
113	David Madison
137	Wendell Metzen/Bruce Coleman Inc.
171	Ira Kirschenbaum/Stock, Boston
197	Joseph R. Pearce/DRK Photo
211	NASA
247	Maresa Pryor/Earth Scenes
281	Keith Gunner/Bruce Coleman Inc.
Cover	Elliott Smith*

*Photos taken expressly for the publisher

Biodot is the registered trademark of Biodots International, Inc., Indianapolis, Indiana.

Alka-Seltzer is the registered trademark of Miles, Inc., Elkhart, Indiana.

This book is published by the Addison-Wesley Innovative Division.

ISBN 0-201-23134-4

BCDEFGHIJKL-AL- 943210

DEDICATION

*This book is dedicated to my mother,
Margaret Helen Hassard, and to the memory
of my father, Russell John Hassard,
who taught me to experience.*

ACKNOWLEDGMENTS

As I put the final touches on *Science Experiences* I find myself reviewing the struggles and joys I experienced during its development. The making of this book has been an *experience*, and the processes it describes were definitely a part of me during the years of writing. In a few days I leave the United States for a three-week journey to the Soviet Union, my sixth trip. I am filled with hope and the desire to strengthen personal and professional relationships that began several years ago. I realize now that these experiences are journeys that involve every aspect of ourselves—our minds, bodies and emotions—and that the bonds we form with people are what make the journey worthwhile. So it was with the development of this book, which took a number of years to write and went through several modifications. At each stage, people helped and shared their insights, and I would like to thank them.

First and foremost was my loyal friend, Joe Abruscato. He provided me with support and encouraged me to see the project to its conclusion.

Three of the chapters of the book were developed by colleagues, whose contributions expanded and embellished my work. Mardy Burgess, a teacher and education consultant in Washington D.C., wrote the materials that are the basis for Chapter 4, The Web of Life. Stan Rachelson, a long-time friend and fellow science educator, wrote the materials that are in Chapter 8, If You Were a Boat. Carol Stangler, a teacher and artist from Atlanta, developed the environmental education materials in Chapter 11.

I also wish to thank Barrie Kelley and Nancy Paule for giving me permission to use some of their environmental education activities in Chapter 10.

Ted Colton, Stan Rachelson, Jerry Allender, and the late John Thompson graciously reviewed an earlier version of the manuscript. Their comments were extremely helpful, their encouragement was essential, and their support in the early stages of the project kept me going.

I especially want to thank my wife, Mary-Alice Hassard, for her professional and personal help during the development of the book. She reviewed the manuscript and provided insight from the vantage point of a professional educator. More importantly, she gave me her encouragement and love, which I cherish more than anything.

Special thanks to Pat and Norman Bowles, Mary and Pedro Diaz, Anne and Bob Lairson, and Claire Murphy on the East Coast and to Paul C. Hannum, Sr., Linda and Craig Hannum, Linda and Tom Hannum, and Carol and Mel Manker on the West Coast.

Although most of the writing was done using a Macintosh computer, Nancy Dinnsen in Hayward, California, and Alex Harris in Atlanta typed various parts of the manuscript; their help was indispensable.

I want to also express thanks to Stuart Brewster of Addison-Wesley who supported my work and was willing to publish the book. Without him, I doubt whether the project would have been completed. And special thanks to Margaret Shanney who directed the development of the book at Addison-Wesley.

J. H.

TABLE OF CONTENTS

INTRODUCTION

During a recent two year period, I had the opportunity to visit over a hundred schools in Arizona, California, Nevada, and Utah as part of a grant I had while at the Far West Laboratory for Educational Research in San Francisco. In the early stages of those visits, I taught science lessons that demonstrated a hands-on approach. As time went on, I realized that talking with the students about their interests and their questions was more rewarding to me and to them. One of the things that struck me was that while teachers and students were interested in science, there was very little evidence of the stuff of science teaching—rocks, straws, hand lenses, terrariums, plants, balances—in the classroom, and only four of the classrooms I visited had a computer.

It became evident to me that an interesting, yet alarming paradox existed with regard to the teaching of elementary and middle school science: Small group, student-involved or led, hands-on science lessons motivate students and help them understand science, yet science lessons are usually teacher-directed to groups of observers. Support for this paradox came from my classroom experiences as well as from the work of science education researchers.

In an analysis of a large group of studies about science teaching in elementary and middle school classrooms, William Kyle reported that lessons involving students, implementing concrete learning materials, and focusing on problem solving helped students develop enhanced attitudes toward science, along with higher-level intellectual skills such as critical thinking, analytical thinking, creativity, and process skills. Furthermore, students in these programs showed enhanced language arts, reading, mathematics, social studies, and communication skills.

In another study, however, Robert Yager found that there was very little evidence of science being taught with a hands-on approach. In fact he reported that most science instruction is in the form of lectures followed by a question-and-answer format and supported only by textbook materials.

Another aspect of teaching that I observed in these school visits was that students worked independently for the most part; it was a rare event to observe students working together in teams on a project or an assignment even though recent research related to improving the teaching of science encourages the reconceptualization of the classroom and stresses the benefits of cooperative learning.

As much as we would like smaller classes, it is evident that money and space will not be made available for this objective, even though research studies show that learning is enhanced as the class size shrinks. We are instead faced with the creative task of improving learning while keeping class size constant. Cooperative, mixed ability group learning offers a solution to the problem of class size. Studies by a number of researchers and practical application in classrooms have led to a mountain of evidence that cooperative learning not only enhances social skills among students but enhances learning and cognitive development in many circumstances. Breaking the class into small cooperative teams of from two to seven students to work on tasks of varying types creates a new topology for the classroom and a potential solution to the paradox stated above.

Science Experiences will help you design classroom environments that provide experiential learning activities for students and will show you how to reconceptualize the classroom into cooperative groups. The learning experiences that have been developed in this book result from the integration of an ecological perspective, the implementation of cooperative learning, and research on whole brain learning. I will say more about these later. First, a few comments about the organization of this book.

The book is divided into two parts. In Part One "Science Teaching and Cooperative Learning," I have laid a framework for science teaching that is based on experiential and cooperative learning. Experiential learning occurs when students are involved in direct and active personal experiences in order to achieve cognitive, affective, or psychomotor goals. The abundance of science lessons that are suggested in this book are based on this approach. Cooperative learning is an educational innovation that emerged during the early seventies and requires students to learn from each other through interaction in small groups. The roots of cooperative learning are found in the work on synergy by Ruth Benedict and Margaret Mead and in the psychological models developed by Abraham Maslow and Carl Rogers. Studies on synergy by Benedict revealed that cooperative actions among persons in a group lead to higher levels of mental health, security, and well-being. Educational practitioners such as David and Roger Johnson, Robert Slavin, and Spencer Kagan reported that cooperative learning resulted in high academic achievement; provided a vehicle for students to learn from each other; gave educators an alternative to the individual, competitive model; and was successful in improving relationships in multiethnic classrooms.

Chapter 1 presents an overview of science teaching and suggests how science should be taught in our classrooms to reflect direct, experiential learning. Chapter 2 shows how to create cooperative learning environments, explains how cooperative learning works, and examines several models of cooperative learning. Chapter 3 presents a kaleidoscope of science lessons based on a whole-brain model of learning. These lessons

are designed to show you how to develop activities favoring physical sensory, right, left, and affective modes of learning, as well as an integration of these learning modes.

Part Two consists of eight science teaching units designed for students in grades four through nine. The eight chapters present science experiences on the web of life, holistic health, astronomy and oceanography, geology, density, the future, energy, and environmental science. The topics chosen deemphasize the normal boundaries of the scientific disciplines, focusing instead on phenomena, everyday examples, and problem-solving activities in order to give students real-world experiences with science. Each unit is an invitation to explore some aspect of science through direct experience and cooperative learning. The units include teacher and student information, as well as reproducible pages for classroom use. The activities in each unit help students become active science learners by becoming members of small, cooperative teams. The activities are grouped into three categories: *Adventures*—experiential activities using a whole-brain model of learning to help students achieve the major goals of the unit; *Side Paths*—interdisciplinary activities in which science is correlated with language arts, reading, mathematics, social studies, art and music; and *Searches*—in-depth science projects for small teams of students.

The philosophy that provides the foundation for *Science Experiences* is derived from a number of educators, psychologists, and scientists. The work of Abraham Maslow and Carl Rogers is important because they helped provide a comprehensive picture of human beings, much as ecology has provided a comprehensive view of nature. Maslow's contribution is embedded in how we view human behavior and motivation. Most contemporary psychologists credit Maslow with developing a new branch of thought in psychology, known as humanistic psychology, presenting a positive theory of human motivation in which psychological development is characterized as being dynamic and unfolding toward self-actualization. Maslow's theory is the guiding concept as we think about the potential of each human being. Organizing students in small cooperative teams has been shown to enhance positive self concepts and to help bring out the potential in each student.

Carl Rogers' person-centered theory is the foundation that guides the role and purpose of the teacher in cooperative learning classrooms. Rogers suggests that the role of the teacher should be a facilitative one, that the teacher should primarily be responsible for establishing a learning environment characterized by trust, positive regard, and empathy. Accepting this role requires a conscious shift of perspective on the part of the teacher, away from authoritarianism and toward coordination of cooperative actions and the facilitation of instruction. Teachers who have incorporated this philosophy into their classrooms orchestrate the students' activities and are masters in securing and creating well-designed, team-oriented tasks.

Bob Samples' work on the metaphoric mind (right brain) fused with the psychological work of Robert Assagioli on psychosynthesis helped create a whole-brain model of learning that is developed fully in Chapter 3. Jack Canfield, who is well known for his book, *100 Ways to Enhance Self Concept*, applied Assagioli's model to education. Canfield developed a holistic model of education that was practical and usable as an educational tool, emphasizing the development of a healthy and positive self concept as the focus for working with students in schools. He further emphasized that because students came to classrooms able to perform tasks using a variety of learning modes—physical-sensory, intuitive, imaginative, cognitive, and emotional—teaching methods should reflect these functions. I have modified Canfield's model and applied it in Chapter 3 and in the eight science teaching units in Part Two.

Three important themes—ecology, cooperative learning, and whole-brain learning—weave their way throughout the book. Ecology, which moves us closer to nature, is the science that looks at relationships, patterns, and natural wholes. Ecology is the one science that places human beings and nature together. Ecology is a comprehensive way of viewing things and provides a holistic model for teaching and curriculum development. The first chapter of the book explores science teaching from an ecological perspec-

tive. An important paper by Rodger Bybee, in which he discussed the role of science education in an ecological society, helped shape my thinking about curriculum planning in this book. Further, the classroom as depicted in this book is viewed as if it were a cultural ecosystem that is shaped by the values and beliefs of the persons involved, the school and its community, and the culture at large.

Cooperative learning manifests itself in several ways throughout the book. I have already mentioned the psychological and sociological implications of cooperative learning on classroom behavior. Cooperative learning is most powerfully realized in the lesson plans and teaching methods advocated in each of the teaching units in Part Two. Many of the applications of cooperative learning in classrooms today are based on having students work together to complete tournaments or games that are designed to prepare them for taking individual or group tests. I have expanded its use to include all aspects of science learning. Thus, the bulk of *Science Experiences* contains units of teaching designed for cooperative learning environments.

Whole-brain learning, which is emphasized throughout the book, is fully developed in Chapter 3. The importance of this chapter lies in the fact that students learn in a variety of ways. For example, some students are better at tactile learning, others at verbal learning, while others prefer kinesthetic learning. You will find an abundance of lessons organized around a whole-brain model of learning. My goal is to provide a variety of suggestions so that you can adapt and apply them to your own classroom.

The three themes—ecology, cooperative learning, and whole-brain learning—carry a common message embodied in the word *whole*. If you are a science teacher, the concept of wholeness should suggest connectedness, unity, synthesis, interrelationships, webs, generalities, systems. *Science Experiences* will be useful to you whether you are a teacher in a self-contained elementary classroom or a science specialist at the upper elementary and middle or junior high school level. You can use the concepts and teaching materials to enhance and expand your current approach to teaching science.

Science Experiences should also have meaning for language arts and reading teachers. There is increasing evidence that a whole language approach should be applied to the teaching of reading and language arts. Researchers and educators in these fields have discovered that a whole language approach enhances literacy. Teachers, of course, have known this for a long time and have realized the importance of integrating reading, writing, drama, and oral learning in the teaching of language. In *Science Experiences*, I have emphasized a whole language approach to learning, especially in the interdisciplinary Side-Path activities for each unit. *Science Experiences* will also provide learning materials for those teachers who are interested in emphasizing other interdisciplinary activities such as writing and reading across the curriculum.

Authors of recent essays have criticized science educators for their lack of nerve in breaking away from old patterns that tend to determine the practice of science teaching. The following are some of the patterns that need to be changed:

1. Too many of us still believe that the reason for teaching science is preparation for the next grade or course in the students' curriculum.
2. There is continued and increasing emphasis on facts, terms, and information and very little on the process of science or the relationship between science, technology, and society.
3. There is a renewed emphasis on state and national testing, which has further reinforced the teaching of facts, terms, and the information of science. This overemphasis on testing has caused a blindness to the real purpose of schooling.
4. Many states have developed curriculum guides and frameworks that list every concept that should be taught—grade by grade—thereby reducing flexibility in curriculum planning.
5. Science teaching continues to be overly abstract, with increasing reliance on theoretical knowledge, furthering an elitist conception of science education.

The patterns listed above overshadow new patterns that have begun to emerge and find their way slowly into the mainstream of classroom science teaching. There is ample evidence to support implementation of the following into the mainstream of science teaching:

1. Science teaching should emphasize the human side of science, thereby acknowledging the importance of human values as well as the practical and social implications of science.
2. There is a growing emphasis on science as a process in which divergent and creative thinking are seen as essential aspects of science teaching.
3. The selection of science content can be a flexible process, resulting in curricula that reflect local needs rather than goals established by remote individuals. Although teachers should think globally, they should act locally.
4. Experiential, participatory learning should replace the overreliance on spectator learning that characterizes much of the teaching in contemporary classrooms.

Science can be an experiential journey, a process of uncovering aspects of ourselves and the universe that can give students immense pleasure and joy. Science teaching, as depicted in *Science Experiences*, can contribute to making science a part of students' lives, related to school for a while and then integrated into everyday life.

Notes

1. William C. Kyle, "Curriculum Development Projects of the 1960s," in *Research within Reach*. Edited by David Holdzkom and Pamela Lutz (Charleston, W.V.: Appalachia Educational Laboratory, Inc. 1984).
2. Robert Yager, "Major Crisis in Science Education," *School Science and Mathematics*. 1984 (3), pp. 189–198.
3. For a discussion of Benedict's and Mead's concepts on synergy, see A. Maslow, *The Farther Reaches of Human Nature* (New York: The Viking Press, 1971).

4. David W. Johnson and Roger T. Johnson, *Circles of Learning: Cooperation in the Classroom* (Alexandria, Virginia: Association for Supervision and Curriculum Development, 1984).

5. Robert E. Slavin, *Using Student Team Learning* (Baltimore, Md: Center for Social Organization of Schools, The John Hopkins University, 1981).

6. Spencer Kagan, *Cooperative Learning: Resources for Teachers* (Riverside, Calif.: University of California, 1985).

7. Abraham Maslow, *Toward A Psychology of Being* (New York: Van Nostrand Company, 1968).

8. Carl Rogers, *Freedom to Learn* (Columbus, Ohio: Charles E. Merrill Publishing Company, 1983).

9. Bob Samples, *The Metaphoric Mind* (Reading, Mass.: Addison-Wesley, 1976).

10. Robert Assagioli, *Psychosynthesis* (New York: The Viking Press, 1971).

11. Jack Canfield and Paula Klimek, "Education in the New Age," *New Age Journal*. February, 1978, pp. 27–37.

12. Rodger Bybee, "Science Education and the Ecological Society," *Science Education*. 63 (1) 1979, pp. 95–109.

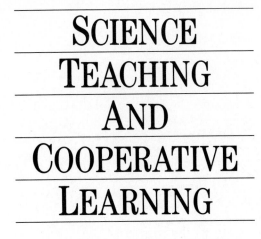

PART ONE

SCIENCE TEACHING AND COOPERATIVE LEARNING

1

The Ecology of Science Teaching

2

Creating Cooperative
Learning Environments

3

Learning and Teaching in
the Cooperative Classroom

THE
ECOLOGY OF
SCIENCE
TEACHING

"Not only does science begin in wonder, it also ends in wonder."

ABRAHAM MASLOW
The Psychology of Science

People seem to agree that there is something wrong with the way science is being taught today. Lewis Thomas, author of several popular books on science, suggests that what has happened is that the fun has gone out of science teaching. I would add that so has the sense of wonder. We have been presenting science in the curriculum for the past 90 years as if it were a collection of unchanging academic subjects. Somewhere along the line we moved science away from nature and into the textbook.

Many students see science as a course to get through and are interested only in their grades. To them, science is a hurdle that prevents them from moving on, rather than a bridge that connects them to the world.

People are turning away from science at the very time when there is an enormous need for them to understand it. I'm not referring to people who will become our future scientists or people who will pursue a science-related career; tens of millions of non-science people are greatly affected by science but are unaware of its impact. More tragic is that so many who have been forced away from science miss the immense pleasure and joy of its mysteries. We need people outside the field of science to appreciate and understand it just as much if not more than we need scientists.

So, welcome to the world of science teaching, and the challenge of capturing students' imaginations. Whether you are a newcomer or an old timer, I hope that this book will provide you with some fresh insights and ideas about science teaching.

The Ecology of Science Teaching— What's It All About?

There is a theory in science called the Gaia hypothesis that proposes that all living things, from whales to bacteria and from evergreens to algae, can be regarded as a single living entity. One of the developers of the hypothesis, British scientist James Lovelock, says that this living entity is capable of manipulating the earth's atmosphere to suit its overall needs.[1] Gaia is an entity involving earth's biosphere, atmosphere, oceans, and soil. If Gaia exists, then we are part of her and therefore part of a whole.

To think in terms of Gaia is to have an ecological view. Ecology is the science of relationships and, as a subject, has more to do with wholes than with parts. Fritjof Capra, a physicist and well-known author, has this to say about an ecological perspective:

> *Detailed study of ecosystems over the past decades have shown quite clearly that most relationships between living organisms are essentially cooperative ones, characterized by coexistence and interdependence, and symbiotic in varying degrees. Although there is competition, it usually takes place within a wider context of cooperation, so that the larger system is kept in balance.*[2]

The classroom is a system, just as a pond or a forest or a desert can be considered a system. (Technically, these are subsystems of a larger system, the whole earth.) We might think of the classroom as a cultural subsystem of the school. There are behaviors exhibited in the classroom that are competitive, and there are many behaviors that are cooperative in nature. An ecological approach to teaching depicts the classroom as a natural cultural ecosystem that is shaped by the values and beliefs of the persons involved, of the school and community, and of the culture at large.

Each system—and therefore each classroom—should be viewed holistically, rather than as separate parts comprised of students and teachers. The important elements of a system are the relationships that exist within it. An ecological perspective places a high priority on relationships and interdependence in the classroom.

The Ecological Classroom—Some Things To Look For

The idea of an ecological classroom is not a new one. Teachers for years have recognized that if learning is to occur in the classroom, they must look beyond subject matter and prescribed teaching behaviors. These teachers know that learning and teaching in the classroom are social activities involving groups.

There are several patterns that characterize an ecological classroom. These patterns are the result of underlying attitudes about learning and teaching.

1. Attention is paid to the interaction of persons with their environment.
2. Teachers help students see relationships between the traditional subject-matter disciplines. An interdisciplinary approach to teaching is at the core of the lesson plan. Science is taught as a subject within the context of the students' total environment. As students get older this environment expands until teaching plans that have a global perspective eventually emerge.
3. Teaching and learning are viewed as a continuously interactive process rather than as a cause-and-effect process. An attempt is made by teachers to deal with the system as a whole rather than attempting to isolate individual effective teaching behaviors.
4. Teachers realize that personal-environmental interactions are seen in relation to other systems that influence the classroom, such as family, community, culture.
5. Attitudes and perceptions of teachers and students (as well as of administrators and parents) provide important data that influences the teaching-learning environment.

Three ideas emerge from an ecological model, and they form the substance and rationale for this book.

Cooperative learning Cooperative learning is a powerful learning model in which groups of students work together to solve problems and complete learning assignments. Cooperative learning is a deliberate attempt to influence the culture of the classroom by encouraging cooperative actions among students. Cooperative learning is a natural approach for the teaching and learning of science and is one that will be shown to be effective with a wide range of students.

Whole-brain learning Students enter our classrooms as whole persons, posssessing a broad range of learning abilities. A whole-brain model of learning is described from a practical-experiential perspective based on the work of brain researchers and students of creativity and problem solving. An inventory of learning modes for the ecological classroom appears in chapter 3, and these modes are integrated in the curriculum materials presented in Part Two.

Experiences In the spirit of an ecological approach, students are provided with experiences that help them search for and discover the world of science. A series of units of instruction, called Experiences, constitute Part Two and are based on this perspective. The Experiences are cooperative learning units designed to help students become science learners. The units invite students to explore diverse topics that deemphasize the normal boundaries of science; a unique list of curriculum topics emerges when these boundaries of science are broken.

This book is a resource for the teacher and is designed especially for implementation at grades 4-9. Because the book deals with topics and approaches not common to all schools and classrooms, a shift in your thinking and your way of looking at things is suggested. One place to begin is to think about your values and attitudes toward teaching and science.

Are You Madly in Love with Science?

In an earlier work entitled *Loving and Beyond,* which I co-authored, it was suggested that loving science is not enough to create a learning environment that will motivate students to learn it. We went on to suggest many strategies that teachers could use to create a humanistic learning environment.

Love is, however, essential; if people hate or are afraid of science, they are going to spend their lives avoiding it. In studies of students' attitudes toward science, it has been revealed that by the end of third grade, nearly one half of American students say they would not like to take another science course; only one in five eighth graders indicated that they would want to take another science course.[3]

Students enter the classroom with a full range of feelings toward science. These feelings are the result of past experiences and opportunities with science. What are your feelings toward science? Look over this list of statements and decide how you feel about science. How do you think your students would respond to these statements?

What are your attitudes toward science and science teaching? Perhaps you distrust science because you do not understand how science works or because you think scientific discoveries are used unwisely. Some people are afraid of science because they have done poorly in science courses and were never given the encouragment that would help them be successful. The complexity and difficulty that people attach to science may be largely due to the way scientists and science teachers convey science to other people.

Science at its core is a wondrous activity of the human mind that all of us are capable of experiencing. Unfortunately, most people are driven away from science during the early years of schooling.

**An Attitude Survey:
Attitudes About Science and Science Teaching**

SA = Strong Agree; A = Agree; N = Neutral;
D = Disagree; SD = Strongly Disagree

	SA	A	N	D	SD
1. I'm afraid of science.	—	—	—	—	—
2. I distrust science.	—	—	—	—	—
3. I find science complex and difficult to understand	—	—	—	—	—
4. I'm turned on to science	—	—	—	—	—
5. I'm interested in science	—	—	—	—	—
6. I'm fascinated by science.	—	—	—	—	—
7. I look forward to teaching/learning science.	—	—	—	—	—
8. Science is essential to our society.	—	—	—	—	—
9. Teaching/learning science is important to our society.	—	—	—	—	—
10. I'm madly in love with science.	—	—	—	—	—

People and Science

Science is a humanistic enterprise. Although scientists use complicated instruments and gadgets to make observations and measurements, the essence of science is having the curiosity to seek answers to questions. In reality, science is a human endeavor full of creativity and wonder, the very qualities that draw many people to literature and art. In *Loving and Beyond*, a humanistic view is presented.

1. Science is a human experience. It involves humans looking out at their world.
2. Science usually involves a cooperative human effort. The scientist, alone, high in an ivory tower, is an inaccurate view of the scientific role.
3. The basic processes of science, such as discovering, valuing, and exploring, are applicable to many of the human social problems people face, problems that include social change and the improvement of interpersonal relationships.
4. Certain products of science, as transmitted through technology, can be used to alleviate human suffering resulting from poverty, disease, and illiteracy.
5. The essence of humanism, as we see it, is that each human being should be encouraged to utilize her or his full human potential, as well as intellectual and social potential.[4]

Each person who enters the classroom has the potential to become fully human. Because science has such a broad vista, the development of myriad human potentialities is at hand in the science classroom. The statements above lead to the following implications for science:

1. Science involves exploration and discovery.
2. Cooperative learning is essential in science.
3. Science is a process that can be used to solve problems in a wide variety of contexts.
4. Science should serve people.
5. Science can contribute to the full development of people.

Helping People Like Science

There is no easy explanation for why some people like science and others do not. Sometimes we simply bore people by choosing uninteresting topics and content. Too often we use methods over and over again that convey the message that the way to learn science is through drill and practice. The following suggestions might get people interested in science.

Focus attention on things that science does not know Years ago, a middle school science curriculum featured a section entitled "Unsolved Problems" at the end of each chapter. Create lesson plans in which students formulate possible theories or explanations to questions such as the following:

- How did life begin?
- What happened to the dinosaurs?
- Will machines ever have consciousness?
- Can we find a cure for cancer or for AIDS?
- Did humans evolve from apes?
- Is there intelligent life elsewhere in the universe?

Teach the puzzles of the origin of the universe Help students realize that there are things going on in the world that still lie beyond comprehension and help them to realize how little is really known. In the Experience entitled "The Third Wave" (Chapter 9), students are introduced to futuristic thinking, another aspect of the unknown.

Teach the life sciences as an alive field of study Help students to discover that there are tiny structures squirming inside our cells that provide all the energy for life, and show them that we have no idea where they came from. Chapter 11, "Investigating the Natural World," will help you meet this challenge. The focus of this Experience is on relationships in nature and on using the senses to find out about life.

Teach ecology starting in Grade 1 Help students realize that life on earth is a system of interdependent creatures and help them understand that we still do not understand how the system works. There are many Experiences in the book that present ecology, including Investigating the Natural World (Chapter 11), The Web of Life (Chapter 4), The Starship and the Canoe (Chapter 6), and Powering the Earth (Chapter 10).

Demonstrate how science, technology, and society interact Technology depends on science, but that is not the reason for studying science. The central purpose of science is to develop a clearer picture of nature, not mastery over nature. Ethical and moral issues abound where science, technology, and people meet. Students should be provided with opportunities to express opinions about important scientific, technological, and social issues. Following are some of the topics from which to develop questions and issues:

- Population growth
- Nuclear technology
- World hunger and food resources
- Air quality and the atmosphere
- Water resources
- Land resources
- Energy shortages
- Hazardous substances such as toxic chemicals
- Extinction of plants and animals
- Depletion of mineral resources

You will find activities in each of the Experiences that deal with scientific, technological, and social issues. For further ideas and examples of lesson plans that deal with the societal implications of science, see Rodger Bybee, et al. *Teaching About Science and Society: Activities for Elementary and Junior High School*, 1984.

There are many other topics that could be used. Running through them, however, is the message that we should convey to our students: Nature is mysterious, and science is full of bewilderment. Science does not have all the answers to our problems. As a field of investigation, it is subject to limitations, just as every other facet of our lives.

Images of Science

Activity is essential to science and teaching, and carrying out this activity is a good place to begin. You will need three or four people, newsprint or construction paper, and crayons. If it is inconvenient to round up other people, go ahead and do the activity by yourself.

> *Make a drawing of a scientist at work. Briefly make a sketch, and then fill in the details with the crayons.*

Well, how did you do? Compare your drawings to the drawing shown here, which was made by a student in elementary school.

This activity has been completed by hundreds of people of all ages, and judging by the results, the following conclusions about peoples' impressions and stereotypes can be drawn.

- The scientist is usually a male caucasian.
- The scientist is either bald or has frizzy, wild hair. On the rare occasions when the scientist is a woman, her hair is in a bun.
- The scientist wears glasses and is dressed in a white lab coat.
- The scientist is shown working alone in a laboratory rather than in nature or in the field.
- The scientist is shown mixing chemicals or doing some kind of chemistry- or physics-related experiment.
- The scientist is shown experimenting with dangerous things and is sometimes shown experimenting on people.

In *Science Anxiety*, Jeffrey Mallow describes one image of science that is very common in our culture:

> *Turn on your television some Saturday afternoon. Find the station with the monster movie. Now settle back in your chair and watch the stereotypes parade across the screen. There goes the beautiful girl. Not far behind her, and gaining quickly, is the monster. And who is that lurking in the shadows: the ugly in the lab coat, with the rimless spectacles and the crazed look on his face? It's the scientist, of course. Brilliant, cold-blooded, seeking to cure humanity's ills but instead unleashing new horrors on the human race, he inspires respect and terror in us at the same time. What he does not inspire in us is the desire to emulate him. And that is the root of science anxiety.*

Mallow's description of the scientist stereotype is prevalent in our society. We think of the scientist as doing secretive things in remote places. Unfortunately, the tendency is to think of the scientist as a person who does not care about people or the effects of science.

There are no simple answers to explain why the stereotype of the scientist persists in our society. The problem we face with regard to the image of scientists and science is multifaceted. Television and the movies have a powerful impact on our perceptions of the world. The Saturday morning cartoon show portraying science fiction and space travel may be a major factor contributing to the image we have of science. Carl Sagan, commenting on children's shows of this nature, made this statement in the April 1979 *TV Guide*:

> *Many of these so-called scientists are moral cripples driven by a lust for power or greed with a spectacular insensitivity to the feelings of others and the message conveyed to the moppet and adolescent audience is that science is dangerous.*

This impression of science is as dangerous as it is unfortunate. Science does not have to be viewed as being dangerous. In the words of Horace Freeland Judson in *The Search for Solutions*, "science is our century's art." Judson portrays science as being oceanic, as providing experiences beyond pleasure, as being the most interesting, difficult, pitiless, exciting, and beautiful pursuit that we have yet found. We should demonstrate to students that science can be a source of pleasure and can create a sense of well-being.

The school curriculum, from kindergarten through college, has had an impact on the cultural view of science. All of our citizens pass through our schools and are influenced by the nature of science teaching, for better or for worse. The curricular innovations of the 1960s and 1970s were generally designed for the elite group of students who would go on to college and probably seek a career in science. Some science educators estimate this to represent about 20% of the population. The courses and programs that were developed were based on the formal structure of science and often had very little to do with the everyday life of the student. Concepts and facts were taught, often with cleverly designed hands-on activities. The abstractness and remoteness of science was reinforced by many of these projects. Did your science curriculum reinforce the stereotypes in your drawings?

The stereotypes in the drawings reveal other impressions of science. Rarely is the scientist seen as a woman. Furthermore, very few students or adults depict scientists as being Black, Hispanic, Asian, or Native American. The implication of this is clear: Role models need to be provided in order to instill in students the idea of possibility and potential. Without role models, we reduce the options for a vital segment of our population.

Changing the Image

The following actions can be taken in order to move away from bias, thereby freeing yourself to work openly with students.

1. Monitor your communication. Avoid utterances of bias and prejudice. How you behave and what you say has more impact on students than the pictures that appear in textbooks.
2. Discuss students' feelings about sexism and other forms of prejudice.
3. Encourage girls to consider careers in science and to keep their minds and options open.[5]
4. Make yourself available as a listener and treat boys and girls equally. Unequal treatment can show up in assignments, expectations, and the choice of content that is presented to students. Girls can enjoy science topics as much as boys do if they are included and encouraged.
5. Provide information about real people in science. Bring guest speakers into the classroom or take students to places where people work in science fields.

The image of science can be changed, but this goal requires the work not only of the education community but of the scientific community as well. The image of science among students in the United States has become more negative in recent years, but the following efforts are being made to reverse this trend.

A New Pattern for Science Teaching

Emerging in our culture is a new pattern for the teaching of science. It is based on an ecological framework and focuses on the nature of learning rather than on the methods of instruction. The learner is foremost, and science content is secondary. Ideas such as how to motivate students to develop a lifelong love affair with science, how to strengthen self-direction in learning, how to awaken curiosity and wonder, and how to encourage creativity are replacing the old ideas of how to achieve norms on tests, how to answer questions correctly, and how to emphasize science facts.

To examine this new pattern, I have compared it to an older but more common pattern of educational behavior.[6]

The new pattern of teaching is ecological. It emphasizes relationships, and views science as a process, a journey. There is emphasis on relating science to the students' world. An interdisciplinary approach is another characteristic of the new pattern. Students should be encouraged to relate science to social problems, to mathematics, and to

Pattern Shifts in Science Education

The Old Pattern	The New Pattern
• The goal of science teaching is to produce scientifically literate people, which implies knowing basic facts, skills, and concepts.	Science teaching emphasizes scientific literacy insofar as science relates to basic human needs, the needs of the physical and natural environment, and the social needs of the planet's human population and other living species; science is seen as touching people; science can provide knowledge in order that we prudently and ecologically care for our planet and can help us realize that our social needs require wisdom and cooperation.
• Science teaching uses a clockwork model of the universe based on Newtonian physics.	Science teaching recognizes relationships in an uncertain universe based on Einstein's physics.
• Science teaching emphasizes the content of science, acquiring a body of the right information during the schooling period.	Science teaching emphasizes inquiry, learning how to learn, how to pose questions, and the search.
• Science is a product, a destination.	Science is a process, a journey.
• Content of science is hierarchical and authoritarian in structure; curriculum is structured and ordered; rigid structure and conformity discourages dissent.	Content of science is relatively flexible; there are many ways to teach and learn science.
• Science curriculum emphasizes lockstep progress and designates appropriate ages for certain science activities; age restrictions, segregation, and compartmentalization are prevalent.	Flexibility and integration of age groupings are encouraged; individuals are not limited by age to certain science learning.
• Priority is given to performance, mastery, acquiring certain knowledge; national test results are very important.	Priority is given to improving self-image; self-concept is an indication of performance; knowledge feeds self-image; the ability to inquire and investigate fuels personal autonomy and self-direction in learning.

The Old Pattern	The New Pattern
• Science content emphasizes the external world, learning what is out there, cognition.	Science content supports the idea that the inner experience is the appropriate context for learning; science teaching methods include visualization, log or journal keeping, right brain learning, attitudinal learning.
• Science learning encourages recall and convergent thinking.	Science learning encourages guessing, estimating, divergent thinking, and the creative process.
• Learning in science is analytical and linear, or left brained.	Learning in science is whole brained; there is a confluence of left- and right-brain learning; holistic and creative thinking is encouraged.
• Children are labeled (remedial, gifted, non-science, science prone, dysfunctional), which leads to self-fulfilling prophesies.	Children are labeled only in unusual situations; attempts are made not to categorize in order to release potential.
• Science presentation relies on abstract, theoretical, or book knowledge; student is spectator.	Science presentation combines experiential knowledge with theoretical knowledge; emphasis is on exciting examples and everyday applications; the student is a participant and explorer.
• Science is taught as a social necessity for a certain period of time in order to inculcate minimum skills and content and to train for specific roles.	Science is seen as a part of a life-long process of learning related to schools for a while but augmented by museum learning, community groups, self-direction, and adult programs.
• The teacher imparts knowledge, and students learn it; communication is generally one way.	The teacher is a facilitator of learning and a learner as well; students are learners and teachers in some situations; networks emerge instead of one-way forms of communication.
• Science is seen as a single subject with little relationship to mathematics, social studies, language arts, art, or music.	Science is seen as part of an interdisciplinary world; emphasis is on relating science to the students' world, which is not compartmentalized.

art. The teacher in this new pattern is a facilitator of learning rather than a dispenser of information.

The new pattern provides a new view of science and science teaching. What should curriculum planners emphasize? How does this new framework affect the lesson plans that we create? What are some of the implications for science education?

Science Teaching—Looking Toward the Future

If you are an active science teacher, you are faced each day with the challenge of developing lesson plans that remove the blahs from learning. Each lesson plan is part of a constellation of plans that constitute the course or subject that you teach. What overall thrust, perspective, or philosophy guides the development of lesson plans?

This section presents six areas that can be used as guideposts for day-to-day planning of science teaching.

Guidepost	Implication
1. Creative and rational thinking	Students should be able to develop and apply creative and rational thinking abilities.
2. Humanistic attitudes	Students should be able to develop values and attitudes that promote ethical and moral thinking, especially with respect to their involvement with the environment and society.
3. Ecological perspective	Students should develop a perspective that promotes the interdependent nature of the environment and the global nature of the planet.
4. Synergic thinking	Students should develop a framework that encourages holistic thinking. Throughout the students' experience in science courses, concepts such as systems thinking, cooperation, global values, and resource management are encountered.
5. Knowledge of science	Students should develop the ability to use science concepts, facts, and principles in the solution of problems.
6. Skills of science	Students should be able to manipulate the materials of science and communicate science information.

Guideposts For Planning—A Closer Look

How can we put guideposts for planning to work, thereby creating the possibility of implementing a holistic framework in the science classroom? Each guidepost is discussed below, and the implications are outlined for application.

Creative and Rational Thinking

Discoveries in science are made by the creativity of human beings. "The creative process which is the ultimate source of all true discoveries has withered away in our super-rational culture," says scientist and educator Ann Palm.[7] She says further that our programs in science teaching produce highly technical, even innovative, experts whose mental abilities dwarf their creative talents. The first challenge, the first goal, for us is to place a new emphasis on creativity in our teaching plans.

Emphasizing creativity implies that the process is more important than the product. Although science curriculum projects that emphasize process to the exclusion of content have been developed, a more balanced and practical approach has been suggested. (In 1985 the State of California rejected the Science Curriculum Improvement Study (SCIS) from the list of recommended elementary science programs. One of the reasons the commission gave was the lack of balance in the SCIS curriculum. It was pointed out that the SCIS program lacked an earth-science strand. The commission only adopted programs that had a balanced approach to curriculum.)

Many science programs have designed their curriculum by integrating process and content. In most programs, the processes discussed below are emphasized and are recognized as the foundation of elementary science process skills. They comprise an outline for the rational thinking skills that can be derived from the science program.

Implications for the Classroom

1. It is not enough to teach about dinosaurs and space exploration; a broad-based approach is required for curriculum planning. As you look over last year's curriculum or look ahead to next year, are you providing balanced lessons that cover earth, life, and physical science topics?
2. Cultivate an atmosphere in which creativity is encouraged and rewarded. Projects and science fairs are excellent ways to facilitate the development of creative thinking.
3. Allow time for creativity. Creativity cannot be forced. Teachers who know this allow time for the incubation of ideas. They let ideas cook by allowing time for making journal or log book entries, letting students go to the library or resource center, and encouraging students to daydream and imagine. Providing structured time for incubation is a productive use of time even though there is a preoccupation with keeping students on task. Encourage students to go away from problems on which they are working, at least for a time. They can return to them later. This process of going away from problems often leads to insights and solutions.

Process-Skill	Definition
1. Observing	Using the senses to identify properties of an object or event.
2. Classifying	Grouping objects and developing classification systems.
3. Communicating	Using written and oral forms of expression, graphs, tables, and constructed models to describe scientific phenomena.
4. Measuring	Making quantitative observations using units of measurement and measuring devices.
5. Predicting	Making forecasts based on observations.
6. Inferring	Drawing tentative conclusions based on observations.
7. Interpreting data	Finding patterns that lead to the construction of inferences or predictions.
8. Formulating hypotheses	Making educated guesses based on evidence.
9. Controlling variables	Identifying variables of a system and choosing those to be held constant and those to be manipulated.
10. Experimenting	Investigating, manipulating, and testing to determine a result.

4. Encourage the use of a variety of sources in the solution of problems. Use questioning strategies that encourage alternative answers to individual questions.
5. Use techniques such as brainstorming to help students generate a variety of ideas. (See chapter 3 for specific suggestions.) As you will see, the cooperative learning model that was developed for the Experiences specifies the use of open-ended discussion and brainstorming at the start of a learning unit.
6. Creativity can be encouraged by focusing on the process skills of science. As you plan lessons, isolate at least one process skill to be emphasized. Note that the lesson plans in the Experiences focus on one or more science process skills.
7. Involve students in long-term learning projects. The cooperative learning units contain suggestions for long-term learning projects.

Humanistic Attitudes

Humanistic attitudes bring us in touch with human values and suggest that science should contribute to the well-being of humanity. Accordingly, the needs of people should always be placed higher than technological innovations. As you think about your science lessons and units of teaching, ask yourself these questions:

- How can science help provide for the needs of each person?
- In what ways can science be used to eradicate the suffering that many men, women, and children endure?
- How are the discoveries and technological innovations used? Are they used for the benefit of humankind or for the destruction of people?

The humanistic guidepost is crucial in an ecological classroom. The attitudes and perceptions of teachers and their students are as important as the test scores that students attain on standardized tests. Students can be taught how to contribute to the solution of problems and how an individual can make a difference. In the Experiences that you will find later in the book, look for examples of projects that encourage students to solve environmental, ecological, and related problems.

Implications for the Classroom

1. Bring students in contact with ways that science can be used in the service of people. Show them how technology has helped alleviate human suffering and how technology and science can be used to help people. Design science lessons in which students question why science contributes to the development of instruments of destruction, such as thermonuclear bombs and chemical and biological agents.
2. Foster an attitude in the classroom in which ethical considerations and values are part of science teaching. Discussions, debates, and writing assignments on moral and ethical issues in science should be a normal part of science teaching.
3. Emphasize the tentativeness of scientific knowledge. It is important for students to realize that there is a range for everything we know. The implication is that there is no absolute knowledge.

4. Provide opportunities for students to express their attitudes and opinions about what and how they are learning. Checklists and opinionnaires can be used to gather student feedback.

Ecological Perspective

Our planet is a living and breathing cell requiring the same attention as a biological cell. Students should learn that the planet earth has to be nurtured just as we nurture ourselves, as some scientists believe.

The earth is a system with all of its parts interconnected. Plants and animals, rocks and soil, water and air are interacting subsystems that constitute the whole earth. The degradation of any one of these can have far reaching affects on the whole system. A plant burning coal in Ohio generates waste products that are associated with acid rain in New England and Canada. The acid rain increases the rate of erosion of sedimentary rocks, which increases the sediment flow in rivers, and so on.

Theodore Roszak, in *Person/Planet*, says that the rights of the person are the rights of the planet and that the needs of the person are the needs of the planet.

This message is best seen in the science of ecology. Even though the old model (science as reductionist and mechanistic) is giving way to a new model (science as a process and based on relationships), the traditional sciences—chemistry, physics, and biology—have held tight to the old model. Ecology, the science that deals with relationships and interdependence, provides insight into this new model. Roszak has this to say about ecology:

> *Ecology is the one science that possesses the ability to recapture the experience of personality in nature. And it comes into its own as a profession at exactly the same time that an intense awareness of personhood enters our political life. We have begun to liberate the earth from her false identity—the mechanistic-reductionist image which has made nature into an object of unfeeling manipulation—just as we begin to fight our way free of the false identities which have made human beings the objects of social power.*

One of the implications for teaching of the ecological perspective is to emphasize the wholeness of the earth and to help students learn how to make ethical decisions about the present and future use of earth and its resources.

Rodger Bybee says that "prudence and stewardship should replace dominion over." If we take an ecological position concerning the future of the earth, science education could be an integral force in affecting that future. Bybee points out that the role of science educators in an ecological society will include the following responsibilities:

- Development of the individual—emphasizes the fullfillment of basic human needs and the discovery of the means of nurturing healthy personal growth.
- Development of environmental quality—includes the protection, conservation, and improvement of all factors that affect individual and community development, including air, water, noise, stress.

- Development of resources—determines what natural resources are to be used and the degree to which they are to be used, recycled, and conserved.
- Development of community—entails greater recognition that groups of humans at local, regional, national, and international levels are dependent on one another for basic requirements of individual growth and that we must cooperate in eliminating racism, sexism, and war.

Implications for the Classroom

1. Create in students an awareness that they are part of a large system and that each part is connected to the whole. "Picking a wildflower causes a star to shudder" is a beautiful metaphorical expression suggested by Ted Colton to explain the interdependent nature of the universe.
2. Remind students as often as possible of the big picture. Use maps, photographs, and pictures showing how an object, event, or area relates to the larger scene.
3. Create a world news bulletin board to bring events of an ecological nature to students' attention for discussion. You might also provide opportunities for students to express opinions and become involved in ecological problems in their local community or in their state.
4. Emphasize the interdisciplinary nature of science by integrating other subjects with science units.

Synergic Thinking

When students are taught the concept of the food web, they are shown that hardly anything is independent and freestanding; everything is part of some larger system. Students begin to think in wholes, to see things holistically. Concepts such as the food web or questions such as the following can lead to holistic thinking:

> *"What would happen if you changed _____?"*
> *"What is the effect of _____ on _____?"*
> *"How do these two factors affect each other?"*

Synergic thinking is another phrase for holistic thinking and should be emphasized throughout the school curricula. Students should be encouraged not simply to recall information, but to combine ideas, show relationships, and develop the big picture.

We need to help students realize the importance of striving for a synergic world, in which wholes are more important than parts. Cooperation rather than competition, interdependence rather than dependence, symbiosis rather than parasitic behavior are concepts that should be included in the science curriculum.

Classrooms in which cooperative learning is used (discussed in detail in the next chapter) are examples of synergic environments. In the cooperative classroom, the teacher's actions are rooted in cooperative and holistic actions. Research studies have consistently supported the hypothesis that classrooms in which peer cooperation is emphasized not only promote academic achievement but enhance social relationships as well.

Implications for the Classroom

1. One of the fundamental concepts presented in this book is cooperative learning. The implication for the classroom is to begin to experiment with this educational format, examining the possibilities in your own classroom. Providing activities in which students have to work with each other in order to solve a task or contribute to the class will help them understand the value of cooperation and will clarify the idea of synergy.
2. Introduce interdisciplinary concepts and use practical examples to help students understand them.
3. Regard each person in the classroom as a high synergy person. As will be discussed, each person should be viewed with unconditional positive regard, as having dignity and worth.
4. Encourage holistic thinking by asking students questions that focus on synthesis and evaluative thinking. Ask them to show how things relate to each other; ask them how changing some variables in a system will affect the whole system.

Knowledge of Science

What knowledge should be included in the science curriculum? Robert Heinlein gives some insight into this problem. In an article in the August 1979 issue of *Omni*, he suggested that a human being living today should be able to complete the following tasks.

1. Change a diaper.
2. Plan an invasion.
3. Butcher a hog.
4. Conn a ship.
5. Design a building.
6. Write a sonnet.
7. Balance accounts.
8. Build a wall.
9. Set a bone.
10. Act alone.
11. Cooperate.
12. Solve equations.
13. Analyze a new problem.
14. Take orders.
15. Give orders.
16. Pitch manure or a tent.
17. Program a computer.
18. Cook a tasty meal.
19. Fight efficiently.
20. Die gallantly.

As far as determining what knowledge will be important, we can conclude that "specialization in living is for insects!"

When you consider what knowledge should be included in the science curriculum, you should make selections in the context of the nature of science. According to many scientists and educators, science is a way of thinking much more than it is a body of knowledge. There are some general principles that might help when you are considering the selection of science knowledge.

The authors of the 1978 Science Framework for the State of California identified the following principles to consider in selecting science content.

Principle 1
Knowledge that enables the
student to verbalize the
thinking processes and skills of
science.

Examples
Students criticize a science
experiment; students
distinguish between the process
of trial and error and more
controlled investigations.

Principle 2
Knowledge that derives from
the basic concepts and structure
of the major disciplines.

Examples
Students identify and describe
living things that grow and
develop in different
environments; students
recognize that the earth is
constantly changing.

Principle 3
Knowledge that is composed of
broad generalizations that
interrelate the many facts,
concepts, and principles of all
the sciences.

Examples
Students identify simple cause-
and-effect relationships;
students identify pairs of
objects with similar
characteristics.

Principle 4
Knowledge of how science and
technology affect society.

Example
Students describe aspects of a
society that tend to encourage
or inhibit the advance of
science; students describe
instances in which a major
scientific or technological
advance has been based on the
work of persons of several races
and/or nationalities.

Implications for the Classroom

1. Concepts are understood when students can apply them to a
   variety of familiar situations. Having students relate concepts to
   their own experiences greatly enhances the utility of science
   concepts.
2. Provide experiences in which phenomena and data conflict with
   the student's conceptual structures. Activities demonstrating
   discrepant events and inquiry problems are excellent examples of
   how to help students deal with cognitive conflicts.

   Here is an example of a simple discrepant event. All you need are
   50 pennies and a full jar of water. Ask students how many pennies
   can be added to the jar without spilling any water. Most students
   will predict that only a few pennies can be placed in the jar, but it
   is possible to put 30 or more pennies in the jar, depending on its
   size. This doesn't make sense to many students, and for them it is a
   classic example of a discrepant event. If you do the experiment,
   students will notice that the surface of the water forms a bulge as
   pennies are added. The surface tension of the water prevents it
   from spilling at first; eventually, the water spills when the force of
   gravity exceeds the forces holding the water molecules together.
3. Introduce students to some of the great unanswered questions in
   science. The questions can be used as a vehicle to help students

explore these areas of science. The following are some of the questions that were suggested in *Science Digest*, October, 1985.

- How did life begin?
- What happened to the dinosaurs?
- Will we ever control the weather?
- Is there a balance of nature?
- Will machines ever be conscious?
- How does the human brain work?
- How does a cell become a complex organism?
- Can we conquer cancer?
- How do plants harness energy from the sun?
- Did humans evolve from apes?
- Do other solar systems exist?
- Is there intelligent life elsewhere in the universe?
- Will computers surpass the brain?
- What is time?
- Is death inevitable?
- How did the universe begin?
- How will the universe end?

Skills of Science

Students should be provided with opportunities to acquire the following kinds of skills.

1. Use laboratory materials and tools in meaningful ways.
2. Develop proper techniques for handling and caring for living things.
3. Gather information needed to develop or test inferences and hypotheses.
4. Record observations in a systematic manner and organize data in a variety of ways.
5. Communicate with others by written, oral, and visual means.

Implications for the Classroom

1. Have students keep a science log in which they record data from activities, experiment results, and summaries of what they are learning. A more complete discussion of using the computer as a writing tool in the science classroom is included in the next chapter.
2. Create situations in which students have to use some of the tools of science: hand lens, microscope, balance, metric ruler. Simple versions of some instruments can be made by the students.
3. Include skill development activities as an integral part of the science program.

These six guideposts of science teaching form a point of view and a philosophy as individual science lessons, units, and courses of instruction are planned.

Toward an Ecological Classroom

Classrooms are complex social environments varying greatly from one to another. Each classroom can be depicted as having a social climate that has an enormous effect on learning. Compare the following classroom situations.

Teacher Talk in Two Different Classrooms

Classroom A	Classroom B
"Which groups are interested in doing the experiment we mentioned yesterday?"	"I like the way Joan and Jim are working. If the rest of you would act like them, we'd all be able to do the experiment."
"How many groups are still working on the Touch the Earth Experience learning contract?"	"You people never finish your work on time. For each day you are late, your grade will drop one letter."
"What are some ways we can all share in the responsibility for learning?"	"Each person is responsible for his or her work. The due date is on the board."
"Has any group solved the problem that was brought in by the iceberg group?"	"Copy the science words from the board and write the definitions on paper."

The environment of these two classrooms differs. In Classroom A, there is a sense of community, characterized by cooperation, trust, warmth, and group responsibility.

In Classroom B, the focus is not on community but rather on a "me-them" mentality, pitting teacher against students. The teacher in Classroom B uses a lot of energy threatening the students to finish their work or to behave properly, while the teacher in Classroom A uses energy to facilitate the work and motivate students.

In the ecological classroom, teachers spend a lot of energy on facilitation and motivation and are interested in relationships, values, and attitudes. Some insights into establishing and implementing an ecological classroom can be derived from studying how classrooms are organized.

Individuals, Teams, and the Whole Class

The following represent three ways to organize and perceive a typical class of students with one teacher.

1. Individuals.
2. Groups of students, or learning teams.
3. The whole class.

The approach advocated in this book is to use all three structures so that the well-being of each individual is achieved in a cooperative climate. To accomplish this, each member in a class is viewed as being an individual, a member of a learning team, and a member of the whole class. The unique abilities of each student are valued and actualized by means of careful conception and management of the learning environment. Understanding how these structures relate to each other will help identify the management and facilitation processes necessary to achieve an ecological classroom.

Individuals Each classroom is composed of many individuals whose uniqueness is enhanced by being members of learning teams and of the whole class. In learning teams, students' unique abilities can be put into action, which helps them realize their individual worth. Personal identity is established through interaction, not through isolation. Seeing and exploring differences in others helps build bridges and at the same time establishes one's unique attributes.

Students in your classroom will vary in every trait imaginable, including cognitive learning style, self-esteem, physical dexterity, emotional maturity, and so on. In a cooperative learning environment, these variations are respected and accepted. Students are not isolated in a cooperative environment, even though there are times when they work alone.

Learning Teams A learning team is a support group composed of up to five students. Learning teams participate in learning activities as a cooperative group to achieve certain goals and objectives. The teams are responsible for setting and reaching goals, solving problems, completing projects and tasks, and showing evidence of their progress.

For team learning to be successful, each member of the group must work cooperatively toward a goal or toward the solution of a problem. Learning teams become integral and central organizing structures of the ecological classroom. With time, each team will develop a personality or set of characteristics, and each student will develop a sense of belonging to the team. A team organization has great advantages from a management standpoint over individual or whole-class organizations, as will be discussed later.

Whole Class Your classroom provides a support group for each individual and an arena in which each of the learning teams functions. It is important that you provide opportunities for the whole class to be engaged in large group instruction and discussion sessions. The approach to cooperative learning advocated in *Science Experiences* suggests frequent class sessions in which groups report to the whole class, the teacher conducts a discussion section, the class begins a unit by brainstorming together, and so on. The periodic bringing together of the class helps students feel part of the whole class rather than part of a small cooperative group. The value of belonging as it relates to large group and team sessions will be discussed later.

Motivation in the Ecological Classroom

The energy source that drives an ecological classroom is intrinsic motivation, the desire to learn, to explore, to find out, to share with others. This sounds idealistic, but evidence from the research presented in the next chapter indicates that students are motivated to work without the external pressures of fear, retribution, or punishment in an ecological classroom. What is motivation, how does it work, and how can it be used in the classroom?

To be motivated is to be active, to be moving, to have high levels of energy that feed into a system, whether it is an individual, a learning team, or a whole class.

According to psychologists, people are motivated by needs—the need to eat, to feel safe, to be loved, to learn, to better themselves. Of particular significance to an ecological framework is the work of Abraham Maslow, who developed a "positive theory of motivation."[8] He believed deeply that hidden away in people was the desire to achieve, to do well, to be kind to others, and to want to be engaged in challenging and meaningful work. He developed a theory that became known as the theory of self-actualization and laid the groundwork for what is now regarded as humanistic psychology.

Maslow believed that human motivation was an ongoing process of development organized into a hierarchy of five stages. In order to progress to a higher stage, the lower stage must first be accommodated. Maslow's stage theory includes the following set of motivations or needs, in which human development progresses toward self-actualization.

Maslow's Motivational Stages		
Level	Motivation	Needs
5	Self-actualization	Personal fulfillment, growth.
4	Self-esteem	Status, prestige, acknowledgment.
3	Social	Belonging, acceptance, love.
2	Safety	Security, order, protection.
1	Physiological	Food, drink, exercise, sex.

Maslow believed that people have a higher nature, and that this nature emerges in environments characterized by trust, acceptance, non-aggression, and cooperation. One of his colleagues, anthropologist Ruth Benedict, studied social behavior in tribal groups and found that where non-aggression was conspicuous, people in the group acted unselfishly and for the good of the group. She characterized such groups as synergistic. In fact, she is credited with introducing the notion of synergy into social science; and Maslow applied this concept to his theory of motivation. He felt strongly that a synergistic environment facilitates the development of healthy individuals.

The evidence from Benedict, Maslow, and others is that a high synergy environment—one based on cooperation and non-aggression—fosters a higher nature in people and creates a climate conducive to the development of higher levels of Maslow's motivation hierarchy.

As will be discussed later, cooperative learning environments provide the kind of ecosystem that fosters the development of healthy individuals, without sacrificing the development of cognitive and intellectual development. In fact, cooperative environments are superior to other environments for developing cognitive skills.

Facilitating Learning:
The Person-Centered Approach

Many writers and researchers maintain that effective teachers manage groups without forgetting the characteristics and needs of the individual students in the class. The most popular teachers tend to be those who are warm, caring, and personal; they use a person-centered approach. Paul George provides the following description.

> *It should not, then, be surprising to note the continuing popularity of what some describe as the person-centered approach to teaching. This approach emphasizes the goals of the student, rather than the goals of the school or the teacher. It prizes decision-making by children and youth rather than restricting the process to adults. It advocates treating pupils as if they were whole human beings capable of contributing a great deal to the direction and management of their own lives, inside and outside the classroom. It focuses on the development of instructional strategies that facilitate rather than direct, and the person-centered approach to teaching aims toward the development of whole human beings in authentically caring communities.*[9]

In order to put the principles of person-centered teaching into practice, Carl Rogers and other person-centered educators suggest acknowledging that the key player is the teacher, who takes on the role of a facilitator of student learning rather than a dispenser of knowledge or information.[10] Three suggestions help to put person-centered teaching into practice:

1. There are qualities in the teacher that facilitate learning.
2. The person-centered approach facilitates inquiry.
3. Specific teacher actions can facilitate learning.

Rogers and others have shown that attitudes can facilitate or inhibit learning, and the most crucial qualities in the facilitation of learning are realness, acceptance and trust, and empathy. In creating a cooperative environment, the interactions among people are given high priority. Rogers, in his many years of research on person-centered therapy and teaching, has discovered that these three qualities keep surfacing in the work of therapists and teachers.

Realness implies that the teacher is genuine and is able and willing to express feelings of all sorts, from anger and sadness to joy and exhilaration. Because students are being asked to work a great deal of the time in learning teams, their feelings are going to be important, and the teacher can set an example by being real with them, though it is not an easy task. Guilt emerges as anger is expressed, but in time, realness will build bonds among the teacher and the class and among the students.

Acceptance of the other person implies prizing the individual and acknowledging that they are trustworthy and can be held responsible for their behavior. Acceptance allows students to be seen as human beings with feelings and attitudes of their own. In cooperative learning environments, you will hear more and see more and come in contact with more dimensions of your students. Being an accepting person will be a nice health and stress insurance policy.

Empathy implies understanding someone else's reactions and feelings from our own experiences. How wonderful it is when someone simply says, "I understand." Empathy is a form of understanding without judgment or evaluation. Empathy in a cooperative climate is an attitude that loosens the bonds of confinement, allowing students to "blossom and grow and learn."

Realness, acceptance, and empathy are not esoteric attitudes; on the contrary, they have been shown in one research study after another to be essential attitudes in the development of classroom climates that exhibit high levels of cognitive learning, as well as effective learning.

Teaching students the process of inquiry is a fundamental goal of science educators. Large-scale curriculum projects to develop inquiry-oriented science programs were funded by the government. One of the things that the developers learned was that in order to implement an inquiry-oriented program, the teacher must create a receptive environment.

Person-centered environments are conducive to teaching and learning the process of inquiry. In these environments, students are encouraged to explore, to discover, and to find out about things in the world that are relevant to them. George outlines the following characteristics of the person-centered environment that facilitate inquiry:

1. A climate of trust is established in the classroom, in which curiosity and the natural desire to learn can be nourished and enhanced.
2. A participatory mode of decision-making is applied to all aspects of learning, and students, teachers, and administrators each have a part in it.
3. Students are encouraged to prize themselves, to build their confidence and self-esteem.
4. Excitement in intellectual and emotional discovery, which leads students to become life-long learners, is fostered.

Inquiry is the process that drives science and is an aspect of motivation. Inquiry is an integral part of the development of self-esteem and self-actualization. If we acknowledge the importance of inquiry at an experiential level, then a climate conducive to inquiry must be established. Some ways to build a climate of inquiry are explored below.

1. Help students select problems, topics of study, and methods of exploring topics. The Experiences provide ample opportunities for students to make decisions about what and how they will learn.
2. Make your classroom an inviting and attractive resource center that contains items such as a microcomputer, science and science fiction paperbacks, video tapes, filmstrips, audio tapes, manipulatives, space for individual and team work, living things, a variety of texts and reference books, newspapers, magazines.
3. Experiment with different models of cooperative learning. Several models are discussed in the next chapter.
4. Give students as many opportunities as possible to engage in experiential learning activities.

The ecology of science teaching depends on your willingness to create a learning climate that is based on person-centered teaching. Cooperative learning strategies have been shown to facilitate a learning climate that is conducive to inquiry. In the next chapter, you will find out about cooperative learning strategies and ways to implement them in your classroom.

Looking Back

A friend of mine said to me recently, "You know, much of the good teaching I know about involves common sense." I said that I agreed, and as I think about this chapter, much of what was discussed is common sense.

The environment has a powerful influence on our attitudes and motivations. If the premises upon which ecological teaching is based are examined, the value of good human relationships is realized. I have always believed that the relationships established in my own classes were as important as the content presented. My desire to create trusting environments in which students felt safe enough to think about and express opinions has always been my primary goal.

I hope this chapter has stimulated you to think about your goals and aspirations as a teacher, and that my views and research on classroom environments and the implications for science teaching will help you realize them.

CREATING
COOPERATIVE
LEARNING
ENVIRONMENTS

"Learning, I believe, can be divided into general types, along a continuum of meaning. At one end of the scale is the kind of tasks psychologists sometimes set for their subjects—the learning of nonsense syllables. Because there is no meaning involved, these syllables are not easy to learn and are likely to be forgotten.

We frequently fail to recognize that much of the material presented to students in the classroom has, for the student, the same perplexing, meaningless quality that the list of nonsense syllables has for us. . . . Such learning involves the mind only. It is learning that takes place "from the neck up." It does not involve feelings or personal meanings; it has no relevance for the whole person.

In contrast, there is such a thing as significant, meaningful, experiential learning. When the toddler touches the warm radiator, she learns for herself the meaning of a word hot; she has learned a future caution in regard to all similar radiators; and she has taken in these learnings in a significant, involved way that will not soon be forgotten."

CARL ROGERS
Freedom to Learn for the 80s

To make learning meaningful for students, we must consider the nature of the environment that we as science teachers create. Is the classroom environment that we create characterized by the learning of material presented as series of "nonsense syllables"? Do students in the classroom interact with each other in meaningful ways and actually discuss the relevance of what they are learning? Are students considered to be intelligent, curious, problem-solving individuals or as empty receptacles in need of a fill-up?

This chapter explores various perspectives on classroom learning environments and focuses on the following goals:

1. Cooperative learning is described and several models of cooperative learning currently being used in classrooms are compared.
2. The steps needed to implement cooperative learning models in the science classroom are identified.
3. The cooperative learning model that is the basis for the science learning units in Part Two is described.
4. The ways in which educational tools and technology—microcomputers, educational television, videodiscs, manipulatives, and print—can be used to humanize the cooperative learning environment are explored.

Cooperative Learning—a strategy for your classroom?

In Chapter 1, I alluded to using cooperative learning as an organizing structure for the classroom. In this chapter I would like you to consider cooperative learning as a potential instructional format for your classroom.

Consider the following questions:

1. What is cooperative learning?
2. What evidence supports using cooperative learning as an instructional format in the science classroom?

Cooperative learning is an instructional format in which students work together in small groups to achieve a particular goal or complete a task. A variety of cooperative learning models have been developed, field tested, and evaluated. Some of them delineate how tasks are structured and how groups are evaluated. In some models, students work together on a single task; in others, members of the group work independently on an aspect of a task, pooling their work when they are finished.

Groups may be evaluated in a variety of ways. In some models, the evaluation is based on the sum or average of individual members' performances; in others, the entire group's performance is evaluated. Methods of evaluation can stretch from traditional testing and grading to self-evaluation.

The reason why teachers are drawn to cooperative learning may include one or more of the following:

1. Cooperative learning is presumed to raise the academic performance of students, because they help and support each

other rather than compete with each other. If teachers reward groups, individuals in the groups will work harder.

2. Students can learn from each other. High-ability students can share their knowledge, and low-ability students can be helped.

3. Cooperative learning is an alternative to competitive learning, which is a disadvantage to slower students or students who have been turned off to school. Stallings and Stipek report that simply being a member of a successful group, regardless of the student's own performance, allows the student some of the advantages of success, such as a heightened perception of their own ability, satisfaction, and peer esteem.[1]

4. Cooperative learning improves relationships between ethnic groups; if students from different ethnic groups work together, they will learn to appreciate each other's strengths and begin to develop friendships. Janet Christ-Whitzel, in an extensive study on multi-ethnic school environments, reported that "small-group cooperative learning methods . . . may have important possible applications and positive results in desegregated settings."[2]

Evidence to Support Cooperative Learning

There is extensive research to support the use of cooperative learning in the classroom. However, it is important to note that even though cooperative learning models have positive effects on cognitive and attitudinal learning, they will be successful only in appropriate contexts, and only if the teacher understands their philosophy and is committed to their use.

Some evidence in support of cooperative learning models is presented below; further evidence can be examined by referring directly to the studies cited in this chapter.

Perhaps the most powerful evidence in support of cooperative learning models is reported by David and Roger Johnson in their work

The Effect of Learning Environment on Cognitive Learning[4]

Cognitive Outcomes	Cooperative	Competitive	Individualistic
1. Mastery of factual information			X
2. Retention, application, and transfer of factual information, concepts, and principles	X		
3. Verbal abilities	X		
4. Problem-solving abilities	X		
5. Cooperative skills	X		
6. Creative abilities: divergent and risk-taking thinking, productive controversy	X		
7. Awareness and utilization of one's capabilities	X		
8. Perspective—role-taking abilities	X		
9. Speed and quantity of work on simple drill activities		X	
10. Individualistic skills			X
11. Simple mechanical skills			X

on cooperation, competition, and individualization.[3] The Johnsons have done extensive research on comparing cooperative learning to competitive and individualistic models of instruction. As seen in this chart from their book, cognitive outcomes are facilitated more in cooperative learning environments than in competitive or individualistic environments. The Johnsons also report that when comparisons are made among these three formats, affective outcomes are favored in cooperative learning environments. They found, for instance that students developed more positive attitudes about themselves in cooperative classrooms. They also found that the following additional affective outcomes were facilitated more favorably in cooperative classrooms.

1. Emotional capacity
2. Enjoyment and satisfaction of learning
3. Positive attitudes toward school
4. Reduction of prejudice and bias
5. Acceptance of and appreciation for cultural, ethnic, and individual differences.
6. Development of interpersonal skills

In *How to Encourage Girls in Math and Science*, Skolnick, Langbort, and Day suggest the use of cooperative groups to help girls overcome their anxiety in science and mathematics:

> *Girls and boys grow confident and able by building on what they have learned to do easily, well, and with interest. From a young age, female socialization emphasizes social skills, a more cooperative style of learning, verbal skills, and a keen interest in relationships and the daily lives of people. If we structure our math and science tasks around these competencies, girls will find their involvement less anxiety-ridden, more interesting and more natural in conjunction with their other activities. Cooperative work will maximize opportunities for talking and interaction among children.*

Skolnick, Langbort, and Day also emphasize that cooperative learning eliminates the feelings of isolation that are often connected with intellectual work, especially in science and mathematics. Furthermore, students feel more comfortable asking questions of each other, rather than adults. They also report success in setting up single-gender groups. They have found that single-gender groups are important because girls may not have had the informal mathematics and science experiences boys have had and may be intimidated by them. They suggest postponing the formation of mixed-gender groups until the latter stages of an activity, after girls have had a chance to gain confidence and support.[5]

Janet Christ-Whitzel did an extensive review of research pertaining to multi-ethnic school environments as part of a larger project to examine teacher training needs in multi-ethnic schools.[6] One aspect of her review was to look at classroom organization. She found that the use of cooperative learning teams was effective in producing enhanced student achievement, positive attitudes toward school and the specific subject matter, and positive attitudes toward others. Her review indicated that Jigsaw and Student Teams-Achievement Divisions (STAD) models of cooperative learning, which are discussed later in this chapter, were most effective.

There is ample evidence to support the use of cooperative learning models to improve cognitive, affective, and interpersonal relationships in the classroom. Cooperative learning is a powerful format for improving teaching in general and science teaching in particular. For further information on cooperative learning, see Appendix A.

Cooperative Learning Models—Putting Theory into Practice

There are many examples of cooperative learning. Which of the following models of cooperative learning are you familiar with? Have you used any of these models in your classroom?

Model	Familiar	Used
1. Student Teams-Achievement Divisions		
2. Teams-Games-Tournaments		
3. Jigsaw		
4. Group Investigation		
5. Co-op Co-op		
6. Team Assisted Individualization		
7. Learning Together		
8. Finding out/Descubrimiento		
9. Experiences		

In a survey I did in an in-service course on science and cooperative learning at the graduate level, only one of the 25 teachers enrolled had heard of any of the cooperative learning models, although they readily indicated that they were familiar with group work. They soon discovered that cooperative learning was more than group work. Let's find out about cooperative learning by examining five models that have been used in a variety of school settings:

1. Student Teams-Achievement Divisions (STAD)
2. Jigsaw
3. Co-op Co-op
4. Group Investigation
5. Experiences

Cooperative Learning Model 1: STAD[7]

If you are interested in implementing cooperative learning in your classroom, STAD is an excellent model with which to begin. I like STAD because you can easily implement cooperative learning into the traditional science curriculum; if a science textbook series is the mainstay of your curriculum, STAD requires little or no modification of materials. You prepare study sheets and quizzes on the material that the cooperative learning teams are studying. Most textbook series are organized very nicely for this approach, since they all include workbooks (skillsbooks, study manuals) and chapter quizzes and tests.

According to its originators—Robert Slavin and his colleagues at Johns Hopkins University—STAD is made up of five components, which are outlined below.

Class presentations The class presentation is a teacher-directed presentation of the material—concepts, skills, processes—that the students are to learn. The presentation can take the form of lecture, lecture-demonstration, or an audio-visual presentation. Many textbook series include hands-on science activities within the text, which could be considered an integral part of the presentation. If the material to be learned is a chapter in the textbook, you will have to plan several presentations.

Teams Teams should be composed of four or five students who represent a balance in terms of academic ability, sex, and ethnicity. The team is the most important feature of STAD, and it is important for you to take time to help the students understand that they will be working together to help each other learn the material.

After the teams are organized, they should complete approximately one lesson working together using prepared study materials. Worksheets and workbook activity pages can be used during the team learning sessions. You could also make up a set of questions, based on the objectives of the chapter, to use for the team learning session. Students should be informed that these worksheets or review sheets are designed to help them help each other get ready for the quiz. Within each team, students should work together to answer each question; they can work in pairs within each team, and then the pairs can share their work. To encourage team members to be responsible for each other, follow these suggestions:

1. Make sure that *each* member of the team can answer each question correctly.
2. Have students answer their own questions, without going outside the group or to the teacher, as often as possible.
3. Insist that team members explain their answers to the questions, especially if they are of the multiple-choice format.

Quizzes After the student learning teams have completed their work, administer a quiz to measure the knowledge they have gained. Students take individual quizzes and are *not* permitted to help each other. Again, this reinforces student responsibility for learning. You can write the quizzes or use the quizzes and tests that accompany the science textbook series.

Individual Improvement Score Assess an individual improvement score to encourage students to work harder from quiz to quiz. Establish a base score—the minimum score on the quiz—for each student; the improvement score is how much the student exceeded the base score on the quiz. Team scores are computed by adding the improvement scores of each team member.

Team Recognition Recognize the work of each team in a newsletter that announces the team scores and indicates the ranking of each team within the class; report outstanding individual performances, too. Sensitivity in reporting is required here. Please note that improvement in learning is as important as the scores students receive on the quizzes. Telling a student directly that he or she did an exceptional job on the last test works wonders for self concept. Use computer technology to create a team recognition newsletter.

Cooperative Learning Model 2: Jigsaw[8]

Jigsaw is a cooperative learning model in which students become experts on a part of the instructional material they are learning about. By becoming an expert, and then, in turn, teaching other members of their team, students are responsible for learning.

Jigsaw can be creatively modified to suit your tastes so that a variety of learning modes are used by students. Furthermore, students can become experts not only by reading information, but by interviewing others, viewing video tapes and film strips, doing hands-on activities, using a computer to connect with on-line information sources. As you read through this section, think about applying Jigsaw to your classroom and let the creative juices flow.

Jigsaw will work well in the science classroom because of the wide range of topics available. The premise of Jigsaw is that students become experts on a part of a topic and then teach what they have learned to other students. The following topics can easily be organized so that individuals on a learning team can focus on a single part:

1. Investigate the systems of the body: digestive, respiratory, circulatory, nervous, skeletal, and muscular.
2. Explore habitats and environments in which different animals live.
3. Investigate the Solar System: the inner planets (Mercury, Venus, Earth, Mars), the outer planets (Jupiter, Saturn, Uranus, Neptune, Pluto), the moons of the Solar System, asteroids, comets, and the sun.
4. Investigate meteorological phenomena: tornadoes, hurricanes, thunderstorms, blizzards.

Other topics suitable for Jigsaw include studying rocks and minerals, classifying plants and animals, identifying renewable and non-renewable energy sources, contrasting theories to explain scientific phenomena (such as the extinction of dinosaurs), comparing chemical elements, identifying types of organisms found in particular environments, learning about contagious diseases.

Three important elements of Jigsaw that you should be familiar with are outlined below.

Preparation of learning materials Develop an expert sheet and a quiz for each unit of teaching. If you are using a standard science text series, this will be relatively easy. First, divide the content into topics for the expert sheets. The expert sheet should communicate what students should do—read, watch a video, do an activity—and an outline of the topic in the form of questions.

Below are some examples of expert sheets used for fifth graders on the topic of oceanography in the *Holt Science* program.[9]

Expert Group 1: **Ocean Resources** **Holt Science, Grade 5**	**Expert Group 2:** **Ocean Life** **Holt Science, Grade 5**
Read pp. 43–45 View video: Exploring the Ocean. Answer these questions: 1. Name four resources we get from the ocean. 2. How would ocean farming help feed people on the earth. 3. What is desalination? 4. What are the main steps in the desalination process?	Read pp. 49–56 Perform activity: Removing oil from water, page 54. Answer these questions: 1. Give three examples of living things found on the ocean bottom near shore. 2. What is a food chain? 3. How does the ocean get polluted?

Teams and Expert Groups In Jigsaw, each student is a member of an expert group and a learning team. Distribute the expert sheets to each learning team and explain that each student will become an expert on some aspect of the topic everyone is studying. Assign each student to an expert group. In order to accommodate a class of 25 to 30 students you will have to create at least five expert groups.

Students should be given time to work on their topics prior to meeting in their expert groups. When the students are ready, have them move into their expert groups; assign different parts of the room for each group.

The activity within the expert groups will vary. Encourage diversity in how the students learn about their subtopics. Your expert sheets will be important; they will direct the students to activities, materials, and questions. Expert groups might do hands-on activities, read from various source books, use a computer for a game or simulation. In each case, the purpose of the expert group is to learn about the subtopic and prepare a brief presentation that they will use to teach the material to members of their respective teams.

Reports and Quizzes When the expert groups have finished their work, students return to their learning teams. Each expert now has the responsibility of teaching the topic to the other members. Encourage students to use a variety of teaching methods. They can demonstrate an idea; read a report; use the computer; illustrate their ideas with photographs, diagrams, charts, and drawings. Encourage the team members to discuss the reports and ask questions; each member of the team is responsible for learning about all the subtopics.

When the experts have reported to their groups, conduct a brief class discussion or hold a question-and-answer session. Encourage the experts to answer the questions.

A quiz should be administered to each individual; students cannot help each other during the quiz time. The same process of scoring and reporting that was described in STAD can be employed in Jigsaw.

As stated above, Jigsaw has great potential in the science classroom. It is superior to STAD because the students are given more responsibility for their own learning and there is a greater emphasis on the process of learning. Students are more actively involved and have to teach other students what they learned. Also students of all abilities are encouraged to be responsible to the same degree, even though the depth and quality of their reports will vary.

Cooperative Learning Model 3:
Co-op Co-op[10]

Co-op Co-op was developed by Spencer Kagan at the University of California, Riverside. (Spencer Kagan actually devised the model to include ten steps. I have abbreviated the steps to five; however I recommend that you examine his book, and use the ten steps if you wish to implement Co-op Co-op. Kagan has also produced two video tapes that explain and demonstrate Co-op Co-op. They are available from Media Resources, Sproul Hall, UC, Riverside 92521.) According to Kagan, Co-op Co-op is based on the following philosophy:

> . . . the aim of education is to provide conditions in which the natural curiosity, intelligence, and expressiveness of students will emerge and develop. The emphasis in this philosophy is on bringing out and nourishing what are assumed to be natural intelligent, creative, and expressive tendencies among students.

Co-op Co-op embodies many of the elements of STAD and Jigsaw. The major difference is that in Co-op Co-op, the goal is for each team to share their learning with the whole class. If you are interested in giving more responsibility to students in terms of what they wish to learn and learning how to learn, then you might want to implement Co-op Co-op in your classroom.

The elements of Co-op Co-op are outlined below.

Student-centered discussions Kagan suggests that students should have more say in what they will be learning. The purpose of the student-centered discussion is to have the students express their own interests in the subject to be covered. Student-centered discussions can follow the introduction to the unit during which time you have made formal presentations; conducted hands-on laboratory activities; assigned some reading on the unit; showed video tapes, slides, or filmstrip programs; and pursued a variety of other direct-teaching strategies. The introduction gives your class a core of information to bring to the student-centered discussion.

I like to encourage brainstorming during the student centered-discussion, followed by a brief discussion of the topics students are interested in. I also find it more effective to keep a record of the brainstorming session using colored marking pens on chart paper rather than a chalkboard. Display the chart on the bulletin board for future reference.

Team selection A comparatively democratic method can be employed to establish the teams for Co-op Co-op, although you should monitor their formation so that students join teams out of interest rather than out of friendship, and so on. However, letting students choose their own groups increases their sense of responsibility, and you can always re-group or discuss problems if they arise.

Topic selection and delegation of work Topic selection may be determined from the student-centered discussion, or you might create a list of topics based on the brainstorming session and have the teams select a topic from the list. It is important to note that the list was generated by the students, not by you. Each team should select a different topic; do not be concerned if there are more topics than groups. The students do not have to learn everything on the first go-around!

The students will need to analyze the topic they have chosen so that it can be broken into mini-topics. Each member of the team will be responsible for gathering information on the mini-topic and sharing it with the team. Students can investigate their mini-topics by gathering library information, doing a computer search, interviewing people, collecting materials, finding experiments that will help demonstrate the central idea. The students should prepare a brief report to be presented to the team.

Team presentations One of the attractive features of Co-op Co-op is that each team will make a presentation to the whole class. Students will have to cooperate to prepare a presentation for the class. In my own experience, student creativity can be facilitated if you encourage a variety of presentations and suggest that the least effective presentation is a lecture. Encourage teams to prepare presentations that involve the audience. Debates, demonstrations, hands-on learning activities, plays, video tape presentations, and computer simulations are effective ideas.

During the presentation, the presenting team is in charge and is responsible for setting up the room, gathering any audio-visual equipment and manipulative materials, and preparing necessary handouts. You should also encourage the teams to allow at least five minutes for questions and comments from the class. In some cases, you facilitate this aspect of the presentation.

Evaluation The approach to evaluation advocated in the Co-op Co-op model of cooperative learning can involve anything from no evaluation at all to a formal evaluation involving quizzes and graded reports. Somewhere between these extremes would be a safe bet. Students can evaluate their own presentations by discussing the strong and weak points, and you can give feedback to each team. A very effective evaluation technique is to have the class evaluate each group presentation. A simple form similar to the one shown below can provide the team with valuable feedback that can be used to improve future presentations. Again, no formal evaluation is required, and in some cases it is a good idea to let the learning and sharing be the reward.

Group Evaluation

Feedback Form[11]

Directions: Evaluate the group's presentation by checking a number for each of the questions below.

	Low	High
1. How effective was the presentation?	1 2 3 4 5 6 7 8 9 10	
2. How interesting was the presentation?	1 2 3 4 5 6 7 8 9 10	
3. How much did you learn from the presentation?	1 2 3 4 5 6 7 8 9 10	
4. What was the quality of the materials used in the presentation?	1 2 3 4 5 6 7 8 9 10	

What did you like about the presentation? _____

_____

What would you suggest the group change in the presentation? _____

_____

Cooperative Learning Model 4: Group Investigation[12]

According to the developers, the Group Investigation method is one of the most complex and ambitious forms of cooperative learning. Its philosophy is to cultivate democratic participation and a somewhat equitable distribution of speaking privileges to group members by the group chairperson. It also encourages differentiated role assignments within groups and between groups.

For Group Investigation, the class is divided into small groups of five students each, although there can be fewer per group. Groups can be formed on any basis you or the students choose. Each group plans their strategy for what and how they will study the topic. Furthermore, individuals or pairs select subtopics and decide how they will pursue them. Individuals or pairs report on their progress and results of their work to the small group. The small groups discuss the individual reports and then prepare group reports to be presented to the whole class.

The six elements that characterize Group Investigation are outlined below.

Topic selection Students choose specific topics in a general problem area. Students organize into small 2–5 member task-oriented groups.

Cooperative planning You and the students plan specific learning procedures, tasks, and goals consistent with the subtopics of the problem selected.

Implementation Students carry out the plans formulated in step 2. Learning should involve a wide range of activities and skills and should lead students to different kinds of sources both inside and outside the school. You counsel the groups by following their progress and offering assistance when needed.

Analysis and synthesis Students analyze and evaluate the information gathered in step 3 and plan how it can be summarized in an interesting manner for a class presentation.

Presentation of final product Groups give an interesting presentation of the topics studied. There is an attempt to get students involved in each other's work and to expand their perspective on the topic. You coordinate the presentations.

Evaluation You and the students evaluate each group's presentation and contribution to the work of the class as a whole. Evaluation can include individual or group assessment or both.

The Group Investigation method places maximum responsibility on the students for identifying what and how to learn, for gathering information, for analyzing and interpreting knowledge, and for communicating and sharing in each other's work. It is very similar to Co-op Co-op, and would have the greatest chance of success after students have had previous experiences in other forms of cooperative learning.

Cooperative Learning Model 5: Experiences

To apply cooperative learning more directly to science, I have developed a series of units and an approach to cooperative learning that I refer to as Experiences. These units place students in the center of the learning model, and encourage scientific investigation. I have chosen topics that deemphasize the normal boundaries of the scientific disciplines, focusing instead on natural phenomena, everyday examples, and problem-solving activities to acquaint students with real-world science. Experiences also emphasize the interdisciplinary nature of science and learning and provide a link between science and social studies, mathematics, language arts, reading, music, and art.

The elements of Experiences are outlined below.

1. Students become active science learners and members of a cooperative learning team.
2. Students develop critical thinking and problem-solving skills in the context of cooperative learning teams.
3. Students explore concepts, questions, and phenomena in one of several areas of science.

Details of how to implement Experiences and the factors to consider for the classroom can be found in the introduction to Part Two. Following is a list of Experiences and the focus of each cooperative learning unit.

Experiences: Science Cooperative Learning Units

Chapter	Experience	Focus
4	The Web of Life	The intriguing world of living things.
5	The "Wellthy" Syndrome	Holistic health and high-level wellness.
6	The Starship and the Canoe	Two vast frontiers: outer space and the earth's oceans.
7	Touch the Earth	The mysterious planet Earth
8	If You Were a Boat, How Would You Float?	Buoyancy and related physical science phenomena.
9	The Third Wave	The future: creating it and developing futuristic thinking processes.
10	Powering the Earth	The earth's energy resources and ecological concerns related to air, water, land minerals, plants, and animals.
11	Investigating the Natural World	Environmental science and ecological concerns.

Technology and the Cooperative Learning Environment

A cooperative learning environment is a special place. It is one in which students work together to answer questions or pose questions and then set out to answer them. In many cases, the only tools available to help students answer questions are textbooks, workbooks, dittos, and other print materials.

Human beings are tool makers and users, and the science classroom should make accessible a wide range of tools to ensure the development of creative problem-solving actions. Five areas of technology should be integrated into the cooperative learning environment: microcomputers, educational television and video tapes, videodiscs, manipulatives, and print materials.

The value of each tool in a cooperative learning environment is discussed below.

Microcomputers

The microcomputer is the perfect tool for enhancing the work of cooperative learning teams. A microcomputer in the learning environment empowers individuals and teams to work on a wide variety of science topics.

The possibility of having at least one computer in the classroom is increasing as time goes on; the discussion that follows is based on the assumption that you have only one. The most advantageous approach is to set up a computer center, housing the following items:

- Computer
- Video monitor
- Printer
- Disc drive
- Modem (optional)
- Software
- Computer literature—books, articles, magazines

Access to the computer center should be controlled by a sign-up system; each team could use the center once or twice a week.

In the cooperative classroom, students should be given more and more autonomy in solving problems and in developing and improving their ability to think, and this should be kept in mind when considering how the computer is to be used in the classroom. Following are some of the uses to consider:

1. The computer as an information tool.

    Suppose students are working on one of the following topics:

    a. Migrating birds in North America
    b. Characteristics of mammals in the Southwestern U.S.
    c. Properties of the ten most common elements
    d. Physical and chemical properties of the five most common elements
    e. Habitats of animals in North America

    Databases such as Scholastic's *Curriculum Data Bases in Life Science and Physical Science* provide the raw information students need in order to investigate each of these. Students can find data to help them answer their questions and easily access the information.

    A more powerful use is the dial-up system in which a modem enables the computer to become part of a telecommunications network. Databases can be accessed from commercial companies, or students can communicate with other classrooms around the country and conduct computer conferences to share information.

2. The computer as a science laboratory.

    The educational software that is now available will enable you to turn your computer into a science laboratory and activity center. The computer can be used to simulate nature quickly without the usual mess, and with the addition of a simple interface box and probes, it can be used to do sophisticated science experiments with ease.

    It is helpful to organize the workspace in the computer area of the classroom so that teams can perform investigations. Students should be encouraged to think in terms of "What if . . ." and be provided with the materials and knowledge that will enable them to set up experiments that test their questions. Simulations allow one or more variables in an experiment to be controlled. High-quality software is available in the areas of weather forecasting, space flight, flight simulation, ecology, volcanology, and other earth phenomena.

    An earth-science simulation called *Volcanos* from Earthware Computer Service allows students to predict eruptions of mythical volcanos. The *Galactic Prospector* from Walt Disney Personal Computer Software gives students access to data gathered from satellites and core drillings as they search for oil, gas, and various minerals.

Although simulations are no substitute for real experimentation, they do help students develop concepts and the ability to solve problems using logical methods. Simulations are also easy to use and apply to the ongoing curriculum and typify a way to use the computer in science teaching for more than drill and practice. For teachers who are looking for a way to start using the computer in the cooperative classroom, simulations and games offer the greatest flexibility and ease of implementation. Cooperative teams can be assigned to the computer for specified work periods. Given the availability of educational software on the market today, you will have no problem finding at least one simulation for each unit you teach.

The names and addresses of the major educational software firms are listed in the Appendix. You can write to them to obtain their latest catalogs.

Some software packages enable students to conduct simulated experiments. One is the *Science Tool Kit* by Broderbund, which comes with a light and temperature probe, an interface box that connects to the Apple game port, and a well-written user's manual and experiment guide. The manual contains a large collection of experiments that students can carry out.

A second product to consider is the *Bank Street Laboratory*, which is a component of the microcomputer software program called "Whales and Their Environment." It is part of the science and mathematics learning package called the *Voyage of the Mimi* published by Sunburst, Inc., Pleasant, New York. The *Bank Street Laboratory* contains hardware and software to convert an Apple computer into a laboratory instrument. With the hardware and software installed, the laboratory can be used to measure light, temperature, and sound. It can also produce light and sound for use in various experiments. The *Bank Street Laboratory* enables teams to conduct experiments indoors and out. Students can use the lab to collect long-term data, often very valuable in science projects. Experiments that are not easy for students to perform can be carried out with the lab. Students can measure the speed of sound and carry out many more sophisticated experiments.

3. The computer as a science writing tool.

Students who are members of cooperative learning teams will have more and more responsibility for communicating what they are learning, writing reports, and keeping track of their progress. Recent research on the use of the computer as a writing tool has shown that it can be used to stimulate written communication. Students ages 9 to 13 can improve their writing if they are given good reasons to write and if they are given appropriate tools. One valuable publication, *Writing and Computers* by Collette Daiute (Addison-Wesley, 1985), has excellent discussions on how to use the computer as a tool to help very young writers, early adolescent writers, adolescents, and college students.

In the cooperative learning environment, I recommend that you make the following tools available to the students to help them improve their writing and at the same time show them how important and interesting writing in science can be.

Word processing programs There are many excellent word processing programs available. The one that I recommend for early adolescent students is the *Bank Street Writer Plus*. This program is very easy for students to master, and it is a fully prompted program every step of the way. It also has options such as a spelling checker and a Thesaurus, two tools that are invaluable for student editors.

Writing formats Students can be helped if they are given specific writing formats—newsletters, articles, stories, book reports, for example. Once they learn a format they can apply it to different topics. Students should have an opportunity to engage in a variety of science writing on different topics using different formats. Writing a newspaper article, a science report, an advertisement, a fictional story, or a book report can be used to explore topics such as "Dinosaurs found in the Galapagos Islands," "A visit to Mars," "The eruption of a volcano."

One of the most valuable formats in the science classroom for students working in cooperative teams is the science log, which can be kept on the computer. From time to time a hard copy can be printed out and added to a loose-leaf notebook. The log should be the main focus of the students' writing experiences. (See pages 48, 49)

Another format that I have found useful is the team newsletter, which can report a variety of each team's activities:

1. Short content articles about the topic the team is studying.
2. Biographies of people who have done work related to the topic.
3. Special columns such as letters to the "super science reporter" or "Dear Scientist."
4. Letters to the editor.
5. Editorial comments about science issues and problems related to the topic.
6. Current events in science that relate to the unit or to special topics.

The Newsroom is a journalistic software program by Springboard that has been used successfully by many teachers. With *The Newsroom* teams can design, write, and illustrate a professional quality newsletter.

Educational Television

Television, including video tapes, is a technology that has been around a long time but has not been used effectively in the classroom. Each cooperative classroom should include a video center equipped with a VCR, television monitor, and video tape library or access to one.

One of the best examples of how educational television can be used in science and mathematics is the *Voyage of the Mimi*, which was developed by the Bank Street College of Education. Organized around a 26-unit television series that depicts the adventures of a floating whale-research laboratory, it combines television viewing with lavishly illustrated books and computer games that simulate the way scientists and navigators work. To some educators, *The Voyage of the Mimi* is the flagship of using television in science learning.

Videotaped programs can be used to great advantage in the science classroom because much of what teachers want to present, especially in the area of life science and ecology, involves natural environments. The camera images can bring topics alive, and students can observe first-hand how scientists work and consider future careers. Quality video programs are highly motivating and can provide the impetus for a team to begin its work.

Videodiscs

One step beyond videotape is the videodisc. Videodiscs are records that can store thousands of frames of information in a quality that is superior to videotapes. For example, every NASA rocket launch can be contained on one videodisc.

Combining videodisc technology with the computer gives students an even more powerful learning tool. In *Children, Computers and Science: Butterflies and Bytes*, Joe Abruscato describes the application and use of the integration of videodisc technology with the computer in the following way:

> *The videodisc offers such great potential because it is able to respond to you. Film can't do this. Videocassettes can't do this. Only videodisc technology coupled with microcomputer technology provides this capability. It is a marriage of technology that brings with it the possibility of having teaching programs that are truly responsive to the learner. The images and sounds encoded on the inner aluminum surface of a videodisc can be instantly projected to our eyes and ears as a response to pressing the keys of a microcomputer keyboard or using some other input device. What it projects depends on what we do. Software programs can be written to cause the videodisc to respond to the student as if the videodisc system had an intelligence of its own.*

Manipulatives

Manipulatives are not often included in a discussion of technologies, yet science materials—rocks, sand, chemicals, water, glassware, balances, thermometers, microscopes, hand lenses—that students will manipulate during hands-on activities are an integral part of classroom technology. All too often, manipulatives are hidden away in storerooms and closets, are given a low priority when budget time comes around, and are considered too messy for the classroom.

Manipulatives can be organized by science topic or unit content and kept in boxes of various sizes. Shoe boxes or cardboard drawers should be labeled appropriately and can be organized into a storage system as shown on the following page.

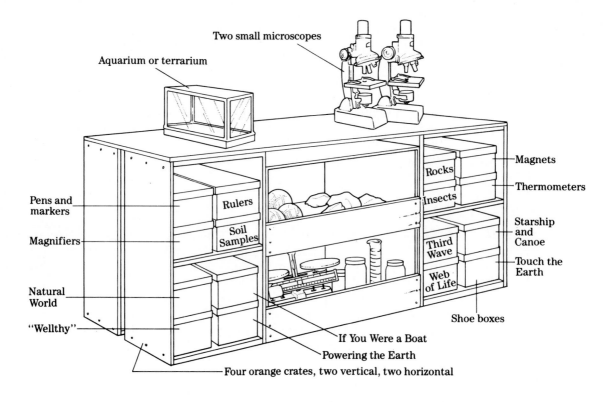

Two small microscopes

Aquarium or terrarium

Magnets

Thermometers

Rocks

Insects

Pens and markers

Rulers

Magnifiers

Soil Samples

Starship and Canoe

Third Wave

Touch the Earth

Natural World

Web of Life

"Wellthy"

Shoe boxes

If You Were a Boat

Powering the Earth

Four orange crates, two vertical, two horizontal

Print materials

A discussion of print materials leads to the topic of reading in the science classroom. In the classroom that I have been describing, reading will be viewed as an integral part of science learning. However, reading materials will include a variety of sources. Too often, the only material that students read in science is the textbook, and more often than not, they read it simply to answer the questions at the end of the chapter.

An excellent source of ideas to help with reading and science is Judith Thelen's book, *Improving Reading In Science*. She offers many suggestions for diagnosing reading problems in science, provides many types of prereading activities, and provides examples of the use of guided material to help students read print material. As she says, the textbook and other print materials are tools to help the students understand science.

In the Experiences that follow in Part Two, a great emphasis is placed on relating science to other disciplines. Language arts and reading are two powerful connections for the science teacher. Literature—science fiction in particular—provides an excellent source of ideas and incentives for developing interest in the cooperative science classroom. Biographies of scientists, adventure books about prehistoric animals, and the literature that deals with ethics, values, and attitudes are powerful additions to your science reading agenda.

Don't let people tell you that reading about science is a thing of the past. Scientists probably spend as much time reading as they do

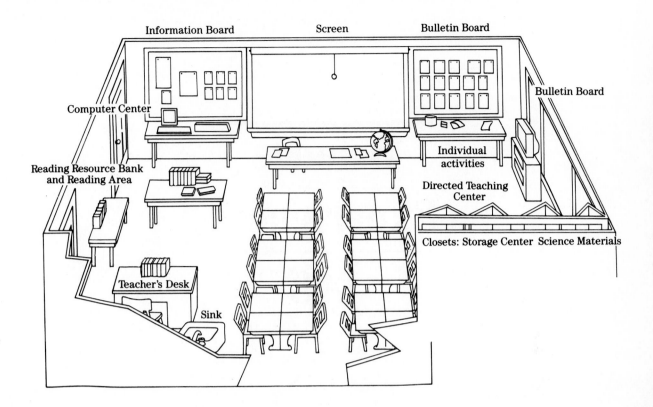

Information Board   Screen   Bulletin Board

Bulletin Board

Computer Center

Individual activities

Reading Resource Bank and Reading Area

Directed Teaching Center

Closets: Storage Center Science Materials

Teacher's Desk

Sink

experimenting, and it is legitimate to encourage reading in the science classroom to the same degree.

The classroom that integrates cooperative learning methods and the technology of teaching and learning will have a special look. The model shown below reflects the following ideas:

1. Arrangement of tables and chairs for cooperative learning teams
2. Provision for whole class learning and discussion sessions
3. Computer center .
4. Videotape, television center
5. Manipulative science equipment storage area
6. Reading resource bank and reading area
7. Bulletin boards
8. Teacher work and preparation area

Looking Back

As I review this chapter I am struck by all that is known about learning environments, especially the superiority of cooperative learning environments over individualistic and competitive ones. But it is the soul of the teacher that creates and determines the nature of the environment rather than the strategies and methods that are used.

Learning environments are created by people, and in this case, you will make the difference. The development of learning environments conducive to cooperative learning will be created by educators who are courageous and forward looking.

Science
Experiences
Log

NAME _____

Science Log

Topic: _____

Date: _____

Page reference: 44

LEARNING AND TEACHING IN THE COOPERATIVE CLASSROOM

The best teachers also know how learning takes place; they know how to apply the principles of learning, and thus they are living embodiments of a parallel principle: all young people can learn. This conviction is at the heart of the teaching profession.

ELIOT WIGGINTON
Sometimes a Shining Moment: The Foxfire Experience

Several years ago, I visited a classroom that had the kind of teacher that Eliot Wigginton speaks of. At the time, Marcia Markwith taught a seventh grade learning disabled class in a school district near Atlanta; she now teaches in Oregon. She told me about the following experience she had with her students:

The game we played had amazing results. I never thought the students would enjoy and learn as much as they did. We divided the class into two teams, with the first assignment that each was to make a cell. First we asked for volunteers to be the cell membrane. The students who became the cell membrane had to encircle everyone else in their group. Those inside were then faced with the problem of choosing who would be the cytoplasm and who would be the cell brain—the nucleus. Students actually bickered over who would be the mitochondria! The nucleus was hoisted aloft on some strong shoulders, then the fun began. Instructions emerged from the nucleus in the form of command statements: "consume that food," "eliminate that waste," "move to the left," "move to the right." We even went through the process of cell division, and to top it off, we had an amoeba race!

Marcia Markwith's experience is typical of teachers who understand how students learn and are willing to plan lessons that take into consideration the wide range of motivational learning activities. Teachers like Marcia approach learning and teaching from a holistic point of view. In the lesson she conducted with her students, feelings and emotions were as important as the content she was trying to teach. The students were engaged in the learning activity, acting out the behavior of a living cell.

In this chapter, learning and teaching will be viewed from a holistic point of view. Holistic teaching is an attempt to synthesize various modes of learning. It is an integrating process in which teachers attempt to plan lessons that combine different types of learning. Feelings and emotions as well as personal opinions about science topics are as important as science facts and concepts in a holistic approach to teaching.

In this chapter I will explore holistic teaching by discussing the concept briefly and then presenting sample lessons from the various learning modes that comprise the holistic model.

Holistic Teaching and Learning

Holistic teaching and learning is a balanced system that addresses the total student. The strategies that are used in holistic teaching encompass a whole-brain learning approach.

In recent years, educators have paid close attention to the findings of brain researchers regarding insights into the way the human brain functions. Some researchers believe that the right and left hemispheres of the brain are involved in quite different aspects of thought. They think that each hemisphere of the brain specializes in the way information is processed. The left brain appears to dominate in linear, time related, and sequential functions; the right brain dominates in special, holistic, pictorial, and nonverbal functions.[1]

Because of the desire to apply research findings and a genuine attempt to improve curriculum, educators have created modes of learning that are related to the brain researchers' discoveries. At least two learning modes have emerged.[2]

Left-mode learning Students who prefer left-mode learning usually organize and analyze information using logic. They frequently must force themselves to grasp the overall concept, to see the broad implications of the new information, and to recognize patterns or cycles.

Right-mode learning Students who prefer right-mode learning look immediately for the whole picture and seek sensory information and the overall implications. They prefer to see the whole before examining the parts. Right-mode learners tend to look for patterns and for purposes.

These two modes will be applied later in this chapter. Two other modes to expand the view of holistic education can be added to left- and right-mode learning.

Physical-sensory mode learning Students who prefer physical-sensory mode learning prefer to come in contact with physical objects. They rely on the sense of touch and motion or movement to experience the world around them and use their keenly tuned sensors—sight, smell, touch, hearing, and taste.

Affective-mode learning Students who prefer affective-mode learning are in touch with their feelings and attitudes and tend to approach learning from a personal point of view. Affective-mode learning fosters the clarification of values and the moral development of the learner.

As with any model, there is the danger of oversimplification. There is much controversy surrounding brain-hemispheric research and its application to teaching. For example, Leslie Hart, author of *How the Brain Works*, says:

> That left and right hemispheres divide the brain's work is now largely beyond question, but exactly how any one brain combines use of the two sides is highly individual and subject to change. While study of hemisphericity has been shown to have practical value for instruction, my associates and I support a broader and deeper approach to adapting education to the ways the brain works.

Barbara Vitale, who has written extensively on the left-right brain issue, had this to say:

> Recently the right-brain, left-brain model has been criticized as too simple. Whether that is true or not, two facts remain. First, schools now emphasize more skills connected to the left hemisphere than those associated with the right. Second, children who are not doing well in school often do better when taught in a whole-to-part approach, which uses visualization, art, music, and movement. Such methods can be as

*simple as showing a completed model of the activity
or using colored overlays in reading. Teachers and
school systems that have tried this approach have experienced improvement in attendance, test scores,
and other measures of achievement.*

A holistic teaching model focuses attention on the fact that learners possess a variety of ways to learn. Holistic teaching is by its very
nature eclectic, and draws upon a wide body of research and practice. The simple schemata shown below identifies the four modes of
learning in the holistic model presented in this chapter. The student is
able to learn using all these modes.

Teaching holistically requires planning and carrying out a wide
range of lessons. In order to provide you with insight into holistic
teaching, I have included brief background information, sample science lesson plans, and pertinent teaching techniques for each mode.

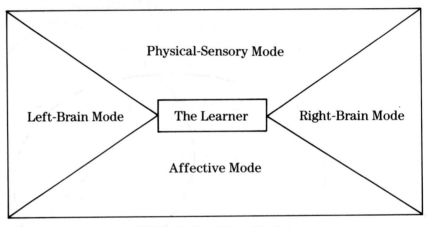

Holistic Teaching Model

Lesson Planning

Lesson planning can be a creative process in which you set a course
for a group of students in the hope that their journey will be enjoy-
able and worthwhile.

Lesson planning is one of the most important aspects of teaching,
yet it is a highly underrated aspect of the teaching process. Successful
teaching is largely dependent on superior planning and the careful
establishment of the learning environment, which was discussed in
Chapters 1 and 2.

Although there are many lesson plans in this book, it is important
that you realize that the most successful teachers create their own
plans, often modifying and adapting ideas they have seen elsewhere.
Following are some suggestions that might be helpful in designing and
modifying science lesson plans.

Examine science lesson and activity sources. Following are several
recommended sources for science lesson ideas:

Abruscato, Joe and Jack Hassard. *The Whole Cosmos Catalog of
Science Activities*. Glenview, Illinois: Scott, Foresman, 1978.

Blough, Glenn O. and Julius Schwartz. *Elementary School Science and How to Teach It*. New York: Holt, Rinehart and Winston, Inc. 1984.

DeVito, Alfred and Gerald H. Krockover. *Creative Sciencing: A Practical Approach*. Boston: Little, Brown and Company, 1980.

Skolnick, Joan, Carol Langbort, and Lucille Day. *How to Encourage Girls in Math & Science*. Englewood Cliffs, N.J.: Prentice-Hall, Inc. 1984.

Stein, Sara. *The Science Book*. New York: Workman Publishing, 1979.

Wolfinger, Donna M. *Teaching Science In The Elementary School*. Boston: Little, Brown and Company, 1984.

Design lessons that help students build confidence. When students are not engaged in activities and lessons that build confidence in their ability to solve problems and learn science, they soon turn off to science. An activity I like to do with students and teachers when I first work with them involves giving them an object—I usually choose a fossil. I place the fossil carefully in their hands and tell them not to look at it. I ask them to list their observations about the object and even draw a picture of it without looking at it. Then I ask them to guess whether they think it is natural or human-made and how old they think it is. After sharing ideas, the students look at the fossil and add observations to their list.

Lesson plans and activities that build confidence, such as the fossil activity described above, have the following characteristics:[8]

- Each student is successful.
- Learning tasks have many approaches.
- Learning tasks have many right answers.
- Guessing and testing is encouraged.
- Estimating is encouraged.

Consider the use of manipulative materials. Manipulative materials and science lessons should go together like peanut butter goes with jelly. It is not necessary to use highly specialized and sophisticated equipment. In fact, as you examine the lessons in this book, you will note the reliance on easy-to-find materials—straws, sand, water, string, paper cups.

You are in good company if you consistently plan lessons that use manipulative materials. Piagetian researchers believe that students need physically to manipulate objects before they are able mentally to manipulate abstract concepts. The experience of manipulating and handling objects such as rocks, mirrors, magnets, and thermometers should not stop at the end of the elementary grades. Junior high and middle school students need the experience of concrete learning, especially if they did not receive adequate exposure to it during their early learning years.

What social arrangement will be used? In this book learning teams are emphasized; however, good teaching employs a variety of arrangements, from working alone to working with the whole class. The social arrangements you use for your lessons will be determined by the goals you have for the students.[10] There are several options open to you. Students can work independently, in pairs, in cooperative teams, or as a whole class.

Independent work can take different forms. In some cases you might have students work at their own pace without pressure in order to improve their skills or ability in some area of science. If you employ the computer as a learning tool, students can be given time to work alone on simulations or models in order to give them confidence in their ability to do things independently.

Other social arrangements are designed to improve communication skills and the ability to get along and work with other people. In designing lessons involving students working together, it will be important to help them identify their roles and responsibilities. If you are doing a whole-class activity, each student needs to know how to interact within that structure. Lessons in which students work in pairs and cooperative teams will greatly improve students' communication skills.

Physical-Sensory Mode Learning

Learning science begins with the senses, and helping students develop an awareness of and the ability to use their senses is an important aspect of science teaching. Sensory awareness is a way of tuning into nature. Students achieve a connection with the environment through their senses. Students are equipped by the time they reach school age with a sensory apparatus that allows them to interact with the environment in many meaningful ways.

It is through sensory interaction with the environment that human intelligence grows and is cultivated. Joseph Pearce in *The Magical Child* emphasizes the importance of this point:

> *Through interaction, intelligence grows in its ability to interact. We are designed to grow and be strengthened by every event, no matter how mundane or awesome. The flow of nature and seasons, people, extreme contrasts, apparent catastrophes, pleasantries—all are experiences of the interaction to be enjoyed and opportunities for learning leading to greater ability to interact.*

Certain science process skills are related to sensory awareness, and you should be cognizant of these as you plan science experiences for your students. These processes—observing, classifying, measuring—are dependent on direct physical contact with physical objects. Thus the senses become important in the learning process.

Science Lessons for Physical-sensory mode learning

Using the Senses: Present a kaleidoscope of activities. The following activities present model lessons that can be used to help students develop and enhance their observational abilities by focusing on the senses. The activities help to review students' abilities to use process skills, or to introduce the importance of the senses to observation skills.

Sensory Activities

Sight	
Grades K–4	**Grades 4–8**
Find a variety of objects and use them to make a classification system. Have students sort objects of a kind—rocks, leaves, buttons, flowers, twigs, pens, shoes—into different groups based on various characteristics such as color, size, shape, feel.	Have students go outside at night and draw patterns of the stars. Ask how many constellations they can recognize. Obtain two small optical lenses or hand lenses. Have students use them individually to look at objects near and far. Have them hold both up to one eye about 12 inches apart and move them around until they are aligned, so that they can see through both of them. They now have a crude telescope. Tell them to look at various objects. Ask whether objects appear to be upside-down.

Taste	
Grades K–4	**Grades 4–8**
Obtain different brands of the same item such as peanut butter, crackers, or orange juice. Have students try to identify differences in each brand of a given substance. Obtain samples of a liquid for each of these four tastes: sweet, salty, bitter, sour. Have students dip a toothpick in one liquid at a time and place a drop at the four corners of their tongues to compare the flavors.	Blindfold a student. Have the student bite into an apple while you hold an onion under his or her nose. Try other combinations and have students discuss the effects. Find your favorite recipes for cooking various foods. Have students taste the foods and identify the dominant tastes.

Hearing	
Grades K–4	**Grades 4–8**
Take the students outside and have them make a list of natural and unnatural sounds. Record sounds in nature with a tape recorder—traffic, voices songs, birds, crickets, dogs, cats. Have students listen to the sounds and try to identify them.	Put blindfolds on students and lead the group on a blind sensory walk. During the walk have the students pay attention to the sounds they hear. How many different sounds can they hear? Can they hear any sounds they cannot identify?

Smell	
Grades K–4	**Grades 4–8**
Blindfold students and have them try to identify unknown substances only by smell. Putting small amounts of the substances in styrofoam cups and covering the cup with aluminum foil is a convenient way to prepare the material. Punch a few holes in the foil with a toothpick when ready to smell. Suggestions: lime, chocolate, pepper, mint, flower.	Give each students a vial containing a small piece of cotton that has been scented with some substance such as lime, chocolate, pepper, mint, vanilla. Prepare two vials for each substance. Tell students to find the vial that matches the smell in the first vial.

Touch	
Grades K–4	**Grades 4–8**
Blindfold students and have them touch various objects such as spheres, rocks, fruit, silky material, sandpaper. Have them describe the feel of each material. Place various objects inside shoeboxes. Cut a hole in the end, and let students stick their hands in to determine what is inside.	Have students dip their hands into water of varying temperatures from ice water to warm water. Have them estimate what they think the temperature of the water is. Give them thermometers to measure the temperature. Provide new bowls filled with water of varying temperatures. Have the students predict the temperature of the water with their hands and then check it with the thermometers.

Observing: Tune in to nature. This activity should be done outside. Find a site where everyone can sit in a circle to tune in to nature. If it is wet, large plastic sacks make excellent mats to sit on. Tell everyone that they are going to explore the environment around them using their eyes, ears, nose, and hands. Have students lie on their backs and begin to explore around them. They can feel the ground around them; they can look skyward to see clouds, birds, trees, or the sides of buildings; they can listen for sounds—birds and other animals, machines, airplanes, conversation; and they can smell things close by.

After a few minutes, have the students sit up and share their experiences: What did you see? What smells did you detect? What percentage of the sky was cloudy? How many different sounds did you hear? What were they?

Observing: Take a sightless walk. This activity involves a little risk; therefore you might want to prepare the students for a blindfolded walk by having them do at least one activity indoors using blindfolds. Give one blindfold to each pair of students in the class. In addition, for each pair prepare a bag that contains a variety of objects: a feather, a rock, a leaf, various pieces of fabric. Have one student in each pair put on a blindfold. Have the other student hold the bag while the blindfolded student reaches in and describes each object, one at a time. Without taking objects out of the bag, have the students reverse roles. They should then compare their observations.

Take a few minutes to allow pairs of students to work together. Have the student that is not blindfolded lead the other student by the hand around the classroom, touching various objects.

After these preliminary exercises, students should be ready to go outside and take a brief walk around the school grounds. Have the seeing students lead the blindfolded students to objects and encourage them to touch, smell, and listen. Be sure to insist that students focus on safety while doing this activity.

When the walk is completed give the students an opportunity to discuss the experience by asking the following questions. How did you feel when you started the walk? How did you feel at the end? What objects did you touch during the walk? Over how many different surfaces did you walk?

Classifying: Make hierarchical systems. Have students classify ten related objects—rocks, leaves, twigs, pencils, combs.

Give teams of students a collection of ten related objects to classify. Encourage them to classify the objects according to physical characteristics. Have them keep a record of their classifications on large pieces of newsprint.

Have the students compare their systems by describing them to each other. Teams can also challenge each other to classify the objects using the system they devised.

Measuring: Understand how water evaporates. Prepare the students for this investigation by showing them a small jar ¾ full of water. Tell them the jar was nearly full two days ago. Ask what happened to the water. Where did it go? How do you know? How could you measure the water that was lost? Accept all answers.

Divide the class into learning teams of three or four. Suggest that each group collect data on one or two of the following conditions:

a. An uncovered container of water.
b. A covered container of water.
c. A container of water half-covered with aluminum foil.
d. Additional containers of other liquids or exposed under different conditions—in sunlight, out of sunlight, on the radiator, away from heat, and so on.

Tell each group to report its results in milliliters or some other unit of measure. Students can collect and record data as shown in the sample chart below.

Evaporation Data

		Level (mL) at the end of			
Container	Original Level	Day 1	Day 2	Day 3	Day 4
c	150 mL	135	122	108	93

Students can also graph their data to discover how fast the water level changes for each condition.

At the end of four days, have each group present its data to the class. Have the students discuss how they measured the change in the water level. What caused the change? What do they predict the level will be on day five?

Right-Mode Learning

In some classrooms, students are involved in activities such as drawing a picture of gravity; creating a symbol for ecology; becoming an atom; walking backward through sand, blindfolded and without shoes; closing their eyes and imagining what it is like to take a space flight; creating a drawing of an improved version of the human body; imagining what it is like to travel backward in time to the age of the dinosaurs. These activities are examples of right-mode learning experiences. Right-mode activities are characterized as being spatial, holistic, pictorial, and nonverbal. Many right-mode activities involve the use of art, music, movement, and visualization. Activating the right brain means focusing more on nonverbal learning. It means, in some cases, substituting pictures and diagrams for words. Following are some sample right-mode lessons that you might want to try in your classroom.

Science lessons for right-mode learning

Flash cards Give each student five large index cards and a set of crayons. Provide a list of the concepts that were presented in the material they have just studied. Have students illustrate each concept and then pair off and challenge each other to interpret the pictures.

Students should be encouraged to draw pictures of concrete concepts (mammal, fish, rock, sediment) and abstract concepts (energy, heat, temperature, freezing point, sound).

Dramatizations There are many occasions when you can help students understand concepts in science by having them act out the behavior of an animal or imagine the dynamics of a phenomenon. Here is a list of ideas, any one of which could be used as a brief review or as the introduction to a concept.

Have students dramatize the gait of different animals in a relay race; a bird in flight; a germinating seed; the water cycle, including runoff, water seeping into soil, evaporation from the sea, condensation, cloud formation, dew, rain, melting snow; white light being separated into component colors by a prism; earthquake waves traveling through the earth; a volcano erupting; a simple chemical reaction such as sulfur combining with oxygen ($S + O_2 = SO_2$)—suggest that students dramatize the smell, too; a wet sheet drying on a clothesline; a rock turning into soil, being plowed, cultivated, eroded, and carried to the sea.

The electric game The following activity is a novel way to introduce the flow of electricity through wire. It takes about 10 minutes and is a nice energizer.

Have students kneel and form two lines facing each other. Students in each line should be holding hands. Everyone except the person at the head of each line should have their eyes closed. Place an object, such as a pencil, at the end of the lines. Flip a coin so that the two students at the head of the line can see. When the coin lands on heads, the students should squeeze the hand they are holding. The squeeze is then passed from hand to hand. When the end person gets the message, he or she should grab for the pencil. The team that gets the pencil earns a point. Rotate positions in the line and repeat so that each person gets a chance to be at the end and at the beginning of the electric line.

Visualization Visualization is an interesting basis for a science lesson. Some educators refer to visualization as guided imagery experiences or fantasy trips. The power of visualization is that it gives students insight into the concepts they have been studying and offers an opportunity to experience science on the right side of the brain.

Most visualization used in science is related to concepts or ideas. Visualization is much like a story; the teacher guides the students through the journey, encouraging them to create images and ideas. Visualization exercises should be done in a quiet, relaxed atmosphere. Some teachers dim the lights or play music and have the students relax quietly at their desks or lie on the floor.

After the visualization, many teachers follow up with some form of expression activity—working with clay, drawing a picture of the experience, writing in the science log, or pairing off and discussing the experience.

The following is an example of a visualization exercise. Read slowly, pausing after each sentence.

The Rock

With your eyes closed, imagine that you are walking in a forest along a trail . . . As you are walking along, you notice a single rock lying on the trail . . . It is the same rock you are holding . . . Imagine that you can make yourself very tiny—so tiny that you become smaller than the rock . . . Imagine yourself crawling around on the rock just like an ant would do . . . Use your hands to grab onto the rock as you crawl over it . . . Feel the rock . . . Is it rough or smooth? . . .

Can you crawl around on it easily? . . . Put your face down on the rock . . . Can you feel the warmth of the sun on the rock? . . . Are any creatures—plant or animal—living on the rock? . . . What are they? . . .

What colors do you see in your rock? . . . Can you dig your fingernails into any of the colors in your rock or is it too hard? . . . Smell the rock . . . What does it smell like? . . . Lie on your back on the rock and look up at the sky and the trees in the forest . . . How do you feel . . . Now carefully climb down off the rock, and when you reach the ground, gradually make yourself larger and larger until you are yourself again . . . When you are ready, open your eyes, and share your experience.

Creating your own visualizations Visualizations are easy to create, and during the course of a year, you will find many opportunities for their use. Some teachers make up visualizations and record them on audio cassette tapes for use by individuals or small groups. Here are some suggestions for creating visualizations.

Science Topic	Key ideas and questions
Paleontology	Living with dinosaurs. Which one is the largest? Which one do you fear the most? Do dinosaurs live in families? How do dinosaurs eat?
Glaciers	Being a piece of frozen water in a moving glacier. What sights might you hear? What effect might you and the rest of the glacier have on the rocks and land you pass over? What might you leave behind?
Hurricanes	Being a cloud traveling near the eye of a hurricane. How fast are you going? What directions do you move? How predictable are you? What damage do you do?
Rocks	Becoming a rock and being tossed along a stream bed. How might this experience change your appearance? Where might you end up? What sights might you see along the way?
Space	Being on board a space ship as it travels to a distant planet. How fast do you go? How does it feel to travel this far? What will you find out about the universe?
Thunderstorms	Being a tiny raindrop in a huge thunderhead. Where did you come from? Where are you going? Where will you fall? How can you change into hail?
Tornadoes	Spinning and spiraling upward with air in a tornado. Is your path predictable? What happens to objects in your path?
Volcanoes	Traveling down the crater of an active volcano. What do you see? What do you smell? How hot is it?
Water	Being an ocean wave crashing on the beach. What do you smell and hear? What kind of work do you perform on the beach? Being a bottle drifting along in the ocean. What fish swim up to greet you? Is the water around you clean and clear, or dirty and oily? Why? What are you doing in the ocean? Are there other bottles floating with you?

Left-Mode Learning

Left-mode learning activities and lessons can be just as inventive and challenging as right-mode activities. The left brain processes information in logical or sequential steps, and learning activities that help students develop this mode will be characterized by logical reasoning. Too often, activities that are indeed left-brain oriented involve such low levels of thinking that they bore students. The types of left-mode learning activities emphasized here are logical reasoning and problem solving.

Logical reasoning is, according to students of Piaget, a human skill that develops gradually during childhood. An important consideration in the science classroom is that students need to learn how to reason using concrete objects before they can move on to abstract reasoning. Physical-sensory mode learning and the use of concrete materials is a necessary prerequisite to logical reasoning.

The following left-mode learning activities are the cornerstones for planning lessons that emphasize logical reasoning.

1. Sorting, grouping, and classifying
2. Using deductive reasoning
3. Using combinatorial reasoning
4. Controlling variables
5. Using probabilistic reasoning

Science lessons for left-mode learning: Logical reasoning

Sorting rocks: In this activity students discover that objects can be sorted according to physical characteristics. You will need about 15 hand-sized rocks, a large sheet of newsprint, and crayons for each team of students. You can design a lesson on sorting in a variety of ways. The following are two methods that you might try.

Give each team the rocks and newsprint and ask them to sort the rocks into a number of groups. Have them put rocks together that they think look alike. Using this method, some groups will stop after grouping the rocks into three or four categories; others will come up with more narrowly defined categories. Have the students keep a record of their categories on the large sheet of newsprint as they group the rocks on the paper. When the rocks have been categorized, have each team give a brief report explaining the reasoning behind their categories.

A second way to do this activity is to direct the students to develop several stages of categories, or a hierarchical system. Have the students group all the rocks in a small circle at the top of the newsprint and tell them to draw a circle around the rocks. Tell the students to sort all the rocks into two categories on the basis of a single property—for example, dark rocks and not dark rocks. They should physically move the rocks to form these two categories. Have them continue separating the piles of rocks into categories by a single property until they cannot divide the rocks further. Again, have each team explain the reasoning behind their system.

Controlling the flight of a paper airplane: Logical reasoning can be encouraged in a lesson in which students learn how to control the variables in a system. A very convenient system to work with is the paper airplane. There is much written about the design of paper airplanes, and an excellent reference is *The Great International Paper Airplane Book* by Jerry Mander, George Dippel, and Howard Gossage (Simon & Schuster, 1967). If you want to go even further with this lesson, there is a computer program for the Macintosh called *The Great International Paper Airplane Construction Kit.*[3] It contains award-winning paper airplane designs and allows you to print them out and even design your own.

Give pairs of students copies of the template for the paper airplane and have them fold the paper following the instructions on the template (pages 77,78). Show students how to make flaps by making small tears in the tail end of the plane.

Students should work with their partners to find answers to a number of questions:

1. How can the distance a plane flies be increased?
2. How can the direction a plane moves—right, left, up, down—be controlled?
3. What modifications can be made in the design of the current plane to make it a better airplane?

Animal life span—using cooperative logic[4] The following is a logic activity that students can solve only by working cooperatively. Divide the class into teams of four to six students. Make one copy of page 79 for each team and cut each sheet apart to make the six separate clue pieces.

Tell students that they will be working on a logic problem and explain that figuring out a logic problem is like solving a mystery. Clues are used to reach the hidden conclusion. The process of using clues is similar to the reasoning used by doctors and mechanics diagnosing medical or mechanical complaints or by detectives solving crimes.

Give the students in each group one clue to the logic problem. If there are more than four students in a group, use the extra clues that are starred(*). All the problems can be solved with the four unstarred clues. The starred clues may be helpful but are not necessary for solving the problem. Students may read their clues to each other but *may not show them to each other.*

Science lessons for left-mode learning: Problem solving

Scientific investigation is at the heart of problem solving in science. Problem solving involves a variety of thinking processes, starting with observation and including asking questions, coming up with ideas, testing the ideas or hypotheses, carrying out experiments, recording results, drawing conclusions, and asking further questions. There are many examples that you can draw on to help students appreciate how scientists develop ideas, and the process they go through. The following activities illustrate how to help students understand the process of problem solving. The first one that should appeal to students because it is a success story and shows how scientific investigation can be helpful in solving important problems.

What is the big picture? In preparation, obtain photographs, slides, or pictures from magazines of whooping cranes and other endangered animals. Make a large drawing of the illustration of the model of science shown below, and make copies of the whooping crane story (pages 80–82) for the students to read along with you.

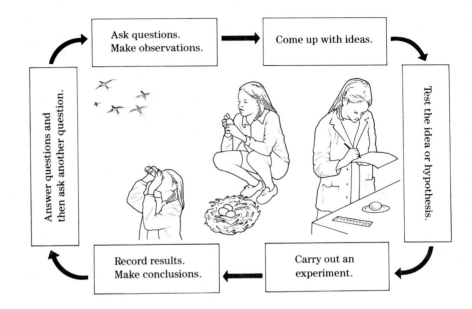

Start the lesson by showing the students a picture of a whooping crane and asking them to list what they know about it. Give a brief overview of the story and then read it aloud as the students read along. When you are finished, lead a class discussion focusing on the following questions:

1. What were some of the ways that Robert Allen studied the whooping cranes?
2. Why were scientists concerned about whooping cranes?
3. What do you think might have happened if scientists like Robert Allen had not studied whooping cranes?
4. Do you have some questions you would like answered?
5. How can this model of science help you answer questions?

Can a mountain last forever?[6] In this activity students perform investigations to find out how materials can be used to make mountains. They then will try to determine which material or combination of materials makes the best mountain—that is, the mountain that is least likely to erode away easily.

You will need to gather together the following materials for each team: paper cups, sand, soil, small rocks and pebbles, newspapers, and aluminum pie pans or trays suitable for collecting water.

Show students how to make a mountain by filling a paper cup with sand, soil, or rocks. Have them experiment making mountains with the various materials. Teams will build mountains with dry sand, moist sand, rocks and pebbles, dry soil or moist soil. Tell the students to determine the size of their mountains by measuring the height of material (sand, soil, rocks) above the top rim of the paper cup.

Have students perform an experiment in which they observe and compare what happens when they pour a cup of water (the amount of water poured on each mountain should be the same—one cup is plenty) over the mountain. Have the students place their cups in the pie pan or tray to collect the rainwater that runs off the mountain. (Note: the students will observe that a few rocks will tumble from the rock mountain, whereas a sand or soil mountain might be completely washed away.) Students can measure the amount of mountain left, and then make a graph comparing the effects of rainwater on different kinds of mountains.

Student teams can continue their investigation by asking questions about mountains or by conducting experiments to answer the following questions:

1. How does the height and steepness of a sand or soil mountain affect of the amount of erosion?
2. To what extent does plant growth affect the amount of erosion on a mountain?
3. Which would last longer, a sandstone mountain or a shale mountain?

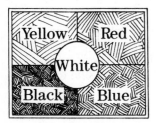

How do mealworms behave? Investigating the behavior of live animals is the focus of this problem-solving activity. You will need to have on hand a supply of mealworms, which are available at your local pet store, or can be obtained from any of the science suppliers listed in the Appendix. You will need to gather together mealworms, oatmeal, colored paper, popsicle sticks, talcum powder, tops of shoe boxes.

Have students design experiments to test the following questions:

> *If mealworms are placed in one end of a box, and a pile of oatmeal is placed in the other, what kind of paths do mealworms take to find the oatmeal? (Sprinkle the box lightly with talcum powder to record the paths.)*
>
> *If 5 to 10 mealworms are placed on a white disk in the center of a box surrounded by four colors, what color do the mealworms prefer?*
>
> *If mealworms are put into a T-maze (built using popsicle sticks), what direction do they turn? Previous experiments lead to the hypothesis that the direction the mealworm turns at the T choice point is related to the direction of the forced turn. Does this hypothesis hold?*
>
> *Do mealworms sense light, sound, or heat?*

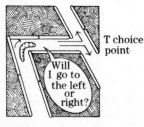
Forced turn
T choice point

Have students design experiments to test their ideas. Follow up the student experiments with a science conference on the behavior of mealworms. Give students time to prepare a brief report on their experiments and their results. They may want to make charts and diagrams to illustrate their oral reports.

Affective-mode learning

Affective-mode learning completes the holistic model of science teaching. Affective-mode learning involves the development of students' feelings, attitudes, values, and emotions. A holistic approach to teaching considers the development of the students' affective side to be as important as the ability to solve problems, think logically, and observe carefully. Emphasizing affective learning in science is not new; however because of the overemphasis on performance testing and achievement scores, little actual classroom time is devoted to affective lessons. As you will see in the Experiences in Part Two, affective-mode learning is given its fair share of time.

Affective science activities help students integrate feelings, attitudes, values, or emotions with cognitive learning. It is indeed possible to have an affective component to every lesson you teach by simply asking an affective question—How do you feel about installing nuclear power plants near highly populated areas? Do you think humans should keep animals in zoos? How do you feel about the topic we just studied?

The affective-mode activities that I have selected for this section will give you an idea of the range of possibilities. Bringing affective-mode learning into the science classroom will liven it up and will help students develop a more complete picture of learning.

Science lessons for affective-mode learning

The dilemma and value sheet[7] A dilemma is a situation that requires choosing among various alternatives. You might find it useful in science teaching to have students use a value sheet to help them deal with a dilemma. The value sheet describes the dilemma and then poses questions for students to ponder and answer. In the cooperative learning classroom, value sheets can be assigned to each learning team first to read about, second to discuss, third to write a brief report about, and fourth to discuss the dilemma with the whole class.

Here are a couple of examples.

Value Sheet: Clean Air

The people in Norway, Sweden, and Finland think that the fish in their lakes are dying because of the air pollution from Britain. Some of the forests in Germany are dying because of air pollution from automobiles. Some countries are making every effort to clean up the air. What is the price of clean, fresh air?

1. Should we continue to pollute the air—even if it means that somebody else suffers?
2. Cleaning the air from power stations and factories is expensive. Would you be prepared to help pay?
3. Since they do not pollute the air with smoke, would nuclear power stations be a better idea?

Value Sheet: Food and Famine

Some people say that the world is overpopulated and there just isn't enough food to go around. But others say that the world produces enough food for every person to have a full and varied diet. The problem is that very often the wrong food is grown in the wrong place. Vast quantities of food in the U.S. are thrown away. In some poor countries, a large portion of food is exported to rich countries.

1. What can be done about the fact that 500 million people in the world are not adequately fed?
2. Is the problem too big for us to solve?

Taking positions There are many issues in science that evoke deep feelings and attitudes. Often, however, students are not given the opportunity to express their feelings about an issue, nor are they given a chance to analyze their position in terms of how others feel. In this activity, students take a position along a line known as the values continuum[8] that is defined by the extreme positions that can be taken on the issue in question.

For example, if students are discussing the issue of cigarette smoking, they could be asked to take a position on the issue of whether smoking should be banned. Using the extremes identified on the issue, students can either mark their position on a sheet of paper, or take their position in line in the classroom.

Smokeless Sam: _____ Lungless Larry:
Refuses to even look   Smoked five packs a
at a cigarette and has   day for 30 years and is
vowed to run anyone   now attached to a
who smokes out of   machine to stay alive.
town.

Once students have taken a position along the smoking continuum, it is important to give them a chance to explain it. Encourage students to listen to each other's positions, rather than argue. Help students understand other points of view by having two students switch places on the line and defend their new positions.

Attitude Survey[9] There will be many opportunities to solicit the opinions and attitudes of your students about a variety of topics. Students can express attitudes about the science course they are taking, the specific topic they are studying, or the textbook they are using.

As an example of an attitude survey, I have selected the fear or anxiety that students have toward mathematics and science. In this activity you will have an opportunity to engage students in a discussion about the fear of math and find out whether boys feel any differently about it than girls do.

Divide the class into learning teams. Give each team a copy of the Math Skill Survey questions (page 83). Tell them that the survey questions represent problems that students in their grade level can solve. Tell the team that they have five minutes to answer the questions as a group. Explain that they will not have enough time to answer all the questions. The students should feel free to talk and discuss the problems among themselves. At the end of five minutes, tell the students to stop working.

Give each team member a copy of the Math Attitude Questionnaire (page 84). Tell them they have five minutes to answer the questions. Explain that they should complete the questionnaire without any help from their teammates. At the end of five minutes, have each team tally their responses. Then have each group report to the whole class what they learned about mathematics attitudes.

Combining modes for learning

The four modes for learning—physical-sensory, right, left, and affective—are theoretical, artificial categories. The discussion and activities highlight the four modes. In many learning situations, more than one mode may be used to solve problems or complete a task. In this section, I would like briefly to describe a few teaching strategies that have been developed to combine modes and facilitate problem solving. Some teachers call them creative problem solving strategies. They use a variety of skills and include brainstorming, networking, synectics, and lateral thinking. You will find many uses for these strategies as you begin to work with the Experiences.

Brainstorming

Brainstorming involves the explosion of ideas on a particular topic or problem, no holds barred. It is a linear process, and its goal is to generate a list of possibilities, alternatives, and choices. During the process, participants—teacher and students—should refrain from criticizing or judging any suggestions.

The first time brainstorming is used, tell the students that it is one method for solving problems. Learning how to use it today will enable them to use it any time in the future.

Have students face a chalkboard or a newsprint pad, and have colored markers or chalk on hand. Then follow this general procedure for conducting a brainstorming session:

1. Choose a problem for the class to work on. For example: How can we make our classroom more attractive and manageable for learning science? What arrangements should we consider for our fieldtrip? What are some subtopics that we might study?
2. Introduce the idea of brainstorming. Tell the class that the idea is to create as many ideas as possible for the topic or question under consideration.
3. Divide the class into groups of about five. Give each group a sheet of newsprint and a marking pen. Each group should select one person to record the brainstorming results.
4. Begin with a practice session. Ask each group to think of things they do in school. The recorder should list the students' remarks. After five minutes, stop the groups and have them count the number of items on their lists.

5. Make sure correct procedures were followed during the practice session by asking if everyone got a chance to participate and if they were able to refrain from criticizing one another.
6. Announce a topic for the groups to work on. You might spend a few minutes clarifying the topic, then tell each group that they have ten minutes to make their brainstorming list. Move around the room; offer encouragement and make contributions as necessary.
7. Ask each group to share its three most important ideas with the class. As they report their ideas, have someone list them on a separate sheet of newsprint for a class discussion.

Networking

Networking is a form of brainstorming that focuses on seeking relationships among items. The heart of networking is making connections. One advantage of the process of networking is that it is closer to the way our brain works, connecting one idea to another.

In networking, you write the topic in the center of a sheet of paper and branch out in all directions as dictated by the central idea, which is very different from starting from the top of a page and working down. Look at the ideas that have been jotted down around the central idea of space travel in the sketch below.

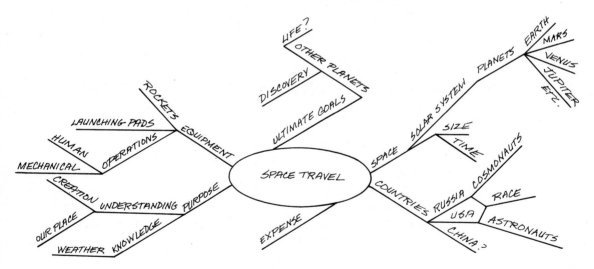

Networking can be used to plan a lesson, think about a topic, write a speech, or consider all sides of a problem. Here are some advantages to using networking with your students:

1. The basic idea is more clearly defined.
2. It is a creative way to think because it is open ended.
3. Each central idea has its own pattern, which will aid in remembering key points about the topic.
4. Information can easily be added, allowing for a richer product. [10]

Here is a networking problem that you can use with your students. Divide the class into teams of four. Identify one environmental problem, such as pollution or littering. Ask students what some examples of these environmental problems are, what causes them, how they can be eliminated. Now tell the students to write "Environmental Problems" in the center of a large sheet of newsprint. Have them create a network on environmental problems that is similar to the network on space travel.

After ten minutes, have a member from each team share the group's product. Display the networks for all students to examine.

Synectics: Making Connections[11]

Synectics was developed by William J.J. Gordon for use in business and industry, but it has also been used as an innovative approach in education. Synectics is a process in which metaphors are used to make the strange familiar and the familiar strange. Synectics can be used to help students understand concepts and solve problems.

According to Gordon, "the basic tools of learning are analogies that serve as connectors between the new and the familiar. They enable students to connect facts and feelings of their experience with the facts that they are just learning." Gordon goes on to say that "good teaching traditionally makes ingenious use of analogies and metaphors to help students visualize content. For example, the subject of electricity typically is introduced through the analogue of the flow of water in pipes."[12] The synectics procedure for developing students' connection-making skills goes beyond merely presenting helpful comparisons and actually evokes metaphors and analogies from the students themselves. Students learn how to learn by developing the skills to produce their own connective metaphors.

Gordon and his colleagues, known as SES Associates, have developed texts and reference materials, and provide training to help teachers implement synectics into the classroom.[13] Here are some examples of synectics.

Invent-O-Rama[14]

In this activity students will use connections to help make guesses about how some things might have been invented.

1. Many famous inventors got their ideas from the world of living things. For instance, think about the hypodermic needle that the doctor uses to give you a shot. It is clear that the idea for this invention came from the mosquito. How do you know? Because when a mosquito bites, it sucks blood up through its hollow nose that is the shape of a needle.

2. The Wright brothers were the famous inventors of the airplane. They got it to fly, but after it was up, they couldn't get it to turn. What use was an airplane that couldn't turn? They were stumped until one day when they happened to be watching a vulture flying above them. They noticed that the vulture lowered one wing when

it wanted to turn. They rebuilt the airplane wings so that they could be lowered and the airplane turned perfectly!

3. Inventors get ideas for inventions from the things they see around them. If you were an inventor, what ideas would these objects give you?

4. Look at the pictures of the things you, the great inventor, see every day. What one might give you an idea for inventing the boat? Explain how the boat idea came to you.
5. What object pictured above might have started you making the first fish net? Tell how your fish net idea and the object are alike.
6. Think of an animal that is not pictured that might have given you the idea of inventing the see-saw. What animal have you chosen? How did this animal give you the idea for the see-saw?

Simple Analogies

Give students analogies and then ask them to explain how the content (the heart) and the analogue (water pump) are alike. Here are some examples:

- The heart and a water pump
- Orbits of electrons and orbits of planets
- The nucleus of an atom and a billiard ball
- Location of electrons in an atom and droplets of water in a cloud
- Small blood vessels and river tributaries
- The human brain and a computer
- The human eye and a camera

Lateral Thinking[15]

According to its originator, Edward de Bono, lateral thinking is closely aligned with insight, creativity, and humor. De Bono believes that "the concept of lateral thinking is insight restructuring and is brought about through the rearrangement of information. *Rearrangement* is the basis of lateral thinking and rearrangement means the escape from the rigid patterns established by experience."

Lateral thinking is an excellent tool for the science teacher. It can be used to help students create new ideas, identify and solve problems, and learn science concepts.

De Bono has developed a vast array of lateral thinking techniques that are primarily designed to help improve the way the mind is used. The most important property of the mind, according to de Bono, is its ability to create patterns. Lateral thinking is a process that helps us break old patterns and generate new ones.

For example, how would you describe the figure shown at the left?

You might have said, "a carpenter's angle," but other descriptions include a gallows upside down, half a picture frame, two rectangles, and so on. As you can see, lateral thinking is a process of looking at something and seeing many alternatives.

Three techniques to bring lateral thinking to the science classroom are described below.

Generating alternatives This is the most basic principle of lateral thinking. It can be stated this way: Any particular way of looking at things is only one of many possibilities. In science teaching, we might think of this as a form of divergent thinking. Science teachers typically like to have students use different methods to solve a problem or come up with multiple answers to a question.

An important strategy when students generate alternatives is to set a quota for each situation. This prevents the students from stopping when a good alternative comes up. Three to five are recommended, depending on the task.

Following are nonverbal and verbal presentations that can be used for a lateral thinking lesson. For a nonverbal lesson, follow these steps:

a. Show a figure either on the chalkboard, overhead projector, or on a handout.
b. Ask students to generate a specified number of alternatives.
c. Ask for volunteer descriptions.
d. Encourage diversity in student alternatives. Do not judge the alternatives.

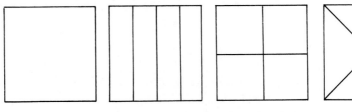

1. How would you divide a square into four equal pieces? What are three alternatives?

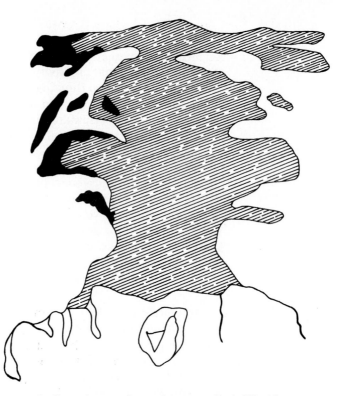

2. Show photographs or pictures, and ask: What do you think is happening in the picture? What three other things could be happening?[16]

Newspaper stories can be used in verbal presentations. For example, a newspaper story reports that an eagle has escaped from the zoo and is proving difficult to capture. It is perched on a high branch and is resisting the efforts of the keepers to lure it back to its cage. Have students describe the situation from the points of view of the ones involved: the zoo keeper, the reporter, the eagle.[17]

Columns such as Dear Abby can also be used. Encourage students to generate alternative ways to state a problem or generate alternative approaches to solving the problem.

Dear Dr. Woods   **September 25**

Dear Dr. Woods,

My sister and I have found four birds on separate occasions near our home. They all are baby birds. How can we help so that the birds do not get separated from their parents?

                               Concerned,

Students should come up with at least three ways of stating the problem .

1. How can we prevent the separation of young from their parents?
2. How can we prevent animals from being lost?
3. How can we return or take care of lost or injured animals?

The why technique The why technique is a game in which students learn to challenge assumptions. Younger students ask why questions because they don't know the answer. In this lateral thinking process, why is asked even when the answer is known.

To play the why game, you make a statement, and the students respond by asking why. You offer an explanation in the form of a statement and the students ask why. The why question can focus on some aspect of the statement. For example:

Teacher: Leaves are green.
Student: Why are leaves green?
Teacher: Because of chlorophyll.
Student: Why?
Teacher: Chlorophyll feeds the tree.
Student: Why does the tree need to eat?
Teacher: I don't know. What do you think?
Student: So it will grow.
Teacher: Why will food help the tree grow?

At any time, you can say, "I don't know. What do you think?" and reverse roles. Why sessions can begin with statements such as the following: The sky is blue. Trees have leaves. Leaves are green. Humans have two legs. The earth rotates. Birds lay eggs.

The design technique An important aspect of lateral thinking, the de-design technique helps students deal with innovation. Projects using design techniques can improve an existing thing, invent something to carry out, or apply science concepts in the design of something.

The following design technique projects can be used in science lessons, homework, or as projects for teams of students.

1. Redesign or improve an existing thing

   - The human body
   - The atom
   - Your aquarium
   - The science classroom
   - A bicycle
   - An airplane
   - A football helmet

2. Design or invent something

   - A sleep machine
   - A time machine
   - A machine to go to the center of the earth
   - A star ship
   - An antigravity machine
   - A perpetual motion machine
   - A fishing machine

3. Apply science concepts

   - Design a way to weigh an elephant (concept of mass and skill in using a balance)
   - Design a solar cooker (concept of solar energy)
   - Design a machine that uses one of the following concepts:

condensation, extinction, reproduction, heat, gravity, time, water pressure, air pressure, electric current

Your role in design technique projects is to encourage the students' work and provide a forum so that the projects can be discussed, examined, and displayed. Provide the students with large sheets of newsprint, colored markers, rulers, and any other measuring and drawing instruments they might need.

Looking Back

This chapter presented some challenges: How can we as science teachers tap the full potential of the students we teach? How can we design lessons that pique the students' curiosity? What kinds of learning activities can we design to pique the students' curiosity?

Each student has a different learning style, and this poses further challenges to us. Can we meet the individual needs of students by creating an environment that is comprehensive enough to include varying styles of learning? The holistic model is one approach with a comprehensive view of learning. Learning includes affective as well cognitive skills and the development of values and feelings as well as sensory encounters. Integrating the modes of learning—physical sensory, left, right, and affective—into the lesson plans and units is our goal.

As you continue in this book, you will find eight units of teaching, called *Experiences*, that were designed using the holistic model. The Experiences put into practice the theory that was discussed and explained in Chapters 1–3.

PAPER AIRPLANE TEMPLATE

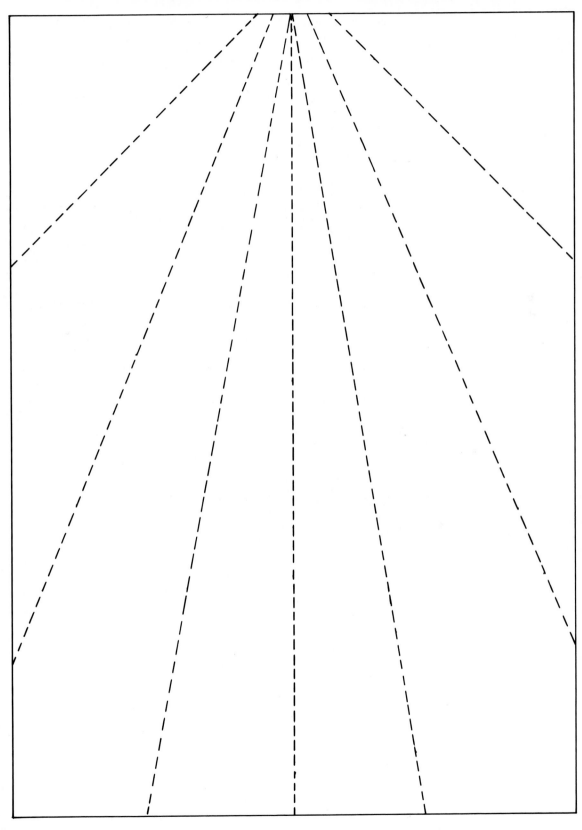

Page reference: 64

PAPER AIRPLANE DIRECTIONS

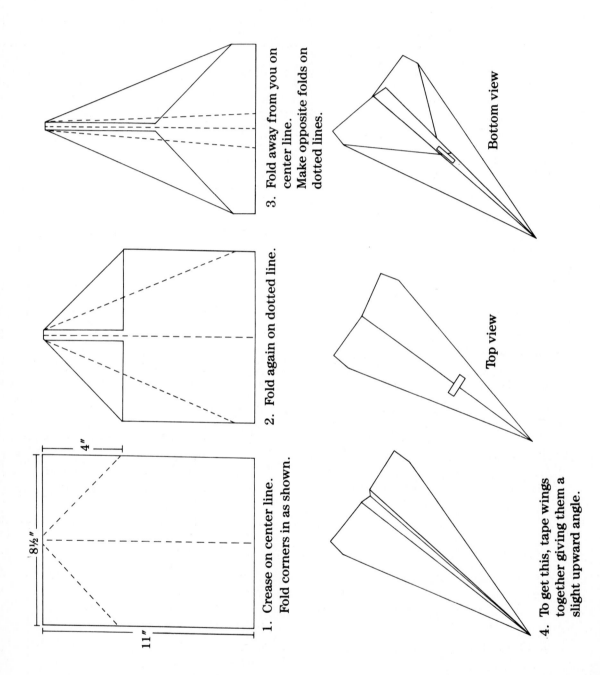

1. Crease on center line. Fold corners in as shown.

2. Fold again on dotted line.

3. Fold away from you on center line. Make opposite folds on dotted lines.

4. To get this, tape wings together giving them a slight upward angle.

Top view

Bottom view

Page reference: 64

ANIMAL AGES[4]

 Camel Giant salamander Gray seal Human Killer whale Tortoise

Animal Ages

These are your clues to help solve the group's problem.

Read them to the group, but, do not show them to anyone.

PROBLEM: Find the longest life span for each animal.
- A giant tortoise has been known to live four times as long as a giant salamander.
- The oldest person on record was a woman who lived to be 113 years old.

Animal Ages

These are your clues to help solve the group's problem.

Read them to the group, but, do not show them to anyone.

PROBLEM: Find the longest life span for each animal.
- A giant salamander lived twice as long as the oldest camel.
- The oldest person lived 23 years longer than the oldest killer whale.

Animal Ages

These are your clues to help solve the group's problem.

Read them to the group, but, do not show them to anyone.

PROBLEM: Find the longest life span for each animal.
- A killer whale lived one year less than the oldest gray seal and giant salamander combined.
- Tortoises are one of the few animals that live longer than people.

Animal Ages

These are your clues to help solve the group's problem.

Read them to the group, but, do not show them to anyone.

PROBLEM: Find the longest life span for each animal.
- The oldest gray seal lived to be 41 years old.
- Giant tortoises have the longest life span of all living creatures except bacteria.

Animal Ages*

These are your clues to help solve the group's problem.

Read them to the group, but, do not show them to anyone.

PROBLEM: Find the longest life span for each animal.
- The oldest tortoise lived almost five times as long as the oldest gray seal.
- People have been known to live over four times as long as the oldest camel.

Animal Ages*

These are your clues to help solve the group's problem.

Read them to the group, but, do not show them to anyone.

PROBLEM: Find the longest life span for each animal.
- The oldest tortoise was over twice as old as the most ancient killer whale.
- Some gray seals live longer than camels.

Answers: giant tortoise (200), human (113), killer whale (90), giant salamander (50), gray seal (41), camel (25).

Page reference: 64

THE STORY OF THE WHOOPING CRANES[5]

Bird counts taken during the late 1930s brought scientists some bad news about whooping cranes. Whooping cranes are tall, white birds that live near the water. The birds were down to a population of about 20. Scientists feared that illness or a bad storm could wipe out the rest.

One flock of these birds spent the winter along the Texas coast. A second flock lived year-round in Louisiana. But no one knew where the Texas birds lived in the summer. And no one knew why the whooping crane population was so low. Wildlife scientists wanted to find out why.

In 1946 Robert Allen was asked to study or investigate the "whoopers." He began his investigation by watching closely or observing a wild flock of whoopers. He observed the birds that wintered at Aransas National Wildlife Refuge in Texas. From sunup to sundown Allen watched the birds. He knew when they slept and what they ate. He watched them care for their young. Like all good scientists, he carefully recorded his observations. Recording information is an important step in investigating.

Next, Allen investigated where the whoopers spend their summers. Each spring the whoopers leave Texas. They head north to breed. They return to Texas in the fall. Allen found out where the whoopers had been spotted over the years. He was able to guess where the cranes went to, or migrated. Making a guess, or hypothesis, is part of how scientists solve a problem. Allen's hypothesis was that the cranes migrated to Canada. In 1952 Allen found the summer home of the whoopers: Wood Buffalo National Park, which is in the Northern part of Canada.

Allen learned many things at the birds' summer home. Whooping cranes lay two eggs each season. Although they are good parents, adult birds raise only one young bird a year. The whoopers also need to be alone. They must have a lot of space around them. Allen's observations led him to make

©1984, 1980 Holt, Rinehart and Winston, Inc. Reprinted by permission of the publisher.

Page reference: 65

these final statements or conclusions: the whooping cranes were dying out because they did not produce enough young cranes each year to make up for the ones that were hunted by people. Also, they were being crowded out of their living space by the growing human population.

Allen's conclusions helped scientists to think of ideas that would help the whoopers. Each idea was carefully studied and tested. One idea was to give the birds more food and protection from outsiders at their winter home. The idea worked. The flock of Aransas whoopers went up from 20 to 70 birds.

Scientists had another idea for increasing the number of whooping cranes. They took eggs from the wild flock to raise in captivity. Later, the captive birds could be released in the wild. Allen had already shown that whoopers raise only one young bird a year. Scientists predicted that taking one egg from a nest would cause no harm. This was tested and proved true. Since 1967, many eggs have been taken from whooper nests in Canada. These eggs have been flown to a research center in Maryland. There, many of the eggs have hatched. Now a captive flock of 25 birds lives there. Scientists have made a good home for the birds. They hope the birds will soon produce eggs on their own.

Scientists now keep a close watch on the whooping cranes. Some birds have been fitted with radio transmitters. From the radio signals, scientists are able to track the cranes' every move.

Page reference: 65

Thanks to the efforts of many scientists, there is more hope now for the whooping cranes than there was in the late 1930s. The work scientists have done with the cranes shows some of the ways scientific investigations are carried out. You have seen how a scientist asks questions and keeps careful records of observations. By observing the same subject over and over again, a scientist notices when changes take place. The observations lead to experiments. But experiments don't always show the results a scientists predicts. The scientist must ask some new questions!

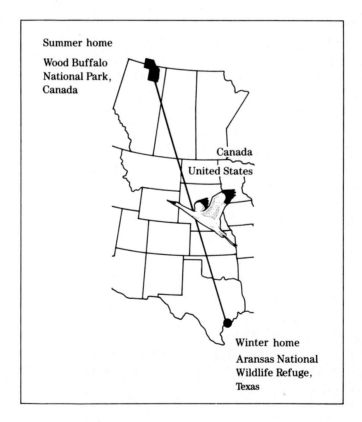

Summer home

Wood Buffalo National Park, Canada

Canada

United States

Winter home

Aransas National Wildlife Refuge, Texas

©1984, 1980 Holt, Rinehart and Winston, Inc. Reprinted by permission of the publisher.

Page reference: 65

MATH SKILLS SURVEY[9]

Group A
____ 1. Round 20.658 to the nearest whole number.
____ 2. Add $714 + 877 + 1301$.
____ 3. Find the area of this rectangle.

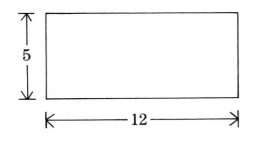

Group B
____ 4. Add $5\frac{3}{4} + 3\frac{5}{8} + 4\frac{1}{2}$.
____ 5. Write 925% as a decimal.
____ 6. Find the value of x: $2x - 20 = 18$.

Group C
____ 7. Divide $\frac{7}{8}$ by $\frac{1}{6}$.
____ 8. Find the value of x: $5x + 7 = 3x - 39$.
____ 9. What number is 20% less than 5?

Group D
____ 10. If an 8-inch pizza serves two, how many will two 12-inch pizzas serve?
____ 11. If the length and width of a rectangle are each increased by 25%, by what percent is the area increased?
____ 12. If Sandy scored 14 baskets out of 20 shots in a basketball game, what is her percentage of accuracy?

Answers: **1.** 21 **2.** 2,892 **3.** 60 square units **4.** $13\frac{7}{8}$ **5.** 9.25 **6.** 19 **7.** $5\frac{1}{4}$ **8.** $x = -23$ **9.** 4 **10.** 3 **11.** 56% **12.** 70%

Page reference: 68

MATH ATTITUDE QUESTIONNAIRE[9]

_____ 1. When handed this math survey, my immediate feeling was:
   a) This is important. I'll do the best that I can.
   b) I'm not going to take this test seriously.
   c) I wish I had stayed home today.

_____ 2. I wondered how my parents would feel when they found out that I had a special test. They might be
   a) very concerned.
   b) a little concerned.
   c) not at all concerned.

_____ 3. If I thought I might not pass the test I would
   a) be very worried.
   b) be a little worried.
   c) not be worried at all.

_____ 4. I thought that the test would be used
   a) to place me in next fall's math class.
   b) for grading me in this class.
   c) for nothing.

_____ 5. If I thought I wouldn't do well on this test I
   a) would try to do the best that I could.
   b) wouldn't try very hard.
   c) would try to find a way to get out of it.

_____ 6. My folks
   a) insist I get good grades in math.
   b) encourage me to get good grades in math so that I can be anything I want.
   c) don't care what grades I get in math.

_____ 7. If another student in class always scored higher than I did on math tests, I would
   a) like to score higher than the student on the test.
   b) like to score higher even though I probably won't.
   c) not really care whether I score higher or not.

_____ 8. On this math survey
   a) the girls would probably do better than the boys.
   b) the boys would probably do better than the girls.
   c) there wouldn't be any difference between how boys and girls in our class do.

_____ 9. When I think about going into a math or science field, I
   a) think of all the possibilities there are in math and science.
   b) don't think I'll be good enough to consider a career in math or science.
   c) am not interested in going into a math or science field.

_____ 10. I think that math tests are
   a) a challenge.
   b) scary.
   c) boring.

Page reference: 69

PART TWO

THE
EXPERIENCES

Cooperative Learning Units
for the Science Classroom

INTRODUCTION

Part Two contains eight Experiences. Each of these Experiences represents a unit of learning for the science classroom, with special emphasis on cooperative learning. The units have been designed for students in grades 4 through 9. The topics chosen deemphasize the normal boundaries of the scientific disciplines. Instead, Experiences focus on phenomena, everyday examples, and problem-solving activities in an attempt to give the students a real-world science experience. Experiences will equip students with the following abilities:

1. They will become active science learners and members of cooperative learning teams.
2. They will develop critical-thinking and problem-solving skills within the context of cooperative learning teams.
3. They will explore concepts, questions, and phenomena in several areas of science.

The Experiences

The chart below lists the eight Experiences and provides information about the focus of each experience and the number of days it will take to complete the unit based on a 45- to 60-minute instruction period.

Experiences: Science Cooperative Learning Units

Chapter	Experience	Focus	Number of Days
4	The Web of Life	The intriguing world of living things.	10
5	The "Wellthy" Syndrome	Holistic health and high-level wellness.	14
6	The Starship and the Canoe	Two vast frontiers: outer space and the earth's oceans.	18
7	Touch the Earth	A discovery and adventure unit about the mysterious planet earth.	17
8	If You Were a Boat, How Would You Float?	Buoyancy and related physical science phenomena.	12
9	The Third Wave	The future: creating it and developing futuristic thinking processes.	16
10	Powering the Earth	The earth's energy resources and ecological concerns related to air, water, land, minerals, plants, and animals.	14
11	Investigating the Natural World	Environmental science and ecological concerns.	18

Organization of the Experience

Each Experience contains two sections: *Teacher Information*, and *Student Information*. The materials in these two sections enable you to implement the Experience.

The *Teacher Information* consists of the following categories:

Background Information

This section outlines the rationale for the Experience and provides some information on the content of the unit to help you develop an orientation lesson.

Overview and Planning Chart

The Overview and Planning Chart provides information on each lesson in the Experience, including science concepts, science processes, learning modes, and attitudes. The chart will aid you in planning specific lesson implementation.

Objectives

The Objectives identify the major cognitive and affective goals for each Experience. Written in terms of performance, they provide an additional planning aid.

Key Concepts

The Key Concepts and a brief definition of each are listed for each Experience; many additional concepts are also developed within each Experience.

Teaching Tips

Teaching Tips vary considerably from one Experience to the next. They may include reminders to order equipment or materials in advance, suggestions for rearranging the classroom furniture, hints about organizing the materials in the unit, and so on.

Teaching Phases

Although you should implement the Experiences in a way that is comfortable for you, I have included a section in the Teacher Information entitled Teaching Phases. The Teaching Phases outline three phases for the implementation of each Experience. The phases answer questions such as: What should I do first? How should I implement cooperative learning formats? How should I bring the experience to a close? Are there some culminating activities to include?

The three teaching phases are as follows:

Phase I. Direct Instruction/Interactive Teaching Recent research has indicated the worthiness and value of active teacher direction and student-teacher interactions.[1,2] The success of the experience will depend upon your taking an active leadership role in getting students involved in the activities of the unit. You will find very specific instructions for each lesson, but all of them are directed at helping you achieve a high level of interaction on all levels.

Phase II. Cooperative Learning One of the principle goals of each Experience is to provide students with a cooperative learning environment. The lesson plans in the experience make specific suggestions to help students work together, solve problems together, and in some cases make group presentations.

Phase III. Culminating Process The Culminating Process provides an opportunity for you to bring the students together to establish what they learned in the Experience. This can be accomplished by having the students present cooperative team projects, by having a discussion session, by taking a field trip, or by having a guest speaker. The important point is to provide an opportunity for closure on the Experience. Closure does not necessarily mean the end, however. You might have students list questions related to the topic, suggest books for further reading, or relate the unit of instruction to the next unit.

A second aspect of the Culminating Process is evaluation. Typically a formal evaluation is given. You could design your own paper-and-pencil test or use some of the ideas found in the Experience. It is also suggested that you obtain feedback from the students on how they reacted to the Experience. A generic evaluation form on page 111 can be used with any of the Experiences.

The *Student Information* is organized into the following sections:

Adventures

Adventures are learning activities that focus on the central science concepts and processes important to the Experience. The Adventures include a range of activities emphasizing the four modes of thinking that were developed in chapter 3: physical-sensory mode learning, left-mode learning, right-mode learning, and affective-mode learning. The Adventures are the core activities of the Experience. Most of the Adventures are written for and designed to be carried out by cooperative learning teams.

Side Paths

Side paths are interdisciplinary activities linking science learning to other subject areas such as social studies, mathematics, language arts, art, and music. Side Path activities can be implemented by individuals or small cooperative learning teams. The activities supplement the Adventures and help students bridge science and other curricular areas.

Searches

Searches are projects that engage teams of students in problem-solving activities that require more time and, in some cases, a greater variety of resources. Some activities involve students in research projects in which they gather data, analyze results, and draw conclusions. In other cases students might design a model of a phenomenon and then present it to the class. These projects can also be used to involve parents in the students' learning.

Evaluation

The Evaluation section suggests ways to evaluate the students' progress in the unit as well as ways to obtain students' reactions to the Experience.

Books for Kids

Each Experience contains a list of related Books for Kids. It is a handy device for students who are working on projects or who wish to do individual work.

Implementing the Experiences

Each Experience is a self-contained unit of instruction that includes a detailed planning chart and specific teacher-oriented information to help implement the unit. The units can be presented in any order.

Here are some guidelines that I think will help enhance the use of the Experience.

Class orientation

Conduct an orientation session each time you begin an Experience. The orientation session should acquaint students with the content and learning possibilities of the unit. Sharing the planning chart is one way to communicate the focus and direction of the Experience. You might combine an activity in the Experience with the orientation session. This is a preferred way to begin because the activities draw the students into the units. Some teachers simply like to have an open-ended discussion to elicit the interests of the students; others prefer to get the students started in an active learning experience.

Learning teams

You can use any approach you wish to form learning teams. You want the students to become active science learners, and this can best be facilitated by giving students choices, not only in learning activities but in establishing learning teams. However, your judgment is most important and should be the final arbiter in making team decisions. Keep the same learning teams throughout the unit, and change the teams with each new unit.

Keep in mind that teams have to learn to work together; if you do not pay attention to this, problems could result. You may have to do some cooperative team building activities each time you form new groups. Since teams will be responsible for carrying out the learning activities in most of the Experiences, giving attention to team building will reap great benefits.

Facilitating learning activities

Many of the learning activities require your active participation in terms of preparing materials and making sure students are aware of what is needed to carry out the activities. Although it is possible to turn some of this responsibility over to the students, you will have to be actively involved in the beginning.

Your role as a learning facilitator is that of a manager of the classroom learning environment. As an effective classroom manager, you will have to have *with-it-ness*, *smoothness*, and *momentum*.[3] With-it-ness means that you communicate to students that you know what is going on at all times. You present the big picture to the students, you are aware of what each group is doing, and you anticipate problems before they happen. Implementing the Experiences will be facilitated by making smooth transitions from one activity to another and having good classroom routines: signal when to begin and end activities, designate a place for science materials, delegate responsibilities for classroom chores, and so on. Finally, the Experiences will be more successful if you build momentum. Running activities at a brisk pace will ward off boredom and keep the students moving at a good pace.

Foxfire reports

Cooperative learning teams will be encouraged to make presentations to the class. Group reports might be brief descriptions of individual learning activities or more involved presentations on projects. The reports that the students share with the entire class are an integral part of learning. Encourage a diversity of reporting styles: debates, mini-conferences, videotape productions, hands-on activities.

In my own classes, I have referred to learning teams as *Foxfire groups* and have called their group reports *Foxfire reports*. The word *foxfire* was borrowed from Eliot Wigginton's *Foxfire Magazine*, and his experiential-community based education approach. Foxfire presentations have on some occasions become elaborate productions, but in the main they represent the variety of learning strategies listed above. If you want to learn more about Wigginton's approach to experiential education, I highly recommend *Sometimes a Shining Moment*, his autobiography of twenty years of teaching in the North Georgia Mountains.

Finally, the preceding comments and suggestions are only guidelines; I encourage you to use these materials in any way that suits you and your students.

THE
WEB OF
LIFE

A Life Science Experience

We need another and a wiser and perhaps a more mystical concept of animals. Remote from universal nature, and living by complicated artifice, man in civilization surveys the creature through the glass of his knowledge and sees thereby a feature magnified and the whole image in distortion. We patronize them for their incompleteness, for their tragic fate of having taken form so far below ourselves. And therein we err, and greatly err. For the animal shall not be measured by man. In a world older and more complete than ours they move finished and complete, gifted with extensions of the senses we have lost or never attained, living by voices we shall never hear. They are not brethren, they are not underlings; they are other nations, caught within ourselves in the net of life and time, fellow prisoners of the splendor and travail of the earth.

HENRY BESTON
The Outermost House

TEACHER INFORMATION

Background Information

Evolution is one of the central and underlying concepts of the life sciences, and students need to be given opportunities to learn what biologists and geologists believe about the evolution of life on the earth and to be able to test these ideas against their beliefs.

This Experience is a journey into the past to find out about the origin of life. Students will be involved in activities in which they imagine how life began to develop on the earth and how cells might have developed into a variety of life forms; and they investigate mammals, the learning animal.

In 1968, an American rocket was shot into space carrying three astronauts on a historic journey to the moon. As they looked back and saw the reflected light of the earth, a precarious spot of life in the universe, they read the story of Genesis—a creation tale about the origin and development of life on the earth.

One of the great questions of this or any century is how life originated on earth. There is a level of mystery attached to it; cultures and religions address the issue and it is a fundamental question of scientists as well, so it is a rich unit of learning for students.

Two broad concepts wend their way through this Experience, and it is important that you communicate these to your students beginning right at the start:

1. The story of life is one of grandeur, a great journey of constant change.
2. We human beings are similar to as well as different from the diversity of life that we observe on the earth.

At the beginning, and at the center is the single cell, the smallest particle that is alive, the building block of life. Scientists speculate that it may have been more than four billion years ago that the first cellular form of life originated in the sea. Single cells divided and perhaps evolved into multicellular forms of life. From this beginning a variety of life forms emerged—protists, animals, plants. Animals were dependent upon plants for food, and they grew in complexity and variety to become sponges, worms, shellfish, and fish. The fish developed lungs to breathe air and legs to move them out of water and onto the land. Life developed and sometimes overflowed, suffering mass extinction many times during geological history.

Some animals, such as dinosaurs and trilobites, became extinct, perhaps because of a cosmic catastrophe. Other life forms developed and changed into a variety of mammals—dogs, cats, horses, whales, rabbits, cows, chimpanzees—that were able to learn from their parents and their environment.

Humans and other living things have a lot in common. People and cells have an outside covering for protection and inside parts that use food. Our digestive system is like that of the worm, we can learn from our experiences as other animals do, and we began life as a single cell. We grew and became people with intelligence, emotions, dreams.

Implicit in the life process is change. We observe change, and our ability to observe makes us different from other living things. This ability is sometimes called consciousness. To be conscious of our similarities to a cell, a worm, or a whale is to see ourselves connected to a web of life. To be conscious of changes in the past will help us make changes in the present and in the future.

In this Experience you can help students realize that the biological story of the origin and subsequent changes in life on the earth can provide a foundation of hope for the future. Life will continue to change and probably needs to change in order to continue. The better students understand change, the better they will be able to make choices that will direct their personal lives.

Overview and Planning

Take a few minutes to review the Overview and Planning chart for the Web of Life. There are five Adventures, three Side Paths, and one Search project in the Experience.

Overview and Planning Chart: The Web of Life

Lesson	Science Concept	Science Process	Modes of Learning	Attitude
Adventures				
1. A Journey of Life	Life on earth evolved from one-celled organisms to multicellular complex organisms.	Observing Inferring	Right Left	Creativity Sensitivity to environment
2. The Cell	Cells are the simplest form of life, consisting of a membrane, nucleus, and cytoplasm.	Classifying Inferring	Right Affective	Sensitivity to environment
3. Life in the Sea	Organisms' physical characteristics and behavior vary.	Observing Classifying	Physical-sensory Left	Objectivity Sensitivity to other living things
4. The Move from Sea to Land	Some animals moved from the sea and adapted to life on land.	Observing Interpreting data	Right Left	Sensitivity to environment
5. Mammals: The Learning Animal	Mammals have relatively large brains and therefore a greater capacity for learning.	Observing Experimenting	Right Left	Sensitivity to environment
Side Paths				
6. The Walking Catfish (Social Studies)	Animals are able to move from one place to another.	Hypothesizing	Left	Curiosity
7. Seeing/Drawing a Bit of Life (Art)	Drawing is a way of observing nature.	Observing	Physical-sensory Right	Creativity Sensitivity to environment
8. Cell Circle (Drama)	Cells have different functions.	Observing	Physical-sensory Right	Sensitivity to others
Searches				
1. Land Snail Terrarium	Artificial environments can replicate a natural environment.	Observing Classifying	Physical-sensory Left	Sensitivity to environment

Objectives

At the end of this Experience, students should be able to:

1. Compare the functioning of a single cell and a human being.
2. Act out various life functions—moving, eating, growing, changing.
3. Compare and contrast the parts and functions of a cell with the human body.
4. Compare and analyze various organisms that evolve in the ocean—clam, scallop, snail, crab, lobster.
5. Discuss how fish may have moved from the sea to become amphibians on the land.
6. Compare and contrast the important structures of the leg and the lung.
7. Describe how a mammal learns from parents and the environment.
8. Observe and evaluate how humans think and choose.

Key Concepts

The following represent the major concepts that students will study:

Cell An organization of living material in which an outer membrane or wall contains the cytoplasm, nucleus, mitochondria, and other components.

Evolution The way scientists believe living things have changed from simple to more complex forms over millions of years.

Adaptation The process by which organisms change to increase their chances of survival.

Instinct Behaviors that animals are born with.

Teaching Tips

In each of the lessons, students are encouraged to observe, experience, identify, and analyze their experiences to reach a general conclusion. To help them personalize and relate this unit to the wider context of life, these strategies may be implemented as you teach this Experience:

1. Have each student keep a daily Web of Life log. At the end of each lesson, give the students a few minutes to write in the log. The focus of the students' writing can be a summary of what they learned. Have the students supplement their logs with drawings, pictures, and newspaper clippings about the origin of life.
2. Create a paper chain of life. Pictures collected by students throughout the lessons can be attached to each other and hung up in the classroom.
3. Create a bulletin board and invite students to bring in newspaper stories related to evolution and life on the earth. This will be an opportunity to relate the subject matter of this Experience to social and societal issues.

Teaching Phases

Following are three phases for implementing the activities in the Experience:

Phase I. Direct Instruction/Interactive Teaching

Most of the lessons will require some direct instruction. It is recommended that for this unit, you move through each lesson in sequence, modifying the procedures to suit your own teaching style. Therefore, direct instruction will be used throughout this unit.

Phase II. Cooperative Learning

The procedures for each lesson in this Experience suggest that students carry out the activity in small group learning teams. You can modify this, of course, and choose to have students work individually or as a class. If you use the learning team format, students will need time to report to the whole class. Thus, you may spend two days on each activity, devoting the first day to the implementation of the activity and the second day to team reports.

Phase III. Culminating Process

As with all Experiences, use a feedback form to gather student opinions about the unit. Use the form that is provided on page 111.

To bring the unit to a close, select one of the evaluation suggestions found at the end of the Experience.

You might have students share their Web of Life logs, reading short passages from or commenting on what they learned about the origin of life on the earth.

Keep your eyes open to the possibility of bringing in a current event story that relates to the origin of life. Use it as a vehicle to culminate the study of the Experience.

STUDENT INFORMATION

Adventures

Lesson 1. A Journey of Life

In this adventure, students will gain an overall perspective of the great story of life—from the Big Bang, to the first cell, to the human baby. By looking at the simplest and earliest form of life, the single cell, and the most complex and the most recent, the human being, students will be seeing the journey of life—a journey that took over four billion years. The story is a simplified version of what scientists have hypothesized. Focus is on the similarities of life functions in the single cell and the human baby, touching briefly on the events in between.

Materials
Paper, pencils, crayons, tape recorder. Record "The Story of Life" prior to the lesson and have the cassette available for learning teams. If you don't use learning teams in the first lesson, you will not need a recording.

Action

1. Explain to the class that they are beginning a unit on the origin of life on earth. In this first activity, they are going to listen to a tape called The Story of Life. It is a special tape that asks students to visualize events and create images about life in the past. They should listen to the tape in a relaxed and comfortable place. Afterward, each team can select from the variety of questions and problems that follow.

   You might want to begin the unit by using a direct or interactive approach instead of beginning with cooperative groups. If this is your first try at cooperative learning, do this lesson with the class as a whole. In this case, you will not need to make a tape. You can read "The Story of Life" to the class and present one or more of the follow-up activities.

2. After presenting "The Story of Life," assign one of the following activities to each of the teams. Students should be given time to work on the assignment and then report to the whole class. Choose from the following activities:

   a. Draw a picture of the cell you visualized. Try to be as detailed as you can.
   b. Write a description of what you visualized. Describe the experience as completely as possible.
   c. Find out about *Amoeba proteus*, the cell that was described in the visualization.
   d. Review the story and describe the feelings you had.
   e. List the things a cell did; make a similar list of what the human did. How do the lists compare?
   f. Brainstorm to list the words and phrases that come into your mind about the visualization. Use the list to write poems about your experience.
   g. Obtain a microscope and examine samples of microscopic life forms or cells from plants or from the inside of your mouth.

The Story of Life
Part I

Once upon a time, there was nothing . . . just blackness. Can you imagine the blackness in your mind? . . . Now you begin to see particles like dust . . . . They begin to move . . . They move faster and faster . . . and farther and farther away from each other . . . until . . .

There's an explosion! (Use a loud and surprising voice.) It is the Big Bang! Dust and sparks of light are whirling themselves into stars and galaxies . . . Now, in all that light and darkness, you see a red ball . . . circling around a medium-sized star at the edge of the galaxy known as the Milky Way. It is the earth orbiting around the sun . . . It is growing as it collects more and more cosmic dust. Now it is turning blue . . .

Now you are moving closer and closer to the earth and you see that the blue is ocean . . .The ocean is moving up and down. It is warm . . . and there are many chemicals in the ocean . . . They are combining in many different ways and separating and combining again . . . Lightning is flashing . . . Over a long, long period of time, something happens . . . Something becomes alive . . . It is a single cell.

Now imagine yourself as that single cell. You are just a blob with no arms or legs or head . . . You're like jello that hasn't quite jelled . . . Feel yourself as a blob . . . You're moving up and down with the waves . . . up and down, up and down.

Now you sense that there is some food nearby . . . You start to move toward it . . . One part of you bulges toward the food and then another part of you moves toward it, and you enclose the food and pull it into you. (Make a gulping sound.) . . . You see another piece of food . . . You are moving toward nourishment.

Something sharp touches you and you move away from the danger, as quickly as possible. There is more food nearby . . . You move toward it, entrap it, and gulp it. (Make a gulping sound.) . . . You are growing bigger and bigger . . . Will you burst? . . . No, you pull yourself into a ball and become very still . . . Something is happening deep inside of you . . . Your center is pulling apart . . . You are dividing . . . Pretty soon you have divided into two cells . . . You have changed . . . Life begins . . . The story continues . . . .

Part II

Some cells become plants and some become animals . . . Some animals begin to eat plants and some animals eat animals . . . and they grow and change, grow and change.

Some are little: worms, snails, lizards, mice . . . Some are big: dinosaurs, alligators, elephants, whales . . . Some disappear forever like the dinosaurs . . . Others continue to grow and change . . . and the earth becomes covered with animals . . . and now you come into being.

At first you don't exist . . . Imagine blackness again . . . Now you are a tiny cell . . . You grow and divide, grow and divide inside your mother . . . Now you are born. You breathe in and out, in and out, and your chest goes up and down, up and down.

You open your eyes . . . The world is bright . . . You try to move away, but you can't . . . You use your voice . . . You grow and change . . . One day you stand . . . You walk and come to school. . . . You sit at a desk . . .You learn. . . .

Lesson 2. The Cell

In this Adventure, students will look at a particular single-celled organism, an amoeba, as an illustration of the first cell and of all single-celled organisms. Students in groups of 10–15 will also build a cell to see how its parts help it to move, eat, grow, and change.

Materials

Cell picture, drawn in lesson 1; pictures, films, or filmstrips of an amoeba or other cells; microscope; microscope specimens for further investigation.

Action

1. Have teams of students study pictures or films of a variety of cells. There are thousands of different kinds of cells that have different shapes and sizes; different habitats (salt or freshwater, soil, plants, animals); different ways of moving (crawling, swimming, flying, walking, running).
2. Have teams of students work together to build a human amoeba. Ten to fifteen students will be needed for each amoeba that is built. The amoeba consists of the following parts:

    a. The outside covering or membrane is the skin that holds the cell together. It allows certain substances, such as food, to pass through it; it keeps out substances that might harm it.
    b. Inside, the nucleus is the center that controls what the cell does. It does not think or plan; it reacts to what is happening around it. The mitochondrion is a sausage-shaped little organ (organelle) in the cell that helps turn food into energy.

3. Have the teams compare a cell to a human being. Use the chart below to lead a discussion. Ask questions such as: How is the cell's membrane similar to parts of a human? The cell's nucleus is similar to what part of a human?

A Comparison of Cell Parts to Human Parts

Cell	Human Part
Membrane	Skin, nails, hair, sense organs
Nucleus	Brain
Mitochondria	Stomach, digestive organs

4. Have students choose parts to make the amoeba. Four to seven students are needed to make the membrane to surround the cell; one student is needed to be the nucleus and direct the actions of

the amoeba; one student is needed to be a mitochonrion in the cell to separate the food into parts; and four students are needed to be one piece of food that will be separated by the mitochondrion into one more nucleus, one more mitochondrion, and two more pieces of membrane. An amoeba eats mostly small cells called ciliates that have tiny hairs they beat back and forth to catch food. The four students in the food group could hold together with one arm each and use the other arm to beat back and forth in order to move; one should also be a nucleus.

5. Provide the following information to each team before having them act out the behavior of an amoeba. You can read the information to the group or you can give a copy to each nucleus to read to his or her team.

Here is how an amoeba behaves. In this activity, only the nucleus can talk; when it sees food, it directs the amoeba to go after it. An amoeba has no up or down, back or front, arms, legs, or mouth. It moves by pushing out a part of its body; then the rest of it moves to catch up. The nucleus senses that there is food nearby and moves toward it. It pushes out one part and then another part to enclose the food and pull it through the membrane. Then the nucleus directs the mitochondrion to take the food and separate it into parts. One part clings to the nucleus, one part becomes another mitochondrion, the rest become part of the membrane. The amoeba has eaten and grown. The nucleus directs the amoeba to prepare to divide. It pulls itself into a ball and becomes very still. Something deep inside is happening. The nucleus pulls apart; it divides and moves to opposite ends. The two mitochondria move to opposite ends. The membrane starts pulling apart, dividing into two groups and reforming into two amoebas. The amoeba has divided and changed.

Use the scenario to prompt the nucleus and suggest that students change it. More students can be food, mitochondria, and membrane; the amoeba can eat several bits of food before dividing; food can be divided in different ways, but the amoeba cannot divide until it has two nuclei and two mitochondria.

6. Have one team at a time take center stage and act out an amoeba. Let each team direct its own actions. After each team has performed, conduct an analysis of the session.

7. To analyze the experience, have teams discuss the following questions:
What actions did your amoeba do?
Why are these life functions important?
How are human functions and actions similar to those of an amoeba?

8. If you are able to get a microscope, set it up and have available either slides of cells or samples of single-celled organisms for students to examine later in small teams.

9. Take the whole class to a spacious area and conclude the lesson with an amoeba race.

Lesson 3. Life in the Sea

When conditions became favorable, the single cell developed into a great variety of life forms. Scientists speculate that life exploded in the seas 580 million years ago. Most early life was four-fifths of an inch to four inches in size. Life crawled on the sea floor or swam slowly and scavenged for food in the mud. Many of these organisms were so successful that their descendants are with us today: the snail (single shelled, or uni-valve), clam and scallop (two shelled, or bi-valve), star-fish (no shell, radial shape), crab and lobster (jointed shells and legs), squid and octopus (no shell). They show great variety in the ways they move and eat. In this adventure, teams of students will investigate a form of sea life living today and compare it to forms in the past.

Materials

Live samples of sea life (clam, scallop, snail, lobster, crab), shells (optional but desirable), books on sea life, films or filmstrips on sea life now and in the past.

Action

1. Explain to students that each learning team will investigate a different form of sea life. Each team should be given a form of sea life, such as a clam or a snail. Each team should prepare a large poster-report that includes a drawing of the animal; observations of the animal; and a description of the animal's habitat, eating habits, predators; and any other interesting facts about the organism. Poster-reports are informal reports that scientists give at conventions. Your students will enjoy creating posters and then using them to report their scientific findings.

2. Have students compare their organism to life in the past. Have them use these questions as a guide:

   - How many of these animals lived long ago?
   - Why do you think relatives of these animals are still around?
   - What does your animal look like? What shape is it? Does it have a hard or soft outside covering?
   - How does your animal move? What parts does it use to move?
   - What sense organs does it have?
   - Does it have a head? Can you see a mouth?
   - How does it find its food and eat it? What does it eat?

3. Give the learning teams time to work on their poster reports. They may need two sessions to complete the work. When the teams are ready, they should present their findings to the class.

Lesson 4. The Move From Sea to Land

The students are to experience the change from fish to amphibian by feeling it as well as understanding it. This should ideally be experienced by moving from a water environment such as the sea or a pool, to a land environment. However, it can also be understood through a movement or a visualization exercise.

There are two theories on how fish may have moved from sea to land to become amphibians. Both theories suggest that fish moved to land from freshwater ponds and rivers. One theory supposes that a fish might have moved out of a pond when it dried up and then struggled across land to find a more permanent body of water, as do walking catfish today (see the Side Paths).

The other theory, which is used in this lesson, suggests that fish could have moved to land to escape from larger fish and to find food.

Materials
Chart paper, colored markers.

Action

1. Conduct an inquiry session using questions and charts to help students understand the role of changing environments and adaptation in the evolution of life on the earth. An approach to this inquiry session is a suggested below.

   a. Discuss that people are used to living on land; walking on the ground; standing in an upright, vertical position; and breathing air. Ask, "What happens when humans move to a water environment? How did you feel when you first learned how to swim? What was difficult? What did you have to learn in order to swim?"

   b. Students should respond with a variety of stories about their experiences.

   c. Explain that fish had to reverse the process. They went from water to land over a very long period of time (80 million years). Ask, "What did fish need that might cause them to go on land?" (food or to escape predators) "What did they have to learn in order to survive on land? What adaptations do you think they made?"

   d. Students should generate a list of things fish had to learn and adaptations they had to make.

   e. Discuss how humans use their arms and legs in water and breathe in water. Ask, "What adaptations have we made to make it easier for us to survive in the water?" (snorkel, mask, flippers, aqualung, weights, wet suit)

   f. Ask, "What two basic adaptations did fish need to make in order to move to the land?" (The first was to develop legs from fins; the lobe-finned fish developed bones in its fins to help it move to the land. The second was to develop lungs from gills in order to breathe.)

   g. Show drawings of animals' limbs, from salamanders to mammals. How do the limbs of these animals compare?

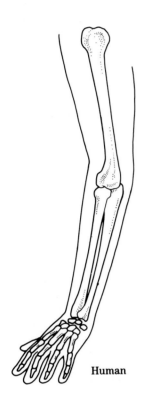

Human

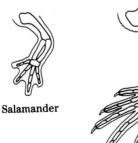

Salamander

Lizard

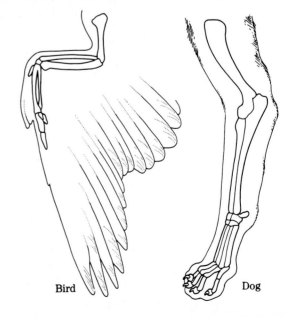

Bird

Dog

2. Have students analyze the story about a fish moving from the water to the land (page 109).

3. After teams have read the story, have them meet and discuss the following questions. Provide a copy of the story for each team for reference.

   a. Have students interpret the experience of the fish in the story. Have them discuss what the fish had to do to move from water to land and what adaptations the fish had to make.

   b. Have students share the most vivid memory they had while listening to the story.

   c. Have students compare the struggle the fish had in moving to the land with the difficulty people would have adapting to a water environment, or the difficulty an astronaut or cosmonaut has in moving from land to outer space.

   d. Explain that scientists believe that whales are the descendants of mammals that originated on the land but moved to and developed in the ocean. Have students discuss adaptations the ancestors of whales would have to make in order to survive in the ocean.

4. Conduct a class discussion after the teams have finished discussing the above questions. You could also have each team report to the class and then use their reports as a basis for the discussion.

Lesson 5. Mammals—The Learning Animal

Most of the animals with four limbs that we know, such as mice, dogs, elephants, cats, and people, are mammals. The following mammalian qualities relate to learning.

1. Mammals have the largest brains and the highest intelligence.
2. Mammals have a long period of childhood to learn how to obtain food and to protect themselves. Mothers protect their babies and feed them with milk from their bodies (from teats or mammary glands, hence the name mammal).

We as mammals have a special ability to observe and then think about our observations. In this lesson, students will observe how a mouse learns to move through a maze through trial and error. They will then compare this to the way they find their way in a new school. This unit helps students learn to choose a behavior in anticipation of a new situation.

Materials
Mouse or other rodent; maze made from corrugated cardboard in a small box; maze map (see page 110); stopwatch.

Action

1. Give each team one copy of the Mammal Pre-Test below. Have members of each team collaborate to try to answer the questions.

Mammal Pre-Test

---

1. What mammal often rides on its mother's back like a jockey riding a horse?

2. What mammal will play "king of the castle"?

3. What mammal will play tag?

4. What mammal will sometimes drop its baby in the water to force it to learn to swim?

5. What mammal squirts milk into its baby's mouth as if it had a squirt gun?

> Answers: 1. A baboon learns by observing the actions of its mother from a safe spot. 2. A goat (king) will stand on a small hill (castle) and butt his enemy with lowered head to practice for defense; a young gorilla will kick his peers and stamp on their fingers as they struggle to dethrone him from his position of leadership. 3. Squirrels learn to balance and jump in trees. 4. A seal baby is born on land and so must learn how to swim to obtain its food. 5. A dolphin needs to breathe air about every 30 seconds; the mother, nursing under water, squirts enough milk for one feeding into the baby's mouth in a matter of seconds so that baby can swim to the surface to breathe.

2. Use the pre-test as a basis for a discussion on how certain behaviors help mammals to learn.

3. Introduce the following four concepts, each of which describes a way that mammals learn. As you introduce each concept, ask students to identify examples. List students' ideas on newsprint.

   a. **Instinct**   Instinct is something that a newborn baby knows without being taught. For example, a baby knows how to suck milk from its mother. Puppies are born deaf and blind but they can smell, taste, and touch, so they can find their mother's milk.

   b. **Teaching**   Animal mothers often teach survival skills to their young. For example, a mother wolf will bring an injured squirrel to give her cub practice in killing. The cub will go on hunting trips with its mother and learn to kill by imitating her.

   c. **Playing**   Babies learn by playing with their peers. For example, bear cubs join in mock battles and wrestling matches to prepare for adult conflicts; kittens pounce on almost anything that moves; colts and calves engage in running games.

   d. **Trial and error**   Animals will try something over and over until they are successful.

4. At this point in the adventure, students are ready to begin a major investigation in which they are going to collect data to test some questions about learning. This part of the adventure will take two or three days.

   Day One: Building the maze

   a. Explain that people behave in different ways when they are faced with something new. Conduct a brief discussion. Ask:

"How would you find your way around a new school? What behaviors would you use?" (observe/ask questions/explore) "How would you feel? How would your actions show your feelings?"

b. Explain to students that a small animal, such as a hamster, gerbil, or mouse, learns to get around a new location in ways that are surprisingly similar to exploring a new school. Explain that students are going to build a maze and observe an animal's behavior in the maze to study how the animal learns its way around a new place.

c. Provide each team with a copy of page 110 on which to draw their completed maze.

d. Each team should construct its own maze according to the following directions:

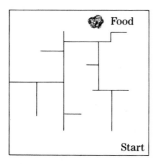

- Using a mat knife, carefully cut corrugated cardboard into strips that are at least 2″ wider than the height of the animal standing on its hind legs, so that the animal cannot escape. Cut slits in the pieces you want to fit together. Do not make the maze too complex; you want to study how the animal moves in a short period of time. The drawing shows a maze as seen from above (a maze map).
- Make a drawing of the completed maze so that you can record how the animal moves.

Day Two: Observing the learning animal

a. Each team should be given one animal to work with. Be sure to discuss beforehand the importance of carefully handling and caring for the animal. Stress that the animal is in a new environment; unnecessary noise and rough handling is unacceptable.

b. Explain to the students that they are going to try to find out how their animal learns its way through the maze. To do this, they should follow this procedure:

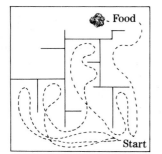

- Place food in the maze away from the starting point (F on the chart).
- Place the animal in the maze at the starting place and start the stopwatch.
- Trace the animal's path on the maze map as it explores. If a video camera is available, you may want to record the animal's behavior and then study it more carefully later.
- Write a report about the animal's behavior. The following questions can be used as a guide:

How does the animal move? Describe its actions.

How do the paths change? Does the animal repeat any paths? Is there any pattern to the animal's movements?

What part of the maze does the animal seem to like? Why?

How many times did the animal return to the starting point?

Did the animal eat the food when it came in contact with it? Why?

How long did it take the animal to find the food and eat it?

c. Some teams may want to investigate further. Here are some
suggestions for the teams to consider:

- Color a part of the maze black. Does the animal avoid this
area?
- Make a graph of the amount of time the animal takes to find
the food in several trials. Plot the data. What conclusions
can be drawn from the data?

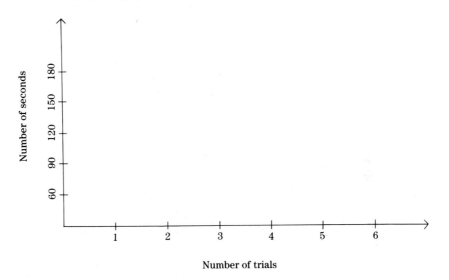

Number of trials

Day Three: Scientific Convention

After the students have had time to investigate, conduct a session
in which they present their findings as if they were at a scientific
convention.

1. Have a representative from each team report their team's findings
Encourage students to show their data on charts and report their
findings, using the questions from above as a guide. Facilitate the
convention by keeping the reports moving along and asking
questions.
2. Conduct a discussion on learning that focuses on the following:

a. Compare observations of how the mouse behaved in the maze
with a student's ability to learn to get around a new school.
b. What can students do that a mouse cannot do?
c. Scientists think that the average human uses only about 8% of
the brain. What new ways do you think we might use our
brains in the future?

Side Paths

Lesson 6. The Walking Catfish (Social Studies)[1]

A number of years ago a tropical fish breeder brought some fish from
Thailand. In their usual manner of breeding fish, they put their new
specimens into breeding ponds in warm southern Florida. The fish
surprised the breeders by climbing out of the ponds and flopping over

land to other ponds. This walking catfish could creep as far as a quarter of a mile between ponds in as fast as five feet per minute. Spines on its lower fins dug into the ground to help it move forward, and its lung-like organ breathed air. Free from its native enemies, this walking catfish thrived in Florida and began to eat up all the more desirable native fish.

Have students make drawings showing what they think it must have been like for the walking catfish to crawl from one pond to another.

After the drawings have been made, have students discuss the following questions and issues.

How might the walking catfish affect the environment in Florida? What effect could the walking catfish have on the fish industry in Florida?

Lesson 7. Seeing and Drawing a Bit of Life (Art)[2]

The purpose of this exercise is not to draw well but to focus one's undivided attention on a living thing, to understand its aliveness with one's eyes and hands, and to have fun.

Take students outside, each with a sketch pad or pieces of paper. Have them sit about five feet from anyone else and be quiet. Tell them to find something in nature that is alive but won't quickly move away. Tell them to observe its shape and the way it moves. Have them notice if it is long, short, bent, or straight. Have them, turn away from the object and imagine it. Have them turn back to the object and notice new things about it.

Now have students start drawing. Have them look at the object and, without looking at the paper or lifting the pencil, draw the complete object. Tell them to let their hands draw what the eye is seeing.

Have students compare their drawings to the objects they observed. What differences and similarities do they notice between their drawings and the object.

Lesson 8. Cell Circle Activities (Drama)

Students should be standing in a circle for these activities.

1. Have students hold hands around the circle and pretend to be nerve cells; the hands are nerve endings. One nerve ending sends a message to the next nerve ending. The message goes around the circle. What affects the speed with which the message is sent around the circle? How is this like the messages sent through the human body?
2. Have students hold hands around the circle and pretend to be muscle cells. The muscle cells extend as students stretch out their arms and contract as they pull their arms into their sides.

Searches

Lesson 1. Land Snail Terrarium

A terrarium is an excellent environment for students to use to observe animal behavior. In this project, students set up a terrarium and then observe snail behavior.

Materials

A large glass fish bowl or fish tank with a lid that has plenty of holes; an inch of soil for the bottom; dead leaves; a stick for snails to climb on; rocks; a small shallow pan of water in which snails can soak; snails.

Action

Have students complete the following steps:

1. Set up the terrarium.
2. Get two or three large snails of the same kind if possible.
3. Take a little bit of vegetation from the place the snails were found and put it in the terrarium.
4. Set the terrarium outside so that the snails can live naturally.

Have the students keep a log of the behavior of the snails in the terrarium.

Evaluation

1. Review Games[3]

   a. **Who Am I?** Pin an animal picture or name card on the back of each student. Have students ask each other questions about the identity of the animal on their back. Questions may only be answered *yes*, *no*, or *maybe*. When students think they know who they are, they write down the name. When all students have written a name, they report who they think they are and why.

   b. **Lobsters and crabs** Divide the class into two teams called the lobsters and the crabs. Have the teams face each other; each has a home-base line about 15 feet behind the team. Make a true/false statement about the content learned in this experience. If the statement is true, lobsters chase crabs, trying to tag them before they cross the home-base line. If the statement is false, crabs chase lobsters. Anyone tagged must join the other team.

2. Essay questions

   a. How does a single cell compare with a human being?
   b. What are some of the chapters in the evolution of life on the earth?
   c. What adaptations would animals have to make if they moved from the sea to the land?
   d. What are some ways that mammals learn?
   e. If humans were forced to live in the sea, what would they have to do in order to live?

3. Affective feedback about the Experience.

   At the end of the Experience, have each student complete a form similar to the one shown below. This form (see page 112) can be used with all of the Experiences that follow.

   Make a class profile of the results. Assign a point value (1–7) to each possible response. Multiply the number of students making each response by its point value, and then divide by the total number of students.

FEEDBACK ON THE EXPERIENCE

Please check the position along the line that reflects how
you feel about the Experience just completed.

The _____(Web of Life)_____ Experience was:

Meaningful	___	___	___	___	___	___	___ Meaningless
Bad	___	___	___	___	___	___	___ Good
Useful	___	___	___	___	___	___	___ Useless
Confusing	___	___	___	___	___	___	___ Clear
Unimportant	___	___	___	___	___	___	___ Important
Simple	___	___	___	___	___	___	___ Complex

Comments:

Books for Kids

Glaser, Michael. *The Nature of the Seashore*. Fiskdale, Mass.: Knicker-
bocker, 1986.

Halstead, Beverly. *A Closer Look at the Dawn of Life*. New York: Glou-
chester Press, 1979.

Malnig, Anita. *Where the Waves Break: Life at the Edge of the Sea*.
Minneapolis: Carolrhoda, 1985.

Michl, Reinhard. *A Day on the River*. Woodbury, N.Y.: Barron's, 1985.

Sabin, Francene. *Swamps and Marshes*. Mahwah, N.J.: Troll, 1985.

Strieber, Whitley. *Wolf of Shadows*. San Francisco: Sierra Club Books,
1986.

THE FISH THAT MOVED FROM THE WATER TO THE LAND

Once upon a time, all the animals were in the water. It became very crowded. As a small fish you had a difficult time keeping away from the bigger fish that wanted to eat you. There never seemed to be enough rocks to hide under or plants to rest in. Here comes a big fish out of the deep water now. Where will you hide? You swim as fast as you can, moving your fins back and forth. The big fish is getting closer. You move toward shallow water where you can turn quickly and swim easily in shallow water. The big fish cannot and turns back to find little fish that have not learned to swim into shallow water.

You rest a minute in the shallow water. You float and let the water hold you up, with your fish-eyes you see something moving on shore. You are hungry and maybe that thing would be good to eat. You try to move toward the shore. Slowly you move your fins along the bottom. Your back is out of the water. You feel so heavy. You can hardly move any more. You can't breathe very well out of water. You pant for breath, but you're very hungry. That food is still moving just in front of you. You take another step with your leg-like fins. They are too weak to hold your heavy body out of the water. You fall back into the water.

Many years pass. You and all the other fish have tried many times to move to land. Finally your fins move forward and hold up your body. The fin muscles have become stronger and they have developed bones. Your backbone has become stronger, too, and can hold up your body when it is out of water. Your flipper-like fins slowly move to land, and at last you can eat that insect larvae, the food you saw moving along the water's edge.
You can stay out of the water for a while. But you need to return to the water at times. You lay your eggs in the water. You have become an amphibian, perhaps a salamander.

Page reference: 102

Page reference: 102

EXPERIENCE EVALUATION

Directions: Please answer the following questions to let me know how you reacted to the Experience we just studied. You do not have to put your name on the paper.

1. How did you feel about this Experience?

2. What was the most important thing you learned from this Experience?

3. What was your favorite activity in this Experience? Why?

4. What was your least favorite activity in this Experience? Why?

5. What would you recommend that I change in this Experience before using it with another group of students?

Page reference: 95

NAME _____

FEEDBACK ON THE EXPERIENCE

Please check the position along the line that reflects how you feel about the Experience just completed.

The _____ Experience was:

Meaningful	___	___	___	___	___	___	___	Meaningless
Bad	___	___	___	___	___	___	___	Good
Useful	___	___	___	___	___	___	___	Useless
Confusing	___	___	___	___	___	___	___	Clear
Unimportant	___	___	___	___	___	___	___	Important
Simple	___	___	___	___	___	___	___	Complex

Comments:

Page reference: 107

THE "WELLTHY" SYNDROME

A Health Science Experience

Everyone participates in his or her health or illness at all times. . . . We use the word participate *to indicate the vital role you play in creating your own level of health. Most of us assume that healing is something done to us, that if we have a medical problem our responsibility is simply to get to a physician who will then heal us. That's true to a degree, but is only part of the story.*

We all participate in our health through our beliefs, our feelings, and our attitudes toward life, as well as in more direct ways, such as through exercise and diet. In addition, our response to medical treatment is influenced by our beliefs about the effectiveness of the treatment and by the confidence we have in the medical team.

O. CARL SIMONTON, M.D.,
AND STEPHANIE MATHEWS-SIMONTON, R.N.
Getting Well Again

TEACHER INFORMATION

Background Information

There is a growing phenomenon in our society. People are expressing their real needs and working towards the attainment of these needs; enjoying their bodies by means of adequate nutrition, exercise, and physical awareness; expressing emotions in ways that communicate what they are experiencing to other people; becoming engaged in projects that are meaningful and reflect their innermost values; enjoying a basic sense of well being, even through times of adversity; and learning to know their inner patterns—emotional and physical—and understanding signals that their bodies give them.[1]

This phenomenon is referred to as the "wellthy" syndrome in this unit (Some people consider good health a form of wealth). The description of the syndrome provides the basis and rationale for this Experience on health science. The Experience emphasizes two important concepts: holistic health, and high-level wellness.

According to Edward Baruman, one of the cofounders of the Berkeley Holistic Health Center, "holistic health is a new name for a very old concept of being." Holistic health, he feels, is a reminder of the unity of all life and the essential oneness of all systems. In his view, healing is nothing more or less than taking care of ourselves throughout the journey of life, and our health is simply a reminder of where we are at any given moment—a reminder of our vitality.[2]

Holistic health focuses on the development of "the joyful expression of good health, not on the achievement of normalcy or balance."[3] A fundamental position of holistic health practitioners is preventive medicine and the development of responsibility on the part of the client. The provider of health care is seen as a guide or facilitator, and the patient is a participant in his or her own treatment.

Wellness is a relatively new term being used to describe our state of health. Wellness begins when a person sees himself or herself as a growing, changing person. According to wellness physicians such as John W. Travis of Mill Valley, California, high level wellness means giving care to the physical self, channeling stress energies positively, expressing emotions effectively, becoming creatively involved with others, and staying in touch with the environment.[4] The concept of wellness described by Dr. Travis is illustrated below:

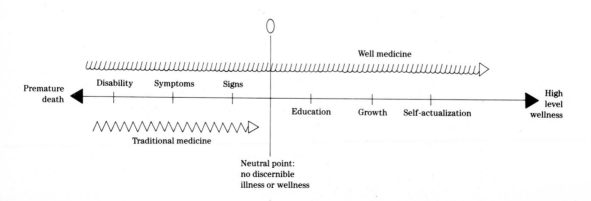

Note that the diagram is a continuum with premature death to the left and high-level wellness to the right. Traditional medicine is concerned primarily with curing disease and bringing the person to the mid-point of the continuum, where no discernible illness is evident. Well medicine starts at any point on the scale and encourages the person—through education, counseling, and treatment—to move as far to the right as possible.

An example of a holistic health approach is found in *Risk Reduction—It's the Name of the Game*, a curriculum guide developed by the Georgia Heart Association for seventh graders. The students develop an awareness of the relationship between five major risk factors—smoking, obesity, high blood pressure, lack of exercise, fat intake—and the increase of arteriosclerosis, which has been shown to increase the risk of heart attack. (For further information about this and other programs write: Schools Program Coordinator, Georgia Heart Association, Inc. 2581 Piedmont Road, Broadview Plaza, Level C, Atlanta, GA 30324.)

Reducing factors that pose a health risk is a fundamental goal of a holistic health and high-level wellness approach. Individual health patterns vary widely and are shaped by the actions and interactions of a series of events that begin at conception.

This Experience will focus on risk factors that fall into three broad categories: heredity, environment, and life style. Let's look at each in detail.[5]

Heredity: Good health or susceptibility to one or more health problems, such as hemophilia, sickle cell anemia, some cancers, heart disease, or certain mental disorders may be inherited. Inheriting a disease is not inevitable, however, particularly in the case of the more common chronic conditions, which often are the result of a combination of factors. Environment and behavior may be just as important as heredity in the development of most illnesses; changing the environment or behavior may help to reduce the risk of inheriting some illnesses.

Environment: Your physical, social and economic environments all affect your health in some way. Physical risks to your health include contamination of air, water, and food; hazards at the workplace and on the highway; noise pollution; radiation exposure; and unsafe consumer products. In the social and economic environment, factors that adversely affect your health include low income, poor housing, unemployment, inadequate education, and incomplete medical services. The family environment is important, too. A stable, loving home contributes to healthy growth and development and anything that causes drastic change—separation, death of a loved one, moving to another city—can affect physical as well as mental health.

Life style: An individual's life style has perhaps the greatest influence on health. Because of this, life style is emphasized in this unit. Many serious health problems are directly related to personal habits or behaviors: smoking, alcohol or drug abuse, sedentary patterns of work and recreation, poor eating habits, excessive exposure to stress and other environmental risks, and failure to buckle seat belts. Statistics show that if people at risk could be persuaded to improve their eating habits, quit smoking, get some exercise, and control their blood pressure, seven of the ten leading causes of death in the United States could be substantially reduced.

It is never too early to educate people about health risks and healthful practices. Early awareness will improve students' chances of maintaining high levels of wellness throughout their lives. The chart on page 131 summarizes information about health risks and healthful practices. It is based on the Surgeon General's Report on Health Promotion and Disease Prevention: *Healthy People*.[6] If you want to share the information on this chart with students, distribute copies of it to the class.

Overview and Planning

Take a few minutes to review the Overview and Planning chart for the "Wellthy" Syndrome. There are six Adventures, five Side Paths, and three Search projects in the Experience.

Overview and Planning Chart: The "Wellthy" Syndrome

Lesson	Science Concept	Science Process	Modes of Learning	Attitudes
Adventures				
1. Looking at Your Health	Knowledge of one's health practices is a first step toward wellness.	Interpreting data	Left Affective	Objectivity
2. The Body is the Hero	The human body consists of several interacting systems.	Measuring Inferring	Right Left	Objectivity Curiosity
3. The Kudzu Kaper	Exercise reduces health risks.	Measuring Interpreting data	Physical-sensory Left	Self-reliance
4. Biofeedback and Health	Relaxation and biofeedback are techniques to reduce stress.	Measuring Controlling variables	Physical-sensory Right	Self-reliance
5. From Yuk to Yum	Proper nutrition reduces health risks.	Classifying Inferring	Physical-sensory Left	Sensitivity
6. Feeling Good About Yourself	Positive self-image reduces health risks.	Interpreting data	Affective	Concern for others
Side Paths				
7. Food Habit Survey (Social Studies)	Evaluate food habits.	Interpreting data	Left	Objectivity
8. Food for a Week (Social Studies)	Eating healthy foods reduces health risks.	Observing Classifying	Physical-sensory Left	Self-reliance
9. Stretch for Health (Physical Education)	Proper exercises reduces health risks.	Observing	Physical-sensory	Self-reliance
10. Making a Nutri-Recipe Book (Language Arts)	Proper diet reduces health risks.	Classifying	Left	Concern for others
11. Visualizing and Drawing the Immune Battlers (Art)	Visualization can positively influence health.	Controlling variables	Right Affective	Self-reliance Creativity

Searches

1. Hazards to Your Health	Environment influences health risks.	Interpreting data Controlling data	Left Affective	Sensitivity to environment
2. Tao Project	Positive addictions can have a beneficial effect on health.	Controlling variables	Physical-sensory Right	Self-reliance
3. Keeping Fit	High-level wellness is positively affected by regular exercise.	Controlling variables Measuring	Physical-sensory	Self-reliance

Objectives

At the end of this Experience, students should be able to:

1. Evaluate their current level of health and set goals for the future.
2. Identify factors that pose health risks.
3. Describe various systems of the body and how they are related to health.
4. Take care of the physical self through regular exercise, proper diet, and stress reduction.
5. Reduce stress through either relaxation or biofeedback.
6. Evaluate the value of food and plan healthy meals.
7. Identify the ways in which emotion affects health.
8. Plan a long-term program of exercise, stress management, and dietary control.

Key Concepts

The following represent the major concepts that students will study:

Wellness A high level of health that may be achieved by giving care to the physical self; channeling stress energies positively; expressing emotions effectively; becoming creatively involved with others; staying in touch with the environment.

Risk reduction A process of creating patterns of behavior that reduce the health risks of smoking, obesity, high blood pressure, lack of exercise, dietary intake of fat.

Teaching Tips

This Experience can be taught in three weeks. During this period, there are some things you can do that will add to the unit and give it a holistic flair.

1. Eat-Ins: If you are really ambitious, you could do this each day of the unit. Instead of having students eat in the cafeteria or school lunch room, have them prepare healthy lunches for the entire class. With the help of parent volunteers, there are many healthy foods that can be served for lunch. Suggest that students consult with the school

dietician. Be sure to get parents' permission in case of dietary restrictions or allergies. As an alternative, you might have one learning team each day be responsible for bringing in a nourishing and healthy snack to share with the class.

2. A Holistic Schedule: Add some healthful practices to the daily schedule. You might begin each day with a classroom meeting. At this time you could lead students in some stretching or yoga exercises, read a story, or discuss the day's teaching plan or some specific topic. Throughout the day allow time for the "pause that refreshes;" students need break times. Think about the transitions that you use when moving from one activity to another. Quieting the mind by simply relaxing is one of the best transitions you can provide your students. It gives them an opportunity to consider what they have just done, as well as time to get ready for what is coming next. Other things you can do for transitions include playing classical music, having students work on their logs, or going outside for a breath of fresh air.

Close each day by assembling students in a circle and leading one of the activities suggested for the morning warm up.

Teaching Phases

Following are three phases for implementing the activities in the Experience:

Phase I. Direct Instruction/Interactive Teaching

The first Adventure, "Looking at Your Health," is an excellent way to begin this Experience. It will give you feedback on the students' knowledge and attitudes toward health science and a vehicle for giving them an overview of the unit.

Most of the Adventures and Side Paths will require some direct instruction, but as you will note, the activities are set up for small cooperative groups.

Phase II. Cooperative Learning

The procedures for most of the lessons in this Experience suggest that students carry out many of the assignments in small cooperative groups.

You might use the three Search projects that are described in this Experience in a cooperative learning format. Explain each project to the class, and then let each cooperative team decide which project they will work on. It is suggested that you begin the projects early in the unit rather than at the end. Students can be working on the projects—health hazard poster, tao project, fitness program—as you engage them in the Adventures and Side Paths.

Phase III. Culminating Process

Use the projects as the major culminating process for this unit. You will need to announce in advance when the students should be prepared to report the results of their projects to the whole class. Explain to students that their reports should involve the class in some way.

Evaluate and obtain feedback on the students' opinions and attitudes toward this holistic health unit. Use the form provided on page 111.

STUDENT INFORMATION

Adventures

Lesson 1. Looking at Your Health

A place to start this Experience is to give your students a health inventory. It will give you information about your students' health practices and will provide a basis for a discussion about health and wellness.

Materials
Make copies of A Health Inventory, pages 132–133.

Action

1. Ask students to brainstorm the topic "Things That Make you Healthy." Write the responses on the chalkboard or chart paper. The responses will vary, but the students will list many of the factors that appear on the health inventory.
2. Organize the class into learning teams. Give each person a copy of the health inventory and have them complete it independently. Tell them this will be used to help them get an idea of their health picture. It is not a test, and it will not be graded!
3. Assign each team a topic from the health inventory to discuss:

    a. Relaxation, awareness, and habits
    b. Exercise
    c. Food, nutrition, and mealtime habits
    d. Mental and emotional health
    e. Social values and relating to others
    f. Environmental health

    Arrange for each team to share ideas about the importance of their topic to overall health.
4. Have each team select a person to participate in a fish bowl discussion. Students should sit in a circle around an empty chair. Students enter the fishbowl to talk by sitting in the empty chair. Have students discuss the health inventories and results of their group discussions.
5. In the fishbowl have each student make a one-minute report on their team discussion. Ask students how they felt about taking the health inventory. Ask whether there were some areas in which they felt they needed to improve.
6. Discuss the title of the unit and then, if you wish, distribute copies of the Overview and Planning Chart to preview what students will be studying.

Lesson 2. The Body is the Hero

How well do students know their own bodies? When students complain of a stomach ache, do they point to their stomachs or lower intestines? In this activity students will help each other trace their bodies and then create a map of their insides.

Materials
Roll of paper with lengths cut for each person, magic markers or crayons, reference book on human anatomy.

Action

1. Inform students that they are going to make maps of their bodies. After they make the maps, they will collaborate in learning teams to fill in the details of one of the following systems of the body.

System of the Body	Task for the Map Makers
Skeletal	Locate and map the major bones of your body—vertebrae, humerus, scapula, radius, pelvis, coccyx, femur, fibula, tibia.
Digestive	Locate and map the esophagus, liver, large and small intestine, mouth, throat, anus
Circulatory	Locate and map the heart, lungs, mouth, throat, major arteries and veins, and kidneys.
Brain and nervous system	Locate and map the brain, spinal cord, and major nerves.

2. Provide time for each student to have his or her body traced by a partner. After all the students' bodies have been mapped, have the teams assemble before continuing.
3. Tell each team they are to work together and help each other out. Their assignment is to identify, map, and label four systems of the body. Each student in the team will pick one system to work on. Make sure all four systems are being worked on in each group. (This adventure fits nicely into the cooperative learning format called Jigsaw (see page 35). Four expert groups could meet to discuss and learn about the systems of the body. After they have had time to examine reference materials and charts, they return to their original teams prepared to teach team members about the body.)
4. Tell the students to pencil in their systems first, saving painting and coloring until later, with the help of their team members before they look at any reference books. Have them consult reference books to improve their maps.
5. When the teams are finished, invite all the students who mapped the same system—for example, the skeletal—to come to the front of the room with their finished maps. They can share and discuss similarities and differences among the final products. Repeat this for each of the systems of the body. Post the maps on the wall.

Lesson 3. The Kudzu Caper

You might be wondering what a Japanese vine, now an exotic plant in the South, has to do with holistic health. Kudzu grows wild in Georgia and through much of the South. To keep it under control, a neighborhood group decided to have an annual race and kudzu clean-up day called the Kudzu Caper. The Kudzu Caper was the first running race I entered after I started jogging. Not only was it a run for fitness, it was also an environmental health activity. There are many activities like this all over the country, each one contributing to personally and environmentally improving health.

This activity is about exercise. Regular exercise has been shown to have positive effects on health and well being, and this activity is designed as a starting point for you and your class. You are encouraged to begin a regular exercise program for yourself (if not already underway) and your students.

The high point of this activity is a class fun run. The run should be held later in the unit after students have had a chance to train for it. You might want to involve the entire school. The race could be held during the school day or on Saturday (to involve the parents) and should emphasize health and exercise. Have students decide on a theme for the race, design and decorate T-shirts, make certificates, and advertise the event in the local newspaper and other media.

You will need a playground large enough to create a 50- to 100-meter race area. Set up two markers 50 and 100 meters apart around which students can run.

Materials

Clock with a second hand, markers or small flags, a copy of the Pulse Chart (page 134) and Personal Training Record (page 135) for each student.

Action
Part A: Taking Your Pulse Rate

Tell students that they will need to record their pulse rates because later in the activity they are going to learn how to raise their pulse rates.

1. Ask students to predict what their resting pulse rates are.
2. The students can find their pulse rates by following these instructions:

   a. Find your pulse at your wrist. Make sure you can find it whenever you want.
   b. Count the number of pulses you feel in exactly 15 seconds.
   c. Take this count three times, and record each one on the pulse chart.
   d. Multiply each count by 4 to find the number of pulse beats per minute.
   e. Find your average pulse rate by adding the three numbers in the "number of pulses per minute" column and then dividing the total by 3.

Part B: Raising Your Pulse Rate

1. Take a clock and the students out to the running area. Be sure to have copies of Personal Training Record and pencils for each student.
2. Tell the students that everyone will run the same distance at the same speed. Tell them that as soon as the run is finished they should start taking their pulse rates and take a 15-second reading every ½ minute for 10 minutes.

3. Lead the race yourself to keep the pace at an easy jog. Run around the two markers until everyone is breathing hard, usually about two minutes.

4. When students are breathing hard, tell them all to sit down and start taking their pulse rate. Each student should have a copy of the Personal Training Record, page 135. Be sure to follow the instructions for recording pulse recovery time. If you think your students will have trouble with this, practice ahead of time in the classroom. The students can jump or run in place for one minute and then measure their pulse recovery time.

5. When the counting is complete, ask the class how long it took their pulse to return to the resting rate. Why do they think the time varies from one person to the next?

6. Further investigation:

   a. Students can explore some of the benefits of running or the advantage of an exercise program, including tones the respiratory system and helps clean the blood of wastes; helps maintain weight; increases muscular strength; clears and relaxes the mind.

   b. Students can find out how running longer distances affects their pulse recovery time.

   c. Students can find out how running at a faster pace affects pulse recovery time.

   d. Start a training program in which students walk/run for 30 minutes three times a week. Each time they train, they should try to increase the amount of time they run and reduce the time they walk until they are running the entire 30 minutes. They should keep a record of their pulse rates before and after running during the training program.

Lesson 4. Biofeedback and Health

Medical practioners feel that good health requires a balance between moving and acting (exercise) and rest and easing of the mind, spirit, and body (relaxation). This lesson will focus on the importance of relaxation and the reduction and control of stress. To help students learn how to control stress, they will be introduced to the relaxation response and biofeedback.

Materials
Biodots® [9]

Action

1. Start the adventure by asking the students to think of situations in which they feel tense. List them on the board. Ask, "How do you feel when you are tense?" List responses on the board. Tell the students that in this activity, they will learn how to deal with stress situations by learning how to relax their bodies. Two methods are presented.

2. Method One: The Relaxation Response

   The relaxation response is a way of relaxing and improving one's health. It was developed and researched by Dr. Herbert Benson at the Harvard Medical School. It is one of the simplest and most useful modes of relaxation.

   a. Dim the lights in the room and place a "Do Not Disturb" sign on the door to create a quiet place.

b. Tell the students to sit comfortably in their chairs. They can sit on the floor if it is carpeted or if they have mats.

c. Tell them to be passive and try to ignore thoughts and images of the past and the future.

d. Tell them to repeat a simple word or sound in order to ward off distractions, puzzles, plans, and the urge to do something. Repeating the word *one* is recommended by Dr. Benson.

e. Have the students close their eyes and repeat the word *one* for five minutes. After this brief period of relaxation, ask the students how they feel. List their responses on the board, and compare them to the list of responses they made when they described being tense.

3. Method Two: Biofeedback

Explain to students that another way to learn to relax is through biofeedback.[10] Explain that the word *biofeedback* comes from *bio,* meaning "life," and *feedback* meaning "sending information back to a system"—in this case the brain. Today students will be sending a message to the brain: "Slow down, relax, cool it."

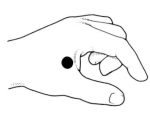

a. Give each student a Biodot and have them place it on their hand between the base of the thumb and the forefinger.

b. Tell students that the Biodot is a little thermometer. It registers temperature as a color change rather than in degrees. Explain that in the laboratory or hospital, very sophisticated machines are used to measure not only temperature, but also blood flow rates, brain waves, and other body functions.

c. In this experiment they will use the Biodot to measure their skin temperature. The Biodot will change color as their internal temperature changes. By telling their brain to warm their hands, they will in fact be telling their brain to direct more blood to that part of the body.

d. Put the following color sequence on the board:

Amber	89.6 F	Tense
Yellow	90.6 F	Unsettled
Green	91.6 F	Involved (normal)
Turquoise	92.6 F	Relaxed
Blue	93.6 F	Calm
Violet	94.6 F	Very relaxed

e. Explain that the temperature range measured by the Biodot is 89.6°F to 94.6°F. Any temperature above or below this range will turn the dot black. Remind students that external skin temperature is lower than internal body temperature.

f. Explain that biofeedback is used to help people relieve headaches, muscle tension, backache, leg cramps, and other signs of stress. If discomfort is due to stress and tension, the cause is usually excess blood flow to an area of the body; the temperature of the hands is lower because there is less blood flowing to them. Using biofeedback, the person thinks "hands warm, hands warm" until the brain hears the message. The brain directs blood flow to the hands, warming them up. Blood flow to the area of discomfort is thereby reduced. The object of biofeedback is not to warm the hands but to regulate the flow of blood through the body. A more relaxed state is achieved when blood is flowing evenly throughout the body than when excess blood is flowing to certain tension areas.

g. Try some of the following exercises with your students using the Biodots:

- Repeat the relaxation reponse activity described in Method A, but this time note the color of the Biodots before and after the relaxation period.
- Have students determine the color of the Biodot and then close their eyes, relax, and repeat the phrase, "Hands warm." After a few minutes, have them check the Biodots.
- Have the students do some exercise, such as jumping in place 20 times to see what color the Biodot shows after exercise.
- Play various types of music—hard rock, country and western, jazz, and classical—and compare the effects by recording Biodot color.

Lesson 5. From Yuk to Yum[11]

An ancient Chinese proverb says "all disease begins in the stomach." What this means is that there are some foods (inappropriate ones) that can make us sick, and there are appropriate foods that make us well. The foods we eat can be one of our best medicines.

Sara Sloan, Director of the Fulton County Schools Nutra Program in Atlanta, has this to say about nutrition:

> *There is currently a nutrition revival abroad in this country as we combine forces with nature in the search for better food, radiant health and reduced environmental hazards. This nutrition revival has caused us to examine what we are eating, what we are not eating and the relationship of our diet to the prevention of disease. We are concerned about the total health of an individual—whether it be of the mind, the body or spirit—because one without the other represents incompleteness. A "healthy mind does exist in a healthy body" and good health is something that we earn by following each day the rules of healthful living. The popular and often quoted proverb, "You are what you eat" should become a challenging concept, provided we believe in it ourselves and practice it in our own lives.[12]*

In this lesson, nutrition revival is stressed through eating some tasty and nutritious snacks and then evaluating foods that we eat.

Materials
Nutritious snacks. See the suggestions below or bring in some of your favorites. Show and discuss a variety of foods beans, seeds, nuts, pasta, berries, candy bar, fruit, canned food, frozen dinner (box).

Suggestions for Snacks

- Peanut butter on graham crackers.
- Peanut butter on celery and carrot sticks.
- Low-fat onion dip and vegetables: Mix one carton low-fat cottage cheese with one package of onion soup mix. Blend until creamy. Refrigerate for 24 hours.

- Yogurt dip served with fruit or vegetables: Mix 2 cups plain yogurt with 4 tablespoon lemon juice, 1 finely chopped green onion, 2 teaspoon paprika, 1 minced garlic clove.
- Fresh fruits
- Unsalted popcorn

Action
Part A. The Tasting Party

Can you think of a better way to learn about good nutrition than to eat good food? Begin with a tasting party. Be sure to obtain permission from parents in case of food allergies or restrictions. Parents may also be willing to help. Prepare the foods in advance and have them spread out on a large table in the center of the classroom. Let students choose snacks and have fruit juices available. After they get their snack, have them sit near the table containing the food. Be part of the group yourself. Then follow the steps below.

1. Sit quietly enjoying the juice and munching on the snacks. Give the group time to enjoy the snack and the break.
2. After a while, ask these questions:

   - How did you enjoy the juice?
   - What was your favorite snack? Why?
   - What is your favorite snack at home?
   - How is it like the snack you just had?
   - How is it different?
   - How are all the snacks you tasted alike?

Part B: Food Awareness

Conceal a variety of foods (see the materials list) in a box for this part of the Adventure. Put away all the snacks that were used in Part A and arrange the class in a circle.

1. Hold up one food item at time and ask a few questions:

   - What is the source of this food?
   - Are you willing to eat food from this source?
   - Was this food once alive? How do you know?
   - How do you feel about eating this food?
   - How do you feel before, during, and after eating it?
   - How is your breath, body odor, sense of taste, and general feeling after eating this food?
   - What is desirable or offensive about this food?

2. After you have gone through most of the foods, have students group them in categories. Let students create their own categories based in part on the questions that were asked.
3. At this point introduce some naturalistic concepts about food:

   - Whole foods are more nourishing than processed foods.
   - Most diets contain too much sugar.
   - Eating three meals a day is customary but not necessary.
   - Reducing salt in the diet is a healthful practice.

Lesson 6. Feeling Good About Yourself

Visualizing yourself as being well—feeling good about yourself—is as important to overall health as proper diet, regular exercise, and personal hygiene.

In their cancer research, the Simontons have found that a patient's self-image is crucial to the recovery-remission process.[13] They identified several personality traits associated with cancer patients:

1. A great tendency to hold resentment and a marked inability to forgive.
2. A tendency toward self-pity.
3. A poor ability to develop and maintain meaningful, long-term relationships.
4. A very poor self-image.

The development of a positive self-image, expressing and letting go of strong feelings, and the ability to form meaningful relationships appears to be an effective health insurance policy. These factors seem to be as important to preventing disease as many of the medical factors affecting health. Here we acknowledge that the mind and the body are one. In this activity the focus will be on self-image and ways to help students feel good about themselves.[14]

Action

There are many things that can be done to focus on your students' self-image. Several are described below. Use them in this Experience and at other times throughout the year.

1. Affirmations
   An affirmation is a positive thought that is consciously chosen and implanted in the subconscious to produce a desired result. Affirmations can help students feel good about themselves, overcome anxiety, and develop a greater sense of self. Affirmations can be said aloud, written down, or repeated silently. Have the students close their eyes and imagine themselves in a particular situation and then begin the affirmation. Some affirmations include:

   - I respect my own uniqueness.
   - I am healthy and well.
   - I am not a failure. I am a total success in all that I do.
   - I am relaxed and alert, and will do well on this test.
   - I am able to put my feelings into words.
   - I know that I can help myself feel better.

2. Today is your day.
   Display a large sign on the classroom door: "Today is _____ _____ Day!" Each student in the room celebrates his or her day sometime during the year. On that day the student is exempt from classroom chores. In addition, classmates are encouraged to do what they can to make the chosen student's day a good one.

3. Collage of self
   Instruct each student to make a collage entitled "Me!" Provide students with 12-inch by 18-inch posterboard and have them collect and cut out pictures, words, and symbols that represent who they are—things they like to do, things they own, things they would like to own, places they have been, people they admire—to paste to the posterboard. Display the finished collages and have students guess who made each one. Then have each student explain his or her collage to the class.

Side Paths

Lesson 7. Food Habits Survey (Social Studies)

Have students take the Food Habits Survey on page 136 and discuss the results as group, or have them use the survey to collect data on the food habits of others.

Lesson 8. Food for Thought (Social Studies)

Have students research recipes that are balanced, nutritious, and appetizing. There are many reference books available that provide ample information. Here are two that are highly recommended:

Sara Sloan, *From Classroom to Cafeteria, A Nutrition Guide for Teachers and Managers*, P.O. Box 13825, Atlanta, GA 30324

Frances Moore Lappe. *Diet for a Small Planet*. New York: Ballantine Books, 1971.

Students could design menus for the recipes they find. With parents' permission and cooperation, students could prepare dishes for a class potluck lunch or dinner.

Lesson 9. Stretching for Health (Physical Education)

Running strengthens the muscles on the back of the leg and lower back, and causes them to tighten. To counter this you should have a regular routine of stretching exercises for those muscles involved. It is also necessary to strengthen the muscles on the front of the leg and stomach to counterbalance the strength of the running muscles.

Have the students do the following stretching exercises as often as possible. The more done, the better. Remind students to stretch slowly, reach a point of resistance, and then back off a little, holding each position for 15 seconds or more. Be sure that they do not bounce or force the muscles at any time.

1. Hamstring Stretch: Sit on the floor. Stretch one leg out at a time. Keeping the knee slightly bent, reach toward your toes. When you feel the pull, back off a little and hold the position for at least 15 seconds.
2. Calf and Achilles Stretching: To stretch the calf muscles, face a wall and lean against it with your hands. Put one leg out behind you and, keeping the knee slightly bent, put your heel on the ground. Hold for 15 seconds. To stretch the Achilles tendon, bend the knee more, raising the heel off the ground. Hold for at least 15 seconds.
3. Back Stretch and Relaxer: Relax your shoulders and back. If you could roll your head into your chest and curl your back into a ball, you could really relax. Since you cannot do that, just roll your backbone forward slowly, vertebrae by vertebrae. When you have rolled as far as possible, roll back up to a standing position.

Lesson 10. Making a Nutri-Recipe Book (Language Arts)

Have students research nutritious recipes, collect them, and then organize them into categories. Provide students with mimeo masters, a typewriter, or a word-processing program, and ask them to create a recipe book that could be distributed to other students in the class and their parents. Note: There are a few commercial computer programs designed for managing recipes.

Lesson 11. Visualizing and Drawing the Immune Battlers (Art)

Teach visualization techniques to help students deal with pain and other ailments.

The body's immune system is our natural protection against disease. Without the immune system, we would be defenseless and would quickly die. The immune system includes antibodies, white blood cells, and the complement system. They flow through the blood.

Students can visualize their immune systems at work, fighting off invading armies of disease. Discuss the following visualizations:

1. Here a white blood cell is going after a source of pain in the body. Note how large the white blood cell is in comparison to the source of pain.

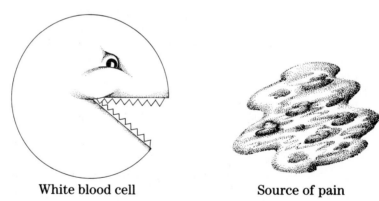

White blood cell   Source of pain

2. Another typical visualization depicts the natural defense system of the body as an army of white cells that rapidly flow through the blood to attack and kill invading diseases.

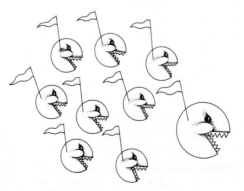   

White blood cell army   Invading disease

3. Here we see antibodies surrounding and destroying an invading antigen.

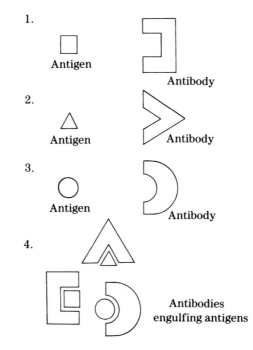

Show students these examples and then have them create their own visualizations. Ask: "How would you picture your body's natural defense system fighting the sources of pain and disease?

Searches

Lesson 1. Hazards to Your Health

Have students make posters that show environmental factors that are health hazards. One way to get started is to collect newspaper and magazine articles that deal with environmental factors and health risks. The final product should be a large poster that is carefully designed to communicate a message about environmental health risks.

Teams should work on one of the following topics:

- polluted air
- polluted water
- disposal of toxic chemicals
- disposal of toxic nuclear materials
- traffic (air and automobile) safety
- alcohol abuse
- drug abuse

Lesson 2. The Tao Project

The word *tao* means "way" or "path." I have had success using the concept of the tao in many of my classes. Students devote 30 minutes per day for three days a week to a tao of their choice. Examples of taos are running, yoga, meditation, keeping a log or journal, drawing, sewing, playing an instrument, listening to music. Have students record the progress of their tao in their log.

Have students record the progress of their tao in their log.

In his work with drug addicts, William Glasser has researched the effectiveness of replacing a negative addiction with a positive addiction. He found that running, meditation, and yoga can be effective positive addictions.[16]

Lesson 3. Keeping Fit

Some students may want to begin a fitness program. A good fitness program will help develop the heart, lungs, and blood system. Long-term health and vitality are determined by maintaining these three vital organs with the help of regular endurance exercises. Your heart is strengthened by steady moderate effort. Your lungs become more efficient in getting life-sustaining oxygen into the blood and removing waste products.

To achieve these results a minimum program of 30 minutes of endurance exercise three days a week is necessary. The more you do, the better. Run slowly enought to enjoy the exercise. It is *distance* that counts, not speed. In fact, recent studies have shown that walking is just as effective in burning calories as running.

Start from where you are and by walking for 30 minutes. Gradually increase your distance by running and walking. Do not increase your running distance by more than 10% each week.

Evaluation

Two surveys in this unit—A Health Inventory (page 132) and A Food Habits Survey (page 136)—can be used to measure students' knowledge and attitudes about health. Both surveys can be administered, first as pre-tests and then as post-tests, to determine knowledge and attitude changes.

Books for Kids

Delton, Judy. *I'll Never Love Anything Ever Again*. New York: Whitman, 1985.

Jacobs, Francine. *Breakthrough: The True Story of Penicillin*. New York: Dodd, Mead, 1985.

Martin, Paul D. *Messengers to the Brain: Our Fantastic Five Senses*. New York: National Geographic Society, 1986.

LeMaster, Leslie Jean. *Cells and Tissues*. Chicago: Childrens Press, 1985.

LeMaster, Leslie Jean. *Nutrition*. Chicago: Childrens Press, 1985.

Settel, Joanne and Nancy Baggett. *Why Does My Nose Run? (and Other Questions Kids Ask about Their Bodies)*. New York: Atheneum, 1985.

Swenson, Judy Harris. *Cancer: The Whispered Word*. Minneapolis: Dillon, 1986.

HEALTH RISKS
AND HEALTHFUL PRACTICES

	Risks	Healthful Practices
Infants	Low birth weight Birth defects	Family planning Pre-natal health care Good nutrition for new born Pediatric care Loving relationships at home
Children	Accidents—45% are highway deaths Tooth decay and periodontal disease Factors associated with heart disease Child abuse Learning difficulties Speech and vision problems	A stimulating, healthy environment Good child care Awareness of children's health Awareness of children's safety Awareness of children's educational needs
Adolescents and Young adults	Automobile accidents Murder Suicide Alcohol and drug abuse Unwanted pregnancy Sexually transmitted disease	Safe driving Avoidance of firearms Good health habits: eating sensibly, not smoking, getting regular exercise, and avoiding drugs Responsible attitudes toward sex Counseling, problem-solving groups, and psychotherapy
Adults	Heart disease Cancer Alcohol abuse Mental health: depression, anxiety, stress Periodontal disease Sexually transmitted disease	Healthy life style: diet, exercise, rest, no smoking, avoidance of alcohol abuse Preventive health maintenance Safety: seat belts, life jackets Environmental awareness: avoid toxic substances Stress management: exercise, meditation Preventive dental care
Older adults	Feeling of helplessness, uselessness Illness Inability to care for themselves Limited activity because of health condition Fear of dependency Chronic illness	Activity: part-time work, active social life Regular physical activity Health maintenance Controlled diet Needs fulfillment: programs, agencies, affordable housing, dietary assistance, transportation services, visiting nurse care

Page reference: 116

A HEALTH INVENTORY[7]

Directions: This inventory is designed to help you find out about your health picture. For each item in the inventory, check one of the five circles. Check 1 if the statement is never true for you. Check 5 if the statement is always true for you. Check 2, 3, or 4 to indicate a position between the two extremes.

1 2 3 4 5   *Relaxation, Awareness, and Habits*

○○○○○   1. I feel relaxed.
○○○○○   2. I am aware of my inner stress/tensions.
○○○○○   3. I do not breathe fully (shallow breathing).
○○○○○   4. I feel rushed.
○○○○○   5. I often feel tired.
○○○○○   6. I am overactive.
○○○○○   7. I feel sleepy during the daytime.
○○○○○   8. I enjoy spending some time without a planned activity.

          Exercise

○○○○○   9. I exercise. Briefly describe how: _____
○○○○○   10. I enjoy the exercises I do.
○○○○○   11. I enjoy doing calisthenics.
○○○○○   12. I am aware of the effect of exercise on my posture.
○○○○○   13. I am out of breath when I walk up a long flight of stairs.

          Food, Nutrition, and Mealtime Habits

○○○○○   14. I enjoy my meals.
○○○○○   15. I take time to taste my food and chew my food well.
○○○○○   16. Mealtimes are free from tensions, conflicts, and disagreements.
○○○○○   17. I use food to reward myself and to escape problems.
          18. My meals include:
○○○○○   fresh vegetables
○○○○○   fresh fruits
○○○○○   raw vegetables
○○○○○   high fiber foods (nuts, seeds, fruits, vegetables, bran)
○○○○○   whole grains (brown rice, millet)
○○○○○   dairy products
○○○○○   fish
○○○○○   poultry
○○○○○   red meat
○○○○○   food supplements
○○○○○   sweets (honey, molasses, sugar)
○○○○○   coffee
○○○○○   regular tea
○○○○○   herbal tea
○○○○○   salt (table salt, sea salt, soy sauce)
○○○○○   refined foods (white sugar, white rice, white flour)
○○○○○   quick-preparation foods
○○○○○   fried foods

[7] ©1985 Berkeley Health Center. By permission of Viking Penguin.

Page reference: 119

19. My fluid intake includes:

○○○○○ tap water
○○○○○ spring/distilled water
○○○○○ vegetable juice
○○○○○ fruit juice
○○○○○ milk
○○○○○ regular tea
○○○○○ herbal tea
○○○○○ coffee
○○○○○ soft drinks

Mental/Emotional Health

○○○○○ 20. My school work brings me satisfaction and a feeling of accomplishment.
○○○○○ 21. I work all the time. I am a "workaholic."
○○○○○ 22. I have difficulty making decisions.
○○○○○ 23. I feel positive about my life.
○○○○○ 24. I do not express my feelings (anger, joy, fear, pleasure).
○○○○○ 25. I find helpful ways to express my feelings.
○○○○○ 26. I am hard on myself. I have high standards for myself.
○○○○○ 27. I feel threatened by criticism.
○○○○○ 28. I generally feel good about myself.

Social Values and Relating to Others

○○○○○ 29. I prefer to be alone.
○○○○○ 30. I have close friends.
○○○○○ 31. I enjoy touching people close to me.
○○○○○ 32. I enjoy being with children younger than I.
○○○○○ 33. I enjoy living in the community I live in.
○○○○○ 34. I belong to several clubs or groups in my community.

Environmental Health

○○○○○ 35. The school I go to has a positive effect on my health.
○○○○○ 36. My home has a positive effect on my health.
○○○○○ 37. The air in my community is clear and smog-free.
○○○○○ 38. I feel my health is related to the health of planet earth.
○○○○○ 39. The rivers, streams and land are free of litter in my community.
○○○○○ 40. I feel that some plants (like nuclear or chemical) could have a negative effect on my health.

Page reference: 119

PULSE CHART

1. Find your pulse at your wrist. Make sure you can find it whenever you want it.
2. Count the number of pulses you feel in exactly 15 seconds.
3. Take this count three times, and record each one on the pulse chart below.
4. Multiply each count by 4 to find the number of pulse beats per minute.
5. Find your average pulse rate by adding the three numbers in the "number of pulses per minute" column and then dividing the total by 3.

Trial Number	Number of pulses in 15 seconds	× 4	=	Number of pulses per minute			
1		× 4	=				
2		× 4	=				Average number of pulses per minute
3		× 4	=				
Add the pulses per minute together.			=		÷ 3		

©Addison-Wesley Publishing Company, Inc. All rights reserved.

Page reference: 121

PERSONAL TRAINING RECORD[9]

Part One: resting pulse

My resting rate today is
_____ pulses per minute.

Part Two: pulse recovery time

1. Find your pulse and get
   ready to count.

2. When your teacher says
   "Count," take your pulse for
   15 seconds.

3. When your teacher says,
   "Stop and record," write
   your count in the box next
   to 0.0.

4. Find your pulse again.

5. Listen for your teacher to
   say "count."

6. Repeat the counting and
   recording procedure.

7. Keep doing this for 10
   minutes, even if your pulse
   reaches your resting rate.

8. If you miss a count, skip that
   box and wait for the next
   count signal.

Minutes After Exercise	Pulses per 15 seconds	x 4 =	Pulses per Minute
0.0	_____	x 4 =	_____
0.5	_____	x 4 =	_____
1.0	_____	x 4 =	_____
1.5	_____	x 4 =	_____
2.0	_____	x 4 =	_____
2.5	_____	x 4 =	_____
3.0	_____	x 4 =	_____
3.5	_____	x 4 =	_____
4.0	_____	x 4 =	_____
4.5	_____	x 4 =	_____
5.0	_____	x 4 =	_____
5.5	_____	x 4 =	_____
6.0	_____	x 4 =	_____
6.5	_____	x 4 =	_____
7.0	_____	x 4 =	_____
7.5	_____	x 4 =	_____
8.0	_____	x 4 =	_____
8.5	_____	x 4 =	_____
9.0	_____	x 4 =	_____
9.5	_____	x 4 =	_____
10.0	_____	x 4 =	_____

Page reference: 121

NAME _____

A FOOD HABITS SURVEY[15]

1. How many glasses of milk do you drink each day?
   - a. 1
   - b. 2
   - c. 3
   - d. 4
   - e. more than 4

2. Did you have breakfast this morning?
   - a. yes
   - b. no

3. Do you ever skip meals?
   - a. yes
   - b. no

4. If the above answer is yes, for what reason do you skip meals?
   - a. not enough time to eat
   - b. to lose weight
   - c. do not care for the food being served
   - d. not hungry

5. Do you eat snacks between meals?
   - a. yes
   - b. no

6. What type of snack foods do you choose?
   - a. soft drinks
   - b. crackers, chips, etc.
   - c. candy
   - d. fresh fruit or juice
   - e. milk or milk products
   - f. hamburger, hot dog, sandwiches

7. Do you think you eat a well-balanced diet every day?
   - a. yes
   - b. no

8. Would you like more information on good nutrition for your age and sex?
   - a. yes
   - b. no

9. How often do you eat lunch in the school cafeteria?
   - a. every day
   - b. 3 days a week
   - c. rarely
   - d. never

10. When you do not have lunch in the cafeteria, what is the reason?
    - a. on a diet
    - b. do afternoon homework
    - c. not hungry
    - d. lines are too long
    - e. menu is not appealing
    - f. to save money
    - g. not enough food to eat

[15] Sara Sloan. *From Classroom To Cafeteria: A Nutrition Guide for Teachers and Managers.* ©1978 Fulton County Georgia Schools

Page reference: 127

THE
STARSHIP
AND THE
CANOE[1]

A Space Science and Oceanography Experience

Freeman Dyson and the others worked out detailed plans for a ship that would quickly carry eight men and a hundred tons of equipment to Mars and back. This solar system model became the heart of the project and most of Dyson's energy went into it. He was personally curious about Mars, and about Saturn as well, for these were places he hoped to visit in the flesh. But Dyson is a man much concerned with human destiny, and his attention soon ranged beyond his own solar system and his own lifespan. Immortality for the human race requires colonization of the stars, he believed, or at very least, of the comets. He sketched out plans for a gargantuan ark, a starship the size of a city and powered by hydrogen bombs. Riding a monstrous concatenation of explosions, thundering silently through the void, leaving behind it a trail brighter than a thousand suns, this vessel would centuries hence take his descendants, frozen if necessary, to Alpha Centauri or another star.

George Dyson, Freeman's only son, has another idea, George wants to build a canoe, a great ocean-going kayak.

KENNETH BROWER
The Starship and the Canoe

TEACHER INFORMATION

Background Information

This is an Experience that involves two vast frontiers: outer space and the oceans. The inspiration for the development of this Experience was a biography of Freeman and George Dyson entitled *The Starship and the Canoe* by Kenneth Brower. It is a gripping story of a remarkable father and son. One searched the stars for meaning, and the other searched the seas. One is a theoretical physicist at Princeton's Center for Advanced Study, and the other is a high school dropout who lives in a tree-house in Vancouver, British Columbia. Freeman Dyson, world-famous astrophysicist, dreams of reaching the stars in a gigantic starship. His son, George, a world-famous kayak builder, dreams of voyaging the earth's waters in a giant kayak.

This Experience is about dreams and how imagination can be used in the world of science. It contains ideas that will encourage you to turn your classroom into a place where the mind is allowed to think freely, where crazy ideas and wild images are allowed to bubble up. In Carl Sagan's television series *Cosmos*, he invented a place called the "ship of the imagination." Using visual and acoustical means, he took his audience on fantastic voyages. I have adapted his concept for this Experience. Ideas will be presented to help you turn your classroom into a ship of the imagination, a vessel for the exploration of the stars and the earth's oceans.

Overview and Planning

Take a few minutes to review the Overview and Planning Chart for The Starship and the Canoe. There are seven Adventures, seven Side Paths, and two Search projects in the Experience.

Overview and Planning Chart: The Starship and the Canoe

Lesson	Science Concept	Science Process	Modes of Learning	Attitude
Adventures				
1. Designing a Logo	Science concepts are visually represented.	Observing Inferring	Physical-sensory Right	Sensitivity to environment Creativity
2. Intergalactic and Oceanographic missions	A vehicle that will take a crew to a distant planet or a vehicle that will sail the oceans for a year is designed.	Identifying variables	Left Right Affective	Value decisions Creativity
3. Investigations of Planet X	"Unknown" material can be described and analyzed to identify its properties.	Observing Interpreting data	Physical-sensory Left	Creativity Curiosity

4. Space Trek	Experience through simulation a space trip and floating in space.	Observing Inferring	Left Right	Creativity
5. Life Cycles of Stars	Stars go through predictable life cycles just as living things do.	Observing Identifying variables Classifying	Left	Sensitivity to environment
6. Life Styles of Sea Organisms	The life style of an organism is related to its environment.	Identifying variables Classifying	Left Right	Creativity
7. Balloon Rockets	For every action, there is an equal and opposite reaction.	Identifying variables	Left Right	Creativity Persistence

Side Paths

8. Capsule to the Stars (Social Studies)	Select artifacts that represent earth societies.	Observing Classifying	Left Affective	Creativity Sensitivity to nature
9. Murmurs from Earth (Social Studies)	Create an audio tape representing sounds of earth.	Classifying	Left	Sensitivity to environment
10. Planetary Race (Physical Education)	Distances to planets are represented in a scale model.	Measuring	Left Physical-sensory	Persistence
11. Save the Whales (Social Studies)	Some whales are endangered, and there are actions that can prevent their extinction.	Observing Classifying	Physical-sensory Left	Sensitivity to living things
12. The Make-a-Dolphin Game (Mathematics)	Energy moves through biological communities by means of food chains.	Observing Classifying	Left	Sensitivity to environment
13. Ocean Tank Beaches (Oceanography)	Wave erosion forms various beach features.	Observing Identifying variables	Physical-sensory Left	Sensitivity to environment
14. Cosmic Telegram (Social Studies)	Design and interpret a message for extraterrestrials.	Interpreting data	Left	Persistence Creativity

Searches

1. Making a Seaquarium	Sea environments can be created in the classroom.	Observing Measuring Interpreting data	Physical-sensory Left	Sensitivity to environment
2. Do-It-Yourself Planetarium and Astrolabe	Constellations are groups of stars.	Observing Measuring Classifying	Physical-sensory Right	Thoroughness

Objectives

At the end of this Experience students should be able to:

1. Demonstrate that adventure and dreaming are part of the process of science.
2. Use imagination to explore outer space and the oceans.
3. Use a variety of creative strategies to solve problems.
4. Design experiments to test unknown materials.
5. Keep a captain's log, recording the results of all activities and daily events.

Key Concepts

The following represent the major concepts that students will study:

Energy The ability to do work.

Change All things are constantly changing and taking different form.

Technology A process in which ideas are used to produce material things.

Ecosystems The basic ecological unit, made up of a community of organisms interacting with each other and the environment.

Teaching Tips

In this Experience, students explore outer space and the ocean in a ship of the imagination. Make minor or major changes in the physical arrangement of the furniture in your classroom to create a ship of the imagination, an environment in which students feel as if they are in an imaginary place, as a planetarium creates an imaginary sky. Your interior design ideas and your willingness to rearrange furniture and put up with a very different looking classroom are your only limitations. This is a great opportunity to involve your students in designing a room plan, making arrangements for obtaining the materials they need, and finally creating a finished product.

You may of course teach this Experience without making any changes in your classroom.

Here are some further suggestions to help you carry through on the theme of imagination. Pick and choose or combine these ideas to suit your taste:

1. Start each lesson with an imagination activity. Here is one you can modify and adapt to your own situation:

   Today we are going to pretend that this room is a special place—one that we can create with our imaginations. I want you to close your eyes and relax . . . Imagine you are walking into a room . . . The walls of the room have special effects . . . One wall has a giant screen on which we shall observe the stars and planets or creatures from the depths of the ocean [Note: on this wall set up a projection screen for movies, slides, filmstrips] . . . Another wall has a control panel and computer to help us direct our ship . . . The other walls have charts and pictures of planets, stars, fish, whales, and ocean waves . . . Imagine that you are in this ship, and you are going to explore both the stars and the oceans . . . Now I want you to open your eyes and get ready to enter the ship of the imagination.

You can rewrite the message depending on the technology you will bring into the classroom and the way in which you will make use of the physical space.

2. Encourage imaginative work by having a ritual each day or at appropriate times during the Experience, such as when you introduce activities on outer space and when you start oceanography activities. It is quite similar to the imagination journey described above, except that props and music are added. Jack Canfield describes this activity in *100 Ways to Enhance Self-Concept* and refers to it as the ''Magic Island Sequence.'' It relates nicely to this activity.

   Identify part of the room to be reserved as the deck of a sailing ship or the flight deck of a spacecraft. A ship's wheel, a picture of the flight deck of the Space Shuttle, and other props could be used to add realism to the deck. To get into this part of the room, students must pass over a gang plank or through an air lock—a refrigerator box works well as an air lock. As the students enter the deck, they are greeted by the captain—you. When all students are on deck, play music that evokes images of the sea or outer space. Suggested music includes:

   Ocean Music: Sailboat/Country Stream Record. Environment Series No. SD 66008, Syntonic Research, 175 Fifth Avenue, New York 10010

   Space Music: The Music of Cosmos, RCA Corporation, New York, NY

   On some occasions you might serve cider, grape juice, cheese and crackers, or space food such as dried fruit and dehydrated fruit juices. After the activity for the day is completed, have the students sit on the deck. Play some music again, and then have them leave via the gang plank or the air lock.

3. Decorate your entire classroom in preparation for the Experience. Here are some suggestions:

   a. Arrange the students' desks in cluster for work and learning purposes. Various learning teams could staff the following areas of the ship: a command room, food preparation and dining area, engine and power station, recreation and exercise room, laboratory and scientific studies area.

   b. Designate one areas as the audio-visual center. Set up a screen for viewing films, slides, and filmstrips. Bring in other technology, such as a VCR, a television, and a microcomputer. There are excellent video programs on space travel and ocean studies and outstanding computer simulations on space flight and space exploration.

c. Paint murals of ocean features and space features: waves, islands, currents, seagulls, dolphins, fish, beaches, stars, planets, comets, asteroids, and a black hole. These can be done as separate art projects by teams of students while the Experience is under way.

d. Decorate the ceiling by hanging objects that relate to the stars and the oceans. You can hang pictures of stars, planets, and ocean creatures, as well as actual rocks and shells. Write to NASA before you begin the unit to obtain an educator's packet containing information about the space program, as well as photographs and other visual aids.

There is a lot of material in this Experience, so that several teams are working on different aspects at the same time. You may want some of the teams to work on the activities that pertain to astronomy and other teams to work on the activities that pertain oceanography so that teams can teach or coach each other.

Teaching Phases

Following are three phases for implementing the activities in the Experience:

Phase I   Direct Instruction/Interactive Teaching

In this Experience, you will engage the class in the study of two vast frontiers at the same time: outer space and the oceans. In the beginning, have all the students work on the same activities together. After they do an activity or two, you may then divide the class into two distinct groups, the Space Trekkers and the Ocean Anglers. Half the class will focus on the study of outer space, and the other half will study the ocean.

To begin the unit, start with Lesson 1, in which the students construct a logo for the Experience. The lesson will give you an opportunity to find out what the students know and what their interests are. Lesson 2 should also be done with the whole class because it involves the design of both a space ship and an ocean ark. At this point, discuss which part of the Experience students would like to work on.

Phase II   Cooperative Learning

Once the class is divided into two groups, you may want to subdivide it into smaller learning teams. The learning teams can then select from among the activities listed below. Students should select at least two of the activities from the list, plus the project. Use the remaining activities for class instruction. In this way, both sets of teams will experience both outer space and ocean activities.

Space Trekkers	**Ocean Anglers**
Investigation of Planet X	Life Styles of Sea Organisms
Space Trek	Save the Whales
Life Cycles of Stars	The Make-a-Dolphin Game
Rocket Balloons	Ocean Tanks
Capsule to the Stars	Project #1
Murmurs from Earth	
Planetary Race	
Project #2	

Phase III   Culminating Process

The Space Trekkers and Ocean Anglers should report the results of their activities in more than a show-and-tell presentation. They should involve the whole class in the activities that they experienced.

Evaluate and obtain feedback on the students' opinions and attitudes toward this unit. Use the form provided on page 111.

STUDENT INFORMATION

Adventures

Lesson 1. Designing a Logo

A *logo* is a distinctive trademark that companies, organizations, and clubs use to identify themselves. Your students will make a logo that will be symbolic of The Starship and the Canoe. Each team could make its own design, students could agree on a class design, or you could have students make their own logos.

Materials
Materials will depend on the type of logo students choose to make. Logos may be made using chart paper, cutouts of The Starship and the Canoe logo shown here, paper, wood, string, paint, water colors, brushes, crayons, hand drill.

Action
Begin the activity with a brainstorming session. Have students list statements or words that answer the following question: What would you like to learn if you could travel either into outer space or around the world's oceans?

Students should work on the question in learning teams. They should write their responses on a large sheet of chart paper. Encourage students to come up with at least five things that they would like to learn about outer space and the oceans. Combine the lists from the various groups to form a master chart. The chart can be used as a stimulus for the creation of logos and for further inquiry during this Experience.

Have students use the following procedures to make logos.

1. Give each student a paper cutout of the logo shown above. They can decorate it, put their names on it, and wear it during the Experience. You can also give them blank circles on which they can design their own unique logos.
2. Have students make logos with a button-making machines. Button-making machines are readily available at teacher centers or can be purchased at a nominal price. Using the design shown here or designs they create, students can make The Starship and the Canoe buttons.
3. Have students make logos from thin slices of wood. Give students pieces of wood and encourage them to design a logo using the brainstorming session for ideas. One group can focus on outer space and another can center in on oceanography. Have students run string through a hole drilled in the wood, so that the logo can be worn as a pendant.

Lesson 2. Intergalactic and Oceanographic Missions

People dream of traveling to the stars or sailing across the vast oceans. In this adventure, students generate a list of survival needs necessary for long-term travel and create a blue print for a spaceship or an ark.

Materials
Poster board, sheets of butcher paper or chart paper, marking pens, pencils, rulers, paints, crayons, masking tape.

Action

1. Divide the class into two teams, one called the Space Trekkers, and the other the Ocean Anglers. Inform them that each team is going to plan a year-long, round-trip voyage, and draw the blueprints for a vessel to send them on their voyage. Establish a story setting for both the Space Trekkers and the Ocean Anglers.

> For the Space Trekkers:
>
> *Scientists at NASA have discovered a new planet that seems almost identical to earth, but the new planet needs to be studied carefully before scientists know if it is safe to land. Your mission is to orbit the planet for one year in a totally sealed spacecraft and then return to earth. Draw the various rooms in the spacecraft and label the things in each room. Be sure to include everything the crew will need to stay alive and well for the whole year.*

> For the Ocean Anglers:
>
> *The Cousteau Society and a local television owner have hired you to explore a series of islands that have never been studied by scientists. Your mission is to study these islands for one year in an oceanographic vessel that you cannot leave. The ship will take you to the island area and return to your home port in a year. Draw the various rooms in the ship and label the things in each room. Be sure to include everything the crew will need to stay alive and well for the whole year.*

2. Instruct students first to draw and label the things that are the most important to stay alive and complete the mission. Explain that they must know what others in the group are doing so that they don't all bring the same things.
3. Pass out a long roll (10 feet) of paper to each group for their blueprints, along with crayons and magic markers. Allow each group to organize the tasks that are necessary to complete the blueprints.
4. Compile the list of things that each group brought. Then have the groups rank the supplies into three categories:

   a. Things that you would die without.
   b. Things that it would be hard or uncomfortable to live without.
   c. Things that would be nice to have but are not necessary.

5. Ask students whether any of their supplies would ever run out. Which ones? How could they make these things last for 10, 50, 100, or 1,000 years? Point out that space cannot be taken up by supplies that are used only once and discarded. Remind students that nothing can be opened to get more supplies in or to dump out wastes. For example, oxygen tanks eventually run out no matter how many you bring, but plants will continue to produce oxygen as long as they are cared for properly; plants will use up soil nutrients if crops are grown over and over without enrichment, but fertilizers will eventually run out no matter how much you bring; if all plant products are composted with manure and all organisms are returned to the soil, the minerals will be replaced; and so on.

6. The blueprints of the spacecraft and ark should be displayed. Interested students and teams can then explore the following topics:

- Space colonies
- Design of space vehicles
- Underwater oceanographic vessels
- Space ports
- Underwater cities
- Space travel
- Sailing adventures

Lesson 3. Investigating Planet X

Present students with the following scenario.

An international space team composed of Soviet, American, Chinese, Indian, Nigerian, and Australian astronauts has successfully traveled to and from a planet orbiting a nearby star. It is the first planet ever discovered revolving around another star. The planet is as yet unnamed; at the present time, it is referred to as Planet X. The planet is earth-like in that it is of similar size, it spins on its axis about once every 24 hours, and it is located about the same distance from its star as earth is from the sun. However, there is one significant difference. Over two thirds of the surface of Planet X is composed of a strange gooey material. Space explorers have brought samples of the material back to earth. You have been asked to analyze it and send a report to the Society of Planetary Leaders and Space Headquarters (SPLASH). Good luck!

Materials

Planet X material: Put a few drops of food coloring into a bowl of corn starch, add water, and stir. The mixture should flow easily but become hard if pressure is added; glass jars; spoons; candle and matches; salt; sugar; soap; salad oil; rubbing alcohol.

Action

1. Read the above scenario to students.
2. Give each team a small amount of Planet X material on a paper plate, and have additional materials available for students to use in their investigation. The teams should be given specific assignments, and each team should write a report of their findings and create a large poster to illustrate their findings. Tell them that each team will participate in a conference where the results will be discussed before they are sent to SPLASH headquarters.
3. When the teams are ready to explore and study Planet X material, select assignments from the following list for each team. You might want to do this over a two-day period. On day one, each team can complete assignment A; on day two each team can solve a different problem from the remaining choices. The investigations that follow were inspired by Alan McCormack's article "Alexander Bort and the Bortian Blobs," *The Science Teacher*, March 1978, pp. 31–33. Please see this article to extend the ideas in this adventure.
4. Investigating Planet X: Problems for study.

   - Have students list as many physical properties of the Planet X material as they can. Have them take about 10 minutes to touch, smell, mix, and examine the material. When the students have completed their lists, conduct a class meeting and have each team report their findings. Compile a new list of the most prominent and important features of Planet X material.
   - Have teams compare the physical properties of Planet X material to water. Provide each team with a copy of page 164. The chart identifies some of the types of comparisons that can be made. Give each team small samples of Planet X material and water, and additional appropriate materials.
   - Have teams find out which common substances will mix with Planet X material and compare that with how the substances mix with water. Have them use very small amounts of the materials identified in the chart on page 165.
   - Have teams investigate special properties of Planet X material using the following methods:

     a. Compare the mass of certain volume of Planet X material with that of water.
     b. Determine the freezing point of each material.
     c. Compare the surface tension of both materials.
     d. Compare the evaporation rate of both materials.

   - Further investigations could include the following:

     a. Does Planet X material burn in a candle?
     b. What floats in Planet X material?
     c. What could Planet X material be used for on earth?
     d. What might life be like living on a planet where the predominant element is Planet X material? Have students write about and draw what they think.

Lesson 4. Space Trek

Visualization is used to take your students on voyages either to outer space or to the depths of the ocean. In this Adventure you will take students on a voyage to outer space.

Materials

Film or filmstrip depicting space travel; chart or drawing paper; marking pens and crayons; photographs of planets, satellites, and space vehicles; audio tape of rocket launch (optional).

Action

1. Prepare the students for the voyage by giving them some visual background on outer space. A film or filmstrip would be very useful, and NASA is a good source for films or videos. Books with photographs of stars, planets, comets, satellites, space ships, and space scenes will aid students in their visualization.
2. Arrange the furniture in the classroom with two or three chairs placed together to help students pretend that they are the flight crew of a spacecraft getting ready to blast off.
3. The visualization that follows can be modified to reflect particular topics in space science. You could make an audio recording of the voyage and let small groups listen to it.

Space Voyage

I want you to imagine that you and the flight crew are seated in your spacecraft on the launching pad . . . Be aware of the seat belt that is holding you in your seat . . . Think about how you feel as you wait for the engines to start. What do you think this trip will be like? . . .

Listen to the sounds of the engines as they begin to fire . . . What is the sound like? . . . Feel the vibrations as the sound gets louder . . . The spacecraft is beginning to rise and roll at the same time . . . Look out the window of the spacecraft and focus on the launching pad. Notice it as it gets smaller and smaller and finally disappears . . . Focus your attention on the seat belt . . . As you climb higher you are traveling faster and faster . . . Your seat belt is getting tighter as you are thrust back in your seat. Imagine there is a string running from your stomach to the center of the earth . . . As you climb higher the string pulls on you harder . . . Feel the tug . . . All of a sudden the string breaks and you no longer feel any pull. How does it feel to have no pull on you? . . . You are now weightless . . . If you were not strapped in, you would float . . . How do you feel?

As you look out the window you realize that you are orbiting the earth . . . While looking out the window you see something . . . Look at it carefully . . . What is it? All of a sudden the object disappears . . . Where do you think it went?

Focus on being weightless . . . Notice that when you hold an object up in front of you and let it go, it just stays there . . . Pretend to unfasten your seat belt . . . Get out of your seat and do a somersault . . . How do you feel? Practice walking with no pull on your feet . . . How well can you keep your balance? . . . Return to your seat and fasten your seat belt . . . Prepare to return to earth.

Listen to the rockets fire to slow the spacecraft for re-entry . . . How do they sound? . . . Feel the pull of gravity on your body as your craft re-enters the atmosphere . . . Feel the string pulling on your stomach again . . . Look out the window and notice the colors from the heat as your craft streaks through the air . . . What colors do you see? . . . Your craft is slowing as it approaches the landing strip . . . Steer the craft in and feel it as it hits the runway . . . How do you feel? . . . How does it feel to return to earth? . . . Slowly open your eyes and come back to this room . . . Unfasten your seat belt, get out of your seat, and get ready to share your experience . . .

After the visualization experience, have students do a follow-up activity from the following choices:

- In small groups have students share their experiences. Have each student take a minute to describe his or her trip and identify at least one highlight of the voyage.
- Have students share their ideas about the most interesting part of the space voyage.
- Provide drawing paper and crayons and ask the students to draw pictures of some of the things they visualized on their space voyage.
- Ask the students to discuss the object that they encountered during their voyage. Have them describe it and explain where they think it went.

Lesson 5. Life Cycles of the Stars

Black holes, neutron stars, and pulsars are all recent discoveries made by astronomers, and each represents a new and fascinating theory about the life cycles of stars. Students may be interested in exploring more of these fascinating new aspects of space science.

Materials
Pictures and charts of stars; chart paper; poster board; old magazines; crayons and marking pens; paints.

Action
Basic information about star birth, main sequence stars, red giants, white dwarfs, neutron stars, supernovae, pulsars, and black holes is provided below. Students can explore any of these topics using the information provided and current books. Encourage them to use their creativity to complete the activities.

1. Have students write a space adventure in which they encounter stars in different life cycle stages.
2. Have students design posters and charts about the various types of stars.
3. Have students read about the life cycles of stars in books and articles and prepare a poster report on their work.
4. Have students make models of the various stars using available materials.

Life Cycles of Stars[2]

Star Birth   Stars are believed to be formed by the condensation of enormous clouds of cosmic dust and hydrogen gas, which is the lightest and most plentiful of the elements. There are many of these clouds in the universe.

The force behind the birth of a star is gravity. According to Newton's theory of universal gravitation, all bodies attract each other in proportion to their mass and distance apart. The gas and dust particles in these vast interstellar clouds attract each other and gradually draw closer together. Eventually the particles form a mass that is bound together by gravitation; the edges of the cloud collapse inward, separating it from the remaining gas and dust in the vicinity. As the cloud shrinks, the core heats up. If the developing star has enough mass, the core will eventually heat up enough to cause nuclear reactions. A star is born!

Scientists believe that stars are still being born today. Astronomers using infrared telescopes to study dense interstellar clouds have discovered many glowing objects that cannot be seen with standard telescopes because of the surrounding dust and gas; these objects are assumed to be developing stars.

Main Sequence Stars   Stars are classified according to their brightness and temperature. When stars are plotted on a graph, most of them fall within a narrow band. This band is called the main sequence of stars.

How long a star remains in the main sequence, burning hydrogen for its fuel, depends largely on its mass. Our sun has an estimated main sequence lifetime of about ten billion years. Cosmologists and geologists estimate that approximately five billion of these years have now passed. Large stars burn fast and hot and may have main sequence lifetimes of as little as a million years. At some point all stars undergo major changes in their size and composition; the life cycle of a star is determined primarily by its original mass.

Red Giants   When the hydrogen fuel in a star's core has been used up, the core starts to collapse. At the same time, the hydrogen fusion process moves outward from the core into the surrounding regions, continuing the process of converting hydrogen into helium and releasing radiant energy as the star grows.

The intense heat of the nuclear reaction now occurring in a shell around the core causes the star's surface to change from white to red. When this happens to our sun, it will grow into a vast sphere, engulfing Mercury and Venus and possibly Earth and Mars. It will then be a red giant.

White Dwarfs.   When there is no nuclear energy left, the star collapses, turning into a small dense star called a white dwarf. Its atoms are packed so tightly together that a fragment the size of a sugar cube would weigh thousands of kilograms. Over several more billion years, the white dwarf cools and gradually turns into a black cinder. This is the fate of our sun and most other stars.

Neutron Stars.   In a star more than about 1½ times the mass of the sun, gravitational forces are so great that they overcome the collective electron pressure that halts the collapse of smaller stars. The compression of the core may continue until its density is so high that its electrons are driven into the atomic nuclei, changing them into neutrons. This creates an atomic nucleus of astronomical proportions—a neutron star.

A neutron star may be as small as 20 kilometers, or 12 miles, in diameter but have a density billions of times that of lead. A cubic centimeter would weigh billions of kilograms because all the space between the atoms in the molecules has been eliminated!

Supernovae. The final collapse of a star to the neutron stage may give rise to physical conditions that cause its outer portions to explode, producing a supernova. The explosion can produce a burst of energy that will temporarily outshine all the hundreds of millions of ordinary stars in a galaxy.

Pulsars. The pulsar was discovered by radio astronomers, who named it after its characteristic pulsing of energy. A pulsar is thought to be a rapidly spinning neutron star that may also give off energy at X-ray and other wavelengths. It is not likely that a pulsar actually turns its radiation on and off; energy is probably emitted from a point on the star that faces toward and then away from earth as the star spins, so that the signal is received for only a small part of each revolution.

Black Holes. Physicists believe that when a star with more than about three times the mass of our sun reaches the end of the gravitational collapse and nuclear burning cycle, it becomes a strange oddity called a black hole. A large, dying star shrinks until it is incredibly dense and its gravity increases in proportion to its size so that nothing, not even light, can escape its surface. It literally becomes a black hole in space. Any matter or light that approaches a black hole is sucked downward to its surface and vanishes.

Lesson 6. Life Styles of Sea Organisms

Looking at an organism's life style, which includes its habitat, behavior, and energy requirements, is a convenient way to study sea organisms. In this activity students will learn about four life styles of sea organisms and use this information to create a viable sea creature.

Materials

Paper cups, plastic spoons, string, paper, paper clips, pipe cleaners, tape, buttons, feathers, tongue depressors, scissors, paint, cardboard.

Action

1. Sea organisms can be classified into four life style groups:

   Benthic life style: Organisms that live in, on, or attached to the ocean bottom.

   Nektonic life style: Organisms that swim under their own power.

   Planktonic life style: Floating plants or animals—they may or may not swim—that are swept about by ocean currents.

   Land and water life style: Organisms that live on beaches or on land near the ocean. They often feed in the ocean.

2. Discuss the four life style groups of organisms. Provide copies of the chart on page 166 and ask questions such as:

   What are some examples of benthic (nektonic, planktonic, land and water) animals?
   How does the life style of a benthic organism differ from that of other organisms?
   What kind of life style does a pelican (porpoise, sea anemone, jellyfish) enjoy?

3. Challenge student teams to create an organism with one of the following sets of characteristics using the materials provided.

   a. The organism meets the requirements of a benthic, nektonic, planktonic, or land and water organism.
   b. The organism has characteristics of nektonic and land and water organisms.
   c. The organism has the characteristics of benthic and planktonic organisms.
   d. The organism has the characteristics of any combination of organisms the students choose.

4. Give each team about 30 minutes to create their new organism. Have them name it using genus and species terminology. Suggest that they look up names of animals to get ideas for species names that describe the organism's characteristics.
5. Assemble the teams of students. Have the students introduce their organisms to the class and describe its life style and characteristics.
6. Display all of the organisms on a large sheet of news print or poster board. Then introduce the idea of a food chain; use the illustration shown here to present the idea.

OCEAN FOOD CHAIN

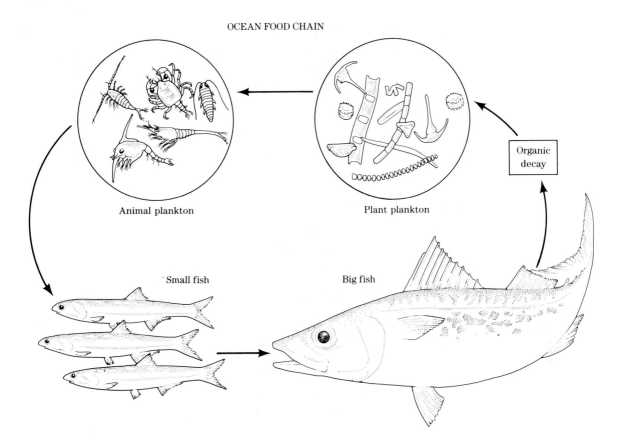

Animal plankton   Plant plankton   Organic decay

Small fish   Big fish

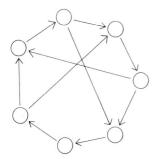

Have each team send one student to the display area at a time; other members of the team can help from a distance. Have students draw arrows showing the organisms their creature will eat and the organisms that will eat their creature.

7. When the food chain predictions are completed, discuss the importance of food chains in the life styles of all organisms.

Lesson 7. Balloon Rockets

A balloon is an excellent device to use to help students understand rocket technology. A rocket gets the push necessary to shoot it into the sky by throwing something out the nozzle. The more that is thrown out and the faster it is thrown, the greater the push. The diagram below illustrates the essential elements in the design of a rocket engine.

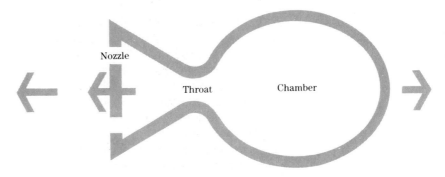

Nozzle

Throat   Chamber

Materials
Balloons, plastic straws, nylon thread, paper clips, string, tape, feathers, toy water rocket and water (optional).

Action

1. Divide the class into teams and challenge each team to design a rocket that will travel the farthest along a test firing line. Establish the line by stretching a 10–15 meter nylon thread between two chairs. Allow each group to test fire their rocket before the final balloon rocket test. Tell the students that they will be limited to one balloon per rocket, but they can use any other materials on hand to improve it.

   One of the most sophisticated balloon rockets I have seen is illustrated below. To control the flow of air out of the balloon, a small piece of straw was taped to the balloon nozzle. When the rocket is fired, the air flows out in a more even exhaust. The balloon does not travel very fast, but it tends to travel for a long period of time. Leave the design and engineering to the imagination and creativity of your students and share your insights during the discussion.

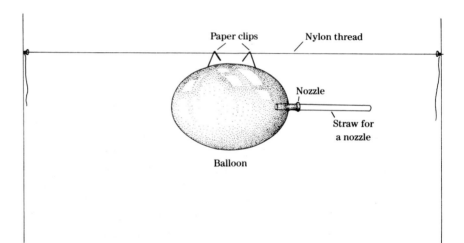

2. When the rocket construction process is complete and each group has had a chance to test fire their vehicle, gather the entire class together to observe the final rocket firing. If you wish to encourage some friendly competition among the groups, you might have a variety of award categories, including the fastest, weirdest, slowest, largest, smallest, and most imaginative rocket.

3. After the rocket firings are finished, have each group draw their rocket design on a large sheet of chart paper or poster board. Ask each group to include information explaining what they think causes the rocket to move. They should do this without referring to books or other sources of information. When each group has completed its design, invite one person per group to enter the fishbowl and take two minutes to explain the group's design. When each spokesperson has had a chance to speak, open the discussion to everyone.

4. Clear up any misconceptions about how rockets work. Provide books and other reference materials for the students to study.
5. Extend this Adventure using plastic toy rockets that are propelled by water. As shown in the drawing below, pressure is applied with a pump. The rocket is pushed off the hand-held launch platform and rises into the air. These rockets are safe, fun, and educationally sound. Combine the use of the water rocket with the astrolabe in Project 2 to determine how high these rockets fly. It is also possible to calculate the velocity of the rocket.

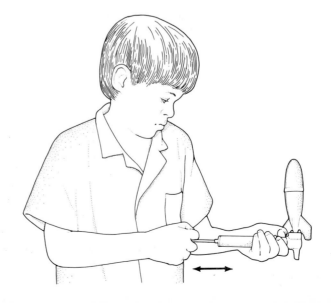

Side Paths

Lesson 8. Capsule to the Stars (Social Studies)

Get a large cardboard carton and cover it with gold wrapping paper or tin foil. Explain that this is a capsule that will be placed in a space probe being sent out of our solar system. Ask students what they would put into the capsule to give extraterrestrials an idea of what earth and its organisms are like.

Have each student draw a picture or glue pictures on paper of what they would like to put in the capsule. On the other side of the paper they should write the reasons for their choices. Place all the items in the box. Then have students pretend that they are extraterrestrials who have intercepted the capsule. Let each person draw one item out of the box, read it to the class, and interpret it.

Lesson 9. Murmurs from Earth (Social Studies)

Have students make an audio tape that would give someone from another planet or star an idea of how earth sounds. You can divide the class into teams, each equipped with a tape recorder. Teams could record sounds from the following categories:

1. Various human languages
2. Bird and animal sounds
3. Sounds of machines
4. Natural sounds of rain, wind, surf, waterfalls
5. Music, ranging from rock to classical
6. Noises
7. Other sounds

When students have completed their recordings, they should play their tape to the class. Have the class evaluate the quality of the recording and discuss how well the sounds represent the categories the team selected.

Lesson 10. Planetary Race (Physical Education)[3]

You will need a bicycle, an empty track, and an assortment of objects to represent the planets. In this activity students use a bicycle to simulate a trip through the solar system, dropping off objects along the way to represent the planets.

The Planetary Lap Chart

Distance in Laps	Planet	Object
Start	Sun	no object
$\frac{2}{5}$	Mercury	fresh pea
$\frac{3}{4}$	Venus	walnut
1	Earth	bigger walnut
1 + 1 step	Moon	dried pea
1½	Mars	bean

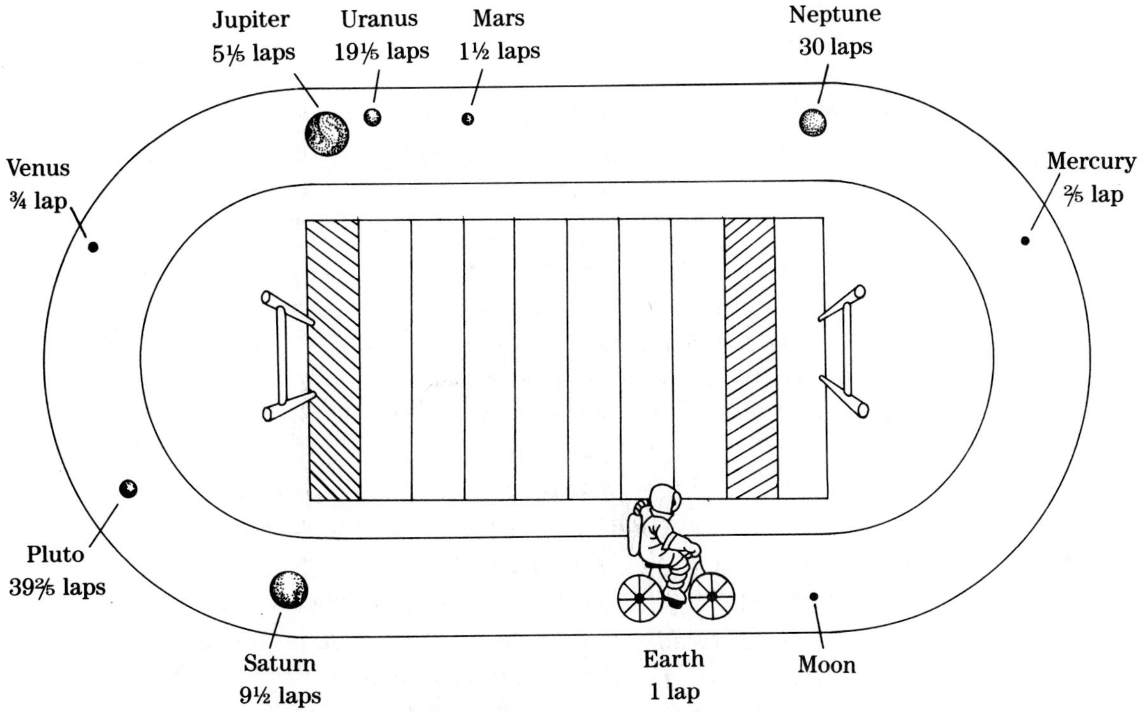

At this point, have students rest. They have gone through the smaller planets and are now ready to consider the more distant planets. When they begin again, they will need to change bikers more often to reach the outer planets.

Distance in Laps	Planet	Object
5⅕	Jupiter	9-inch cabbage
9½	Saturn	8-inch cabbage
19⅕	Uranus	orange
30	Neptune	grapefruit
39⅖	Pluto	bean

Students should be impressed that the moon is only one step from the earth whereas Saturn, an outer planet, is 9½ laps away! Be sure students understand that the closest star would be thousands and thousands of laps away!

Note: If you do not want students to do actual bicycle laps, you can use distances of the laps in meters. For example, Mercury would be ⅖ of a meter from the sun, and Jupiter would be 5½ meters from the sun. Students will be able to appreciate the vast distances that exist between the planets by using either method to do the activity.

Lesson 11. Save the Whales (Social Studies)

The whale, which is the common name used in the order of mammals known as Cetecea, includes sperm, bottle-nosed, beaked, killer, humpback, and pilot whales; dolphins; and porpoises. There are several studies that your students might be interested in exploring. For example, *Voyage of the Mimi*, developed by the Bank Street College of Education, combines television, computers, and print materials to present an exciting dramatization and documentation of how scientists study whales.

1. Have students write letters to various wildlife groups, government agencies, and politicians for information about what is being done to protect whales. This could lead to a Save the Whales campaign in the school or neighborhood.
2. The ability of cetaceans to see with sound is called "echolocation." Have students investigate and find out what echolocation is and how whales, dolphins, and porpoises use it to see.
3. The language of whales, porpoises, and dolphins has been recorded and studied by several groups of scientists. Recordings of whale songs and communications are readily available in local libraries. Obtain copies of these whale sounds so that students can listen to them and speculate about what they mean.

Lesson 12. The Make-a-Dolphin Game (Mathematics)[4]

The purpose of this game is to create a 40-pound dolphin using the following food chain: diatoms, copepods, oysters, crabs, and fish. Each feeding level of the chain represents a different amount of food material. Since only 10 percent of the material at each level is used to build the organism at the next higher level, it will take 4,000,000 pounds of diatoms, 400,000 pounds of copepods, 40,000 pounds of oysters, 4,000 pounds of crab, and 400 pounds of fish to make one 40 pound adult dolphin.

Preparing for the Game

In advance, make copies of the Make-a-Dolphin game board (page 167) and glue it onto cardboard. Push a brass fastener through the center of the board to hold a spinner and cut out a piece of cardboard in the shape of an arrow. For each game board, make four sets of cards (pages 168, 169), so that up to four persons can play at each game board.

Rules

1. To play the game, two-to-four players need a game board and a set of cards for each player.
2. One player is chosen to keep score and hand out food chain cards.
3. Players spin to see who goes first. The highest number starts.
4. Each player starts with a diatom card.
5. Players move through the food chain by collecting the amount of weight written on the cards.
6. The value of the units on each card is determined by the numbers on the gameboard. For instance, a 2 on the game board equals 2 times the value of a unit on the food chain card. A player holding a diatom card would receive 2 x 100,000 = 200,000 lbs and on the next turn would need only 2 to receive a copepod card.
7. As each player reaches or exceeds the amount on the next food chain card, he or she obtains the card from the scorekeeper.
8. The first player to move through the entire food chain to the dolphin is the winner.
9. Each player is allowed one spin at a time.

Lesson 13. Ocean Tank Beaches (Oceanography)

The patterns that are created along our shorelines are works of art. These patterns can be made and observed in a portable ocean tank. It is a waterproof box containing water, dirt, sand, and gravel. It can be used to simulate ocean waves, beaches, beach erosion, beach construction, and a variety of geological features.

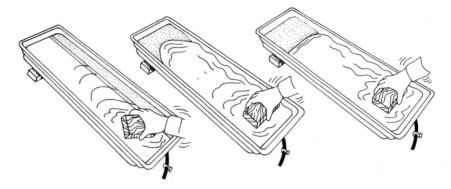

Set up an ocean tank for the duration of the Experience so that students can study ocean processes. You will need only one tank, and you can obtain an inexpensive one (under $20) from Science Kit, Inc.

Students can use the tank to perform a variety of experiments.

1. Provide photographs of ocean features and challenge the students to create the processes in the ocean tank that would cause the feature. A series of excellent photographs are available from Webster Division, McGraw-Hill Book Company in the guide and cards for "Stream Tables", which is one of the Elementary Science Study (ESS) units.
2. Obtain topographic maps of beach areas and have students recreate the area in the ocean tank.
3. Use colored dye in the ocean tank to study currents and water motion.
4. Have students simulate the action of waves by gently pushing down on a wood block placed in the ocean tank and investigate the effect of ocean waves on the profiles of beaches.

Lesson 14. Cosmic Telegram (Social Studies)[8]

Communication with extraterrestrials may be possible, and scientists have already begun to attempt doing so. The diagram shown on page 160 appeared in *Discover Magazine*. It contains nine distinct messages and was designed by Professor Frank Drake. Give a copy of it to your students and have them try to figure out the messages.

After students have had a chance to work on the diagram, give them the decoding key. Let them work for a while to see if they can figure out the logic behind the system.

As a follow up, students can write to NASA and ask for information on the search for other intelligent life in the universe. Students might keep a Starfolk Notebook containing newspaper and magazine articles on UFOs, close encounter reports, and radio astronomy communication. They can also read and review books about attempts to communicate with extraterrestrials.

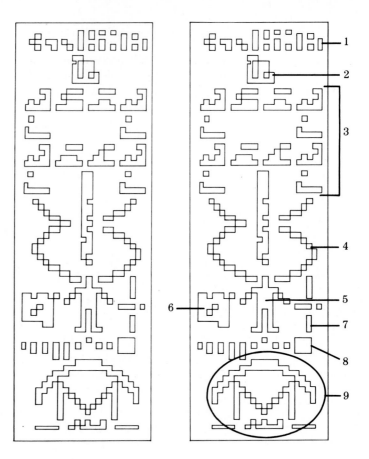

Cosmic Telegram Decoding Key[5]

Code Number	Message
1	From right to left, binary representations of the numbers one through ten.
2	In binary number form, the atomic numbers (numbers of protons in the nucleus) of hydrogen, carbon, nitrogen, oxygen, and phosphorus—the chemical elements essential for life.
3	Twelve blocks that give the chemical formula for DNA, the key life molecule on earth.
4	A picture of the DNA molecule—the famous double helix.
5	A human being
6	In binary notation, the population of earth, about 5 billion.
7	The height of a human being.
8	The sun and its nine planets, with the third planet (earth) slightly displaced to show where the message came from.
9	A diagram of the Arecibo telescope.

Searches

Lesson 1. Making a Seaquarium[6]

A seaquarium is an aquarium that can support sea life. It can be made by adding saltwater, crushed shell, a thermometer, and an aerator to an aquarium with a top. The following illustration shows a simplified way to set up a pair of seaquariums.

Students working on this project should visit a local pet shop that specializes in marine life to obtain plants and sea life. You could also invite someone from a local pet shop to your class and in advance purchase a starter supply of marine life for the seaquariums.

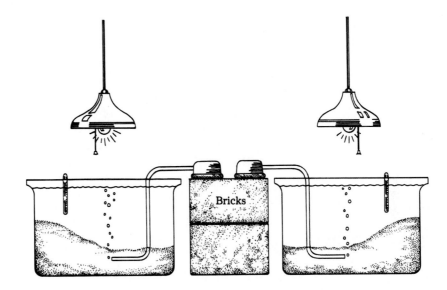

Bricks

Lesson 2. A Do-It-Yourself Planetarium and Astrolabe Kit

For this project, students can make a simple planetarium, which is nothing more than a star projector, using a tin can. Cut both ends out of a two-pound coffee can. Have them trace constellations on black paper and punch holes in the paper with a pin or nail. The size of the holes can be varied to show the relative brightness of each star in the constellation.

When the patterns are complete, darken the room and project the constellations onto the ceiling of the classroom by placing a flashlight in the open end of the can.

Black paper

Coffee can

Flashlight

Students working on this project can make a catalog of constellations, with a single constellation on each sheet. Other students can learn the constellations using the Do-It-Yourself Planetarium.

To extend this activity, have students follow the directions below to make a star sighter, called an astrolabe. Students will need string, a washer, a brad, a straw, and an astrolabe template (see page 170).

1. Tape the straw to the top of the astrolabe.
2. Push the brad through the astrolabe template and attach a piece of string to the brad. Tie a washer to the end of the string.
3. To use the astrolabe, point to an object and sight through the straw. Read the angle on the astrolabe. This number tells you how high the object is above the horizon.

CAUTION: NEVER POINT OR LOOK AT THE SUN WITH THE ASTROLABE.

Evaluation

To evaluate the progress of students' understanding of the concepts developed in this unit, you can ask any one of the following questions. These questions can be answered in writing, or in a mock conference in which teams of students collaborate before giving a response.

- Why is it important to explore outer space? Is this something that humans should continue to do?
- What should people know about space and space exploration? Why is this knowledge important?
- Scientists and officials of the United States and Soviet governments are seriously thinking of planning a joint mission to Mars. Do you agree or disagree with this mission. Why?
- If you were to give a talk to students in the third grade about the importance of the earth's oceans, what would you tell them?

Books for Kids

Starship Books

Barrett, N.S. *Astronauts*. NY: Watts, 1985.

_____. *Spacecraft*. NY: Watts, 1985.

Billings, Charlene W. *Crista McAuliffe: Pioneer Space Teacher*. NY: Enslow, 1986.

_____. *Space Station: Bold New Step beyond Earth*. NY: Dodd, Mead, 1986.

Branley, Franklyn M. *From Sputnik to Space Shuttles: Into The New Space Age*. NY: Crowell, 1986.

Cannon, Robert L. and Michael A. Banks. *The Rocket Book: A Guide to Building and Launching Model Rockets for the Space Age*. Englewood Cliffs, NJ: Prentice-Hall, 1985.

Gunston, Bill. *Aircraft*. NY: Watts, 1986.

Lord, Suzanne and Jolie Epstein. *A Day in Space*. NY: Scholastic, 1986.

Maurer, Richard. *The NOVA Space Explorer's Guide: Where to Go and What to See*. NY: Clarkson N. Potter/WGBH Boston, 1985.

McPhee, Penelope and Raymond McPhee. *Your Future in Space: The U.S. Space Camp Training Program*. NY: Crown, 1986.

Ride, Sally with Susan Okie. *To Space & Back*. NY: Lothrop, 1986.

Swiggins, Don. *Flying the Space Shuttles*. NY: Dodd, Mead, 1985.

Canoe Books

Arnold, Caroline. *Bodies of Water: Fun, Facts, and Activities*. NY: Watts, 1985.

Gilbreath, Alice. *The Continental Shelf: An Underwater Frontier.* Minneapolis: Dillon, 1986.

_____. *River in the Ocean: The Story of the Gulf Stream*. Minneapolis: Dillon, 1986.

Glaser, Michael. *The Nature of the Seashore*. Fiskdale, MA: Knicker-
    bocker, 1986.

Green, Carl R. and William R. Sanford. *The Great White Shark*.
    Mankato, MN: Crestwood, 1985.

_____. *The Humpback Whale*. Mankato, MN: Crestwood, 1985.

Hanmer, Trudy J. *Water Resources*. NY: Watts, 1985.

Malnig, Anita. *Where the Waves Break: Life at the Edge of the Sea*.
    Minneapolis: Carolrhoda, 1985.

Mitgutsch, Ali. *From Sea to Salt*. Minneapolis: Carolrhoda, 1985.

Sabin, Louis. *Fish*. Mahwah, NJ: Troll, 1985.

Sabin, Frances. *Whales and Dolphins*. Mahwah, NJ: Troll, 1985.

Seymour, Peter. *What Lives in the Sea*. NY: Macmillan, 1985.

COMPARING PHYSICAL PROPERTIES

Comparing the Physical Properties of Planet X Material with Water

Property:	Planet X Material	Water
Color		
Clearness		
Odor		
Feel		
Flowing properties		
Shape of drops on wax paper		
Other		

Page reference: 146

COMPARING MIXING PROPERTIES

Comparing the Mixing Properties of Planet X Material with Water

Materials:	Salt	Sugar	Cornstarch	Soap	Water	Rubbing Alcohol
Dissolves in Planet X material						
Does not dissolve in Planet X material						
Dissolves in water						
Does not dissolve in water						

Page reference: 146

LIFE STYLE GROUPS OF SEA ORGANISMS

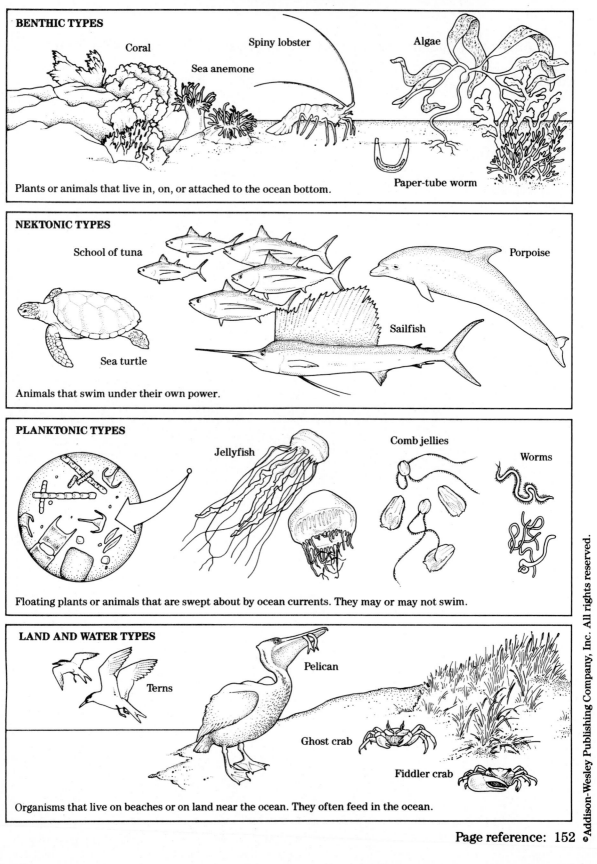

BENTHIC TYPES

Coral

Spiny lobster

Sea anemone

Algae

Paper-tube worm

Plants or animals that live in, on, or attached to the ocean bottom.

NEKTONIC TYPES

School of tuna

Porpoise

Sea turtle

Sailfish

Animals that swim under their own power.

PLANKTONIC TYPES

Jellyfish

Comb jellies

Worms

Floating plants or animals that are swept about by ocean currents. They may or may not swim.

LAND AND WATER TYPES

Pelican

Terns

Ghost crab

Fiddler crab

Organisms that live on beaches or on land near the ocean. They often feed in the ocean.

Page reference: 152

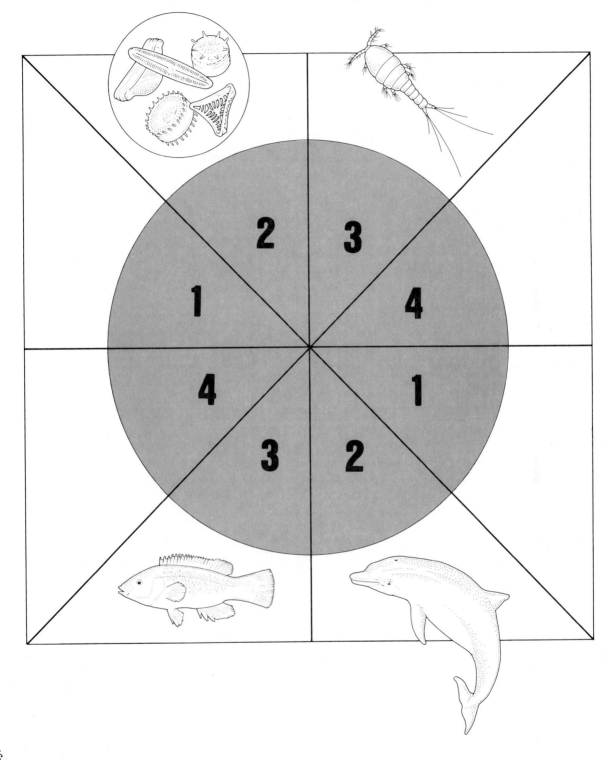

[3] The Dolphin game was developed by the Sea Grant College Program, Texas A&M University.

Page reference: 158

Make-A-Dolphin Game, page 2

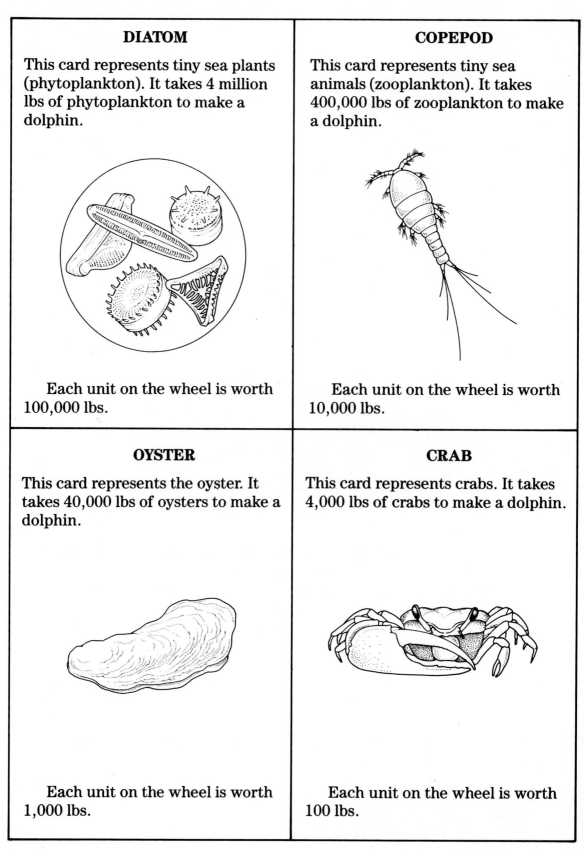

DIATOM

This card represents tiny sea plants (phytoplankton). It takes 4 million lbs of phytoplankton to make a dolphin.

Each unit on the wheel is worth 100,000 lbs.

COPEPOD

This card represents tiny sea animals (zooplankton). It takes 400,000 lbs of zooplankton to make a dolphin.

Each unit on the wheel is worth 10,000 lbs.

OYSTER

This card represents the oyster. It takes 40,000 lbs of oysters to make a dolphin.

Each unit on the wheel is worth 1,000 lbs.

CRAB

This card represents crabs. It takes 4,000 lbs of crabs to make a dolphin.

Each unit on the wheel is worth 100 lbs.

Page reference: 158

The Dolphin game was developed by the Sea Grant College Program, Texas A&M University.

Make-A-Dolphin Game, page 3

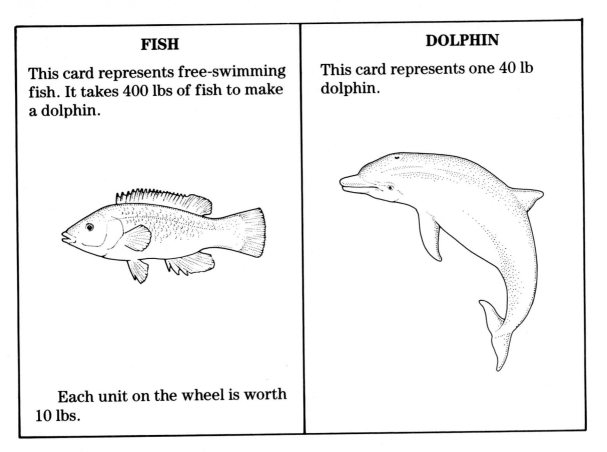

FISH	**DOLPHIN**
This card represents free-swimming fish. It takes 400 lbs of fish to make a dolphin.	This card represents one 40 lb dolphin.
Each unit on the wheel is worth 10 lbs.	

Rules

1. To play the game, two-to-four players need a game board and a set of cards for each player.
2. One player is chosen to keep score and hand out food chain cards.
3. Players spin to see who goes first. The highest number starts.
4. Each player starts with a diatom card.
5. Players move through the food chain by collecting the amount of weight written on the cards.
6. The value of the units on each card is determined by the numbers on the game board. For instance, a 2 on the game board equals 2 times the value of a unit on the food chain card. A player holding a diatom card would receive 2 x 100,000 = 200,000 lbs and on the next turn would need only a 2 to receive a copepod card.
7. As each player reaches or exceeds the amount on the next food chain card, he or she obtains the card from the scorekeeper.
8. The first player to move through the entire food chain to the dolphin is the winner.
9. Each player is allowed one spin at a time.

Page reference: 158

The Dolphin game was developed by the Sea Grant College Program, Texas A&M University.

DIRECTIONS FOR MAKING
AN ASTROLABE

To make an astrolabe you will need: string, a washer, a brad, a straw, and the astrolabe template below.

1. Tape the straw to the top of the astrolabe.
2. Push the brad through the astrolabe template and attach a piece of string to the brad. Tie a washer to the end of the string.
3. To use the astrolabe, point to an object and sight through the straw. Read the angle on the astrolabe. The number tells you how high the object is above the horizon.
CAUTION: NEVER POINT OR LOOK AT THE SUN WITH THE ASTROLABE.

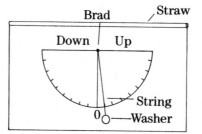

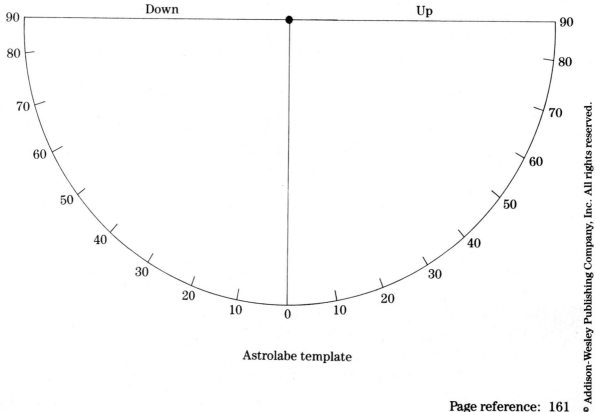

Astrolabe template

Page reference: 161

TOUCH
THE
EARTH

A Geological Experience

"The crust of the Earth is dynamic. Every few hundred million years the continents are rearranged and the ocean floors are made anew. Life must adapt its drama to the shifting stage. Every rock, every pebble, every grain of sand has a story to tell of the earth's past."

CHET RAYMO
Biography of a Planet

TEACHER INFORMATION

Background Information

Learning about the earth can be fun. Imagine giving pairs of students a bag for collecting rocks and instructions to find the following:

1. A rock smaller than the fingernail on your pinky.
2. A rock bigger than your fist.
3. A rock with something growing on it.
4. A square rock.
5. A round, smooth rock.
6. A rock with more than one color.
7. A rock that makes you feel good.
8. A very rough rock.
9. A rock that would make a good paperweight.
10. A rock that would make a nice gift for someone special.

Touch the Earth is a unit of discovery and exploration of earth's geology. Rocks and fossils are clues to help us unravel pictures of the earth's past. Geology is like detective work. The geologist examines rocks and fossils just as a detective examines footprints, tire marks, and fingerprints. Interpreting these clues is the business of both detectives and geologists. At times the work these people do can be tricky and dangerous. Following is a comparison of the processes used by a paleontologist—a geologist who studies fossils—and a detective. Note the similarities used by these searchers.

Geologists and Detectives at Work: A Comparison

Process	Fossil Evidence	Criminal Evidence
Reconstruction	Paleontologists piece together fragments of an animal's skeleton.	A police artist recreates a face from a skull or from a description.
Deduction	Knowledge that bears could not survive in a region's climate eliminates the possibility of finding a fragment of a bear's skeleton.	Knowledge of the whereabouts and actions of a person when a crime is committed eliminates that person as a suspect.
Location	After finding tool-like objects, the paleontologist looks for fragments of human bone.	After finding evidence of a forced entry, the detective looks for evidence of a crime.
Technology	Paleontologists use chemical dating techniques (C14) to determine the age of objects they find.	Detectives use fingerprints to identify unknown suspects and victims.
Recognition	Paleontologists distinguish one type of bone from another.	Detectives tentatively rely on eyewitness identification of suspects.

Rocks, patterns in the rocks, and fossils are examples of evidence that geologists use to develop theories of the earth. Such theories help to explain how rocks are formed; the various stages of earth history; the sequence in the development of life on earth; the origin of ocean basins, continents, and mountains.

In order for geologists to assemble evidence, it is often necessary to dig into the earth to find what is needed. In fact, the word *fossil* is derived from the Latin word meaning "dug up." Many human activities, such as road and building construction, reveal layers of earth not otherwise visible. Drilling machines can expose a cylindrical core of rock, giving us a glimpse of earth we would not have been able to see otherwise. In exploration for oil, minerals, and building materials, the mysteries of the earth's interior are often revealed.

Overview and Planning

Take a few minutes to review the Overview and Planning Chart for Touch the Earth. There are six Adventures, seven Side Paths, and four Searches.

Overview and Planning Chart: Touch the Earth

Lesson	Science Concept	Science Process	Modes of Learning	Attitude
Adventures				
1. Touching Rocks	Rocks are natural materials that can be described using the senses.	Observing	Physical-sensory	Sensitivity to environment
2. Bits and Pieces of Earth	Physical properties are clues to the history of a rock.	Observing Classifying	Physical-sensory Left	Objectivity Thoroughness
3. Being a Geological Detective	Physical properties are clues to the history of a rock.	Observing Classifying	Physical-sensory Right Left	Curiosity Objectivity
4. Older Than You Think	Events in the geological history of earth can be represented on a geological time line.	Inferring Classifying	Physical-sensory Left	Curiosity
5. A Fossil Dig	Fossils are the remains or traces of animals or plants that have been preserved in the earth's crust.	Observing Classifying	Physical-sensory Cognitive	Creativity Persistence

Overview and Planning Chart: Touch the Earth

Lesson	Science Concept	Science Process	Modes of Learning	Attitude
Adventures				
6. A Crusty Puzzle	The earth's surface is covered by thin plates that move over the materials beneath.	Inferring Formulating hypotheses	Left Right	Creativity
Side Paths				
7. Continental Drift Flip Book (Geography)	Over time, the continents have drifted away from a supercontinent to their present locations. This movement is called continental drift.	Observing Inferring	Physical-sensory Left	Creativity
8. Home Inventory (Social Studies)	Many materials found at home are made from rocks and minerals.	Observing Classifying	Physical-sensory Left	Objectivity Sensitivity to environment
9. Values and the Environment (Social Studies)	Attitudes about the environment depend on one's beliefs and values.	Interpreting data	Left Affective	Sensitivity to environment
10. Gravel Art (Art)	Earth materials can be used as art media.	Classifying	Physical-sensory	Sensitivity to environment
11. Clay Models (Art)	Earth materials can be observed and described using the senses.	Observing Inferring	Physical-sensory	Creativity
12. Creating Stories (Language Arts)	Past ecologies can be inferred from fossil evidence.	Inferring	Left Right	Creativity
13. Writing About Science (Language Arts)	The senses are the foundation for further observing and interpreting.	Observing Interpreting data	Physical-sensory Left	Creativity
Searches				
1. Locating Earthquakes	Most earthquakes occur along the edges of moving plates.	Observing Interpreting data	Left	Sensitivity to environment

Lesson	Science Concept	Science Process	Modes of Learning	Attitude
2. Shells as Architects	Shells have diverse properties.	Classifying	Physical-sensory Left	Curiosity
3. Mineral Madness	Minerals can be classified on the basis of physical characteristics.	Classifying	Physical-sensory Left	Sensitivity to environment
4. To the Field!	Experiences in the field are the real world of geology!	Observing	Physical-sensory Left	Sensitivity to environment

Objectives

At the end of this Experience students should be able to:

1. Develop inquiry techniques to ask questions about rocks, fossils, and geologic features.
2. Appreciate the outdoors as a natural geological laboratory.
3. Carefully observe objects such as rocks and fossils.
4. Make inferences based on observations.
5. Create art forms about geology using poetry, painting, sculpture, and dioramas.

Key Concepts

The following represent the major concepts that students will study:

Rocks Any natural material formed of minerals; rocks are grouped into three classes: igneous, sedimentary, and metamorphic.

Fossil The remains of an animal or plant preserved in a rock; fossils are found as a cast, impression, or trace.

Paleoecology The study of fossil animals and plants in relation to the conditions under which they lived.

Fossil Community A group of fossils found in the same place where they lived.

Evolution The process by which new forms of living things may develop from earlier forms by passing on small changes from one generation to the next.

Plate tectonics The theory that the earth's surface is covered by a number of relatively thin plates that move over the material below.

Teaching Phases

Following are three phases for implementing the activities in the Experience:

Phase 1. Direct Instruction/Interactive Teaching

Rocks, minerals and fossils are objects that students enjoy observing and experimenting with. In this Experience, you might want to do the Adventures in sequence and then choose activities from the Side Paths for enrichment. The Adventures in this Experience will give students opportunities to examine and study minerals, rocks, and fossils, as well as investigate geologic time and plate tectonics.

Phase II. Cooperative Learning

All of the Adventures are designed for students in cooperative groups. After you get the students involved in the Adventures, you might present this option. Explain to students that there are four different projects from which to choose. Conduct a session in which you discuss each of the projects, and then provide time for the teams to decide which project they will do.

Phase III. Culminating Process

The students will collect and make a variety of artifacts during this Experience. One thing that is very effective is to set up a display of all the objects that are made and collected and any other products created during the Experience.

The student projects should take one or two days. Encourage diversity and creativity among the teams as they prepare for their class presentations.

Evaluate and obtain feedback on the students' opinions and attitudes toward this unit. Use the form provided on page 111.

STUDENT INFORMATION

Adventures

Lesson 1. Touching Rocks

This activity introduces students to the essence of geology by providing an opportunity for finding rocks, handling and playing with them, and relating geology to music and language arts.

Materials
Before the lesson, scout an area in the school yard for a place that your students can find at least one rock. If this is not possible, have a box of assorted rocks available.

Action

1. Take the students outside to the site that you have chosen. Tell the students that each of them is to find one rock. After a few minutes, gather students together and form a circle. Have the students observe their rocks using their senses. To encourage good observations, ask questions such as:

   - What colors do you see in your rock?
   - What does your rock smell like?
   - How big is your rock?
   - How heavy is your rock?

2. Tell students to form a circle so that they can play a game called "Find Your Rock." Have each person pass his or her rock to the left. Have them continue passing the rocks, one at a time. After three or four passes, have everyone in the circle change positions. Then tell the group that the object of the game is for each person to get his or her own rock back but that they are not allowed to look at the rocks as they are passed. Have students continue passing rocks. As they identify their rocks, they should remove themselves from the circle. The game ends when everyone has their original rocks.

3. In their science logs, have each student make a list of as many observations of their rocks as they can. Then have them use the data to write a rock *syntu*. A rock syntu is a five-line Japanese poem. The lines are written according to five simple rules:

   > Line 1—Name the object.
   > Line 2—Identify an observation of the object.
   > Line 3—Identify a feeling about the object.
   > Line 4—Identify another observation about the object.
   > Line 5—Close with a synonym for the name of the object.

   Have students experiment with writing syntus about their rocks, and have them write their final poems on construction paper for a classroom display.

4. To complete the lesson, ask students what questions they have about rocks, fossils, and the earth. Help generate questions by writing *Who*, *What*, *Where*, *Why*, and *How* on the chalkboard. Accept all questions. Refrain from trying to answer them or making comments about them. The idea is for students to come up with as many questions as they can in a short time. Display questions on a large piece of butcher paper in a prominent place.

Lesson 2. Bits and Pieces of Earth

Rocks are marvelous storehouses of information waiting to be examined and explored by students. Each rock has its own story, its own history. This lesson gets students started on a rock exploration. There are several interdisciplinary activities and projects that you can use for class or team follow-up activities. In all of these activities, you are encouraged to use rocks found in the surrounding area to help the students appreciate rocks and minerals as important local natural resources.

Materials

5-by-7-inch index cards; chips of the following rocks and minerals: granite, sandstone, shale, limestone, gneiss, marble, quartz, feldspar, mica, calcite; glue; a variety of rocks, one for each student.

Action

1. Take students on a guided adventure to explore a rock. Have the students prepare for a very short guided imagery experience by relaxing, and as they do so, give each student a small rock. Tell students to examine the rock by touching it but instruct them not to look at it. Explain that they are going to use their imaginations to explore and discover more about their rocks.

   Some students may wish to record their experience in their science log. Have copies of the visualization on page 188 on hand to help the students recall their experience.

2. The students are now ready to make their own rock identification cards.

3. Have students pick up an index card, and one of each rock and mineral chip you have prepared. The rocks and minerals suggested are the most common in the earth's crust and should be readily available, but any others may be substituted. To prepare the chips, crush a few hand samples with a hammer. Put the chips in separate labeled containers.

4. Students should glue their chips on the card as shown below. Some students may want to classify the rocks and separate them from the minerals. The rocks can be arranged on the cards in the following groups:

Halite	Mica	Feldspar	Quartz
Granite	Gneiss	Sandstone	Limestone
Slate	Shale	Calcite	Marble

5. When the rock identification cards are completed, have the students examine each of their samples by making observations and recording them in a chart (pages 189, 190).

Lesson 3. Being a Geological Detective

This lesson encourages students to use the processes of observation and classification to make inferences about rocks. After carefully looking at and performing simple tests on rocks found in the field, students are asked to make decisions about the kinds of rocks they have.

Materials
Several small bottles of vinegar (acid); magnifying glasses; porcelain pieces (used to determine the color of a mineral's streak); small pieces of flat glass; rock samples: sandstone (sedimentary), shale with fossils (sedimentary), limestone (sedimentary), granite (igneous), pumice (igneous), gneiss (metamorphic), marble (metamorphic), slate (metamorphic); mineral samples: quartz, feldspar, mica, calcite, chalk, coal, soapstone.

Action

1. Have the students imagine that they are geologists who have just returned from a field expedition to several places around the United States. Tell them that it is up to them to make careful observations about the rocks and minerals they found so that they will be able to identify them later. Give each learning team a set of samples that have been placed in small burlap bags to add a bit of suspense, magnifying glasses, vinegar, porcelain, and glass. It is recommended that you number the minerals and the rocks.
2. Have the students investigate the rocks and minerals and record their observations on the charts on pages 189 and 190.
3. Give the students the Rock Identification Key on page 191 and have them use it to classify the rocks in their samples.
4. Have the correct identifications available so that the students can check their work. Have several mystery samples in each grab bag. Challenge students to identify one or two of the mystery samples by using their charts and the rock identification key.

Lesson 4. Older Than You Think

Most students are fascinated by such things as the age of the earth, when dinosaurs roamed the earth, when life began on earth, and the amazingly short time that humans have been around. In this lesson, which integrates art, mathematics, and science, the students will construct a geological time line to help them understand the vastness of time and the myriad life forms that have evolved and disappeared.

Materials
Five meters of butcher paper per team, meter sticks, crayons, paints, small rulers, pencils, pens, assorted materials such as cotton, cloth, cardboard, magazine pictures, one or two fossils per team (use a variety such as crinoids, brachiopods, trilobites, dinosaur bones).

Action

1. Roll out five meters of butcher paper and fasten the ends down with tape. Tell the students that one end of the paper represents today and the other end represents when the earth was formed

(about five billion years ago). Have them label both ends of the paper.

Give each student a fossil and tell them that it was an animal or a plant that once lived on the earth. Tell them that they are to guess how old the fossil is and then stand along the time line at a place where they think the age of the fossil is represented. Give students a few minutes to get into position. Then have several volunteers explain why they chose their positions along the time line and ask what kind of fossil they think they have.

Students will not have much information upon which to base their decisions. Tell them that in this activity they will discover more about the history of the earth and when various groups of animals and plants lived on the earth.

2. Divide the class into learning teams. Give each team a History of the Earth chart (page 192), five meters of butcher paper, a meter stick, and crayons. Before the students begin making their time lines, show them how to divide the paper into time units and how to use the meter stick. Have them divide the paper into five sections one meter long to represent one billion years. Explain that since the meter stick is divided into 100 centimeters, each centimeter equals 10 million years and each decimeter equals 100 million years.

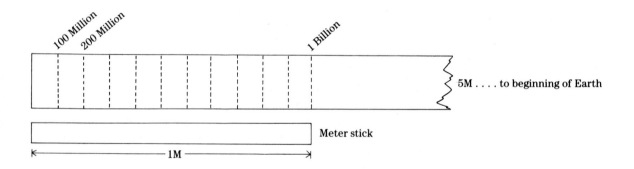

3. Have students label each section on their time line: 1 billion years ago, 2 billion years ago, and so forth. Then have them divide the first billion years into 10 equal parts and label each part: 100 million years ago, 200 million years ago, and so on.

4. Refer the students to the History of the Earth chart and ask the following questions:

   • What are the names of some of the geological periods?
   • What is the earliest period shown on the chart?
   • How many years did the Paleozoic era last?
   • When were the trilobites abundant?
   • When did the dinosaurs first appear on the earth?
   • When did the dinosaurs disappear from the earth?
   • When did humans first appear?

5. After you feel confident that the students can read the chart, tell them they are to label all the geological periods on their time line and then highlight each period with drawings and labels for major events or happenings in the history of the earth.

6. Display the completed time lines. Turn students' attention to the fossil you gave them earlier. Ask them to stand along a time line at the point that represents the age of this fossil.

Lesson 5. A Fossil Dig

One of my favorite activities is to take students fossil hunting, but unless there are fossiliferous sedimentary rocks close by, the venture is impractical. The solution is to bring the fossils into the classroom and simulate a fossil hunt. Bury fossils in containers and have students dig to find them.

Materials

Bury the following items in five half-gallon milk cartons filled with soil and sand: pieces of a wooden dinosaur from a hobby or school supply store (do not bury the complete animal, and be sure to spread the pieces among the five boxes); chicken and fish bones; twigs, stones, leaves; fossils. Provide pictures or books about dinosaurs and a plastic bag, a magnifying glass, a plastic spoon, one sheet of newspaper, a box to discard sand, and a map of the classroom dig area for each group.

Action

1. Introduce the lesson by showing students pictures of dinosaurs or a filmstrip or film about dinosaurs. Refer the students to the time lines they made, and have them identify the Mesozoic Era, when dinosaurs lived on the earth—from about 200 million years ago to about 65 million years ago.
2. Explain to the students that they are going to pretend to be paleontologists (scientists who study fossils) in search of dinosaur fossils. Give each group a plastic bag containing a spoon and a magnifying glass, as well as a sheet of newspaper, a box, and a geologic map of the classroom. Assign one group to each of the classroom dig sites.

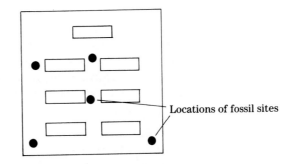

Locations of fossil sites

3. At each dig site students should carefully remove sand and objects they find using only their spoons. Have them put the sand in the box and the objects on the sheet of newspaper.
4. Have the students classify the material into various groups according to the physical characteristics of the objects. Make sure one of the categories is dinosaur bone. They should also make a list of all the objects they find and record the information on the map.

5. Encourage each group to fit the dinosaur bones together to find out whether they have a complete dinosaur or to discover what parts they have. Each group will be missing many parts. Bring the groups together to share what they found and select one person from each group to work together to construct the dinosaur using all the pieces. Have students use pictures in their reference books to identify the dinosaur.

6. Discuss the following questions:

   • What happened to the missing pieces of the dinosaur skeleton?
   • How did the dinosaurs and other animals and plants become extinct?
   • Are animals and plants becoming extinct today?
   • Could humans become extinct?

Lesson 6. A Crusty Puzzle

One of the most exciting ideas in geology today is the theory that the earth's crust consists of gigantic plates that are moving, colliding, rubbing, and sliding around. The idea is known as plate tectonics; many will recognize it as an extension of the continental drift theory. Like any theory, plate tectonics is a unifying concept that helps explain and predict earthquakes, volcanos, the formation of mountains and oceans, and many other geological processes. This lesson introduces students to the theory.

Materials
Tracing paper, map of the continents (page 193), globes, 3-by-5-inch index cards.

Action

1. Show students a map of the world or a globe and point out that most of the continents are separated by oceans. Point out the outline of North and South America, Africa, and Europe. Then take your students on this imagery experience.

Close your eyes and relax. Imagine you are lying on a magic carpet that is able to travel anywhere . . . Pretend that you leave the room on your carpet and that you are climbing high into the sky . . . You climb high enough to see the continents of North and South America, Africa, and Europe . . . You can see the ocean that separates them . . . Then magically the continents start to move closer and closer together . . . Watch them move until they join to form a single giant continent . . . Now watch as the continents slowly drift apart . . . Can you see the ocean water filling in the spaces as the continents drift apart? . . . Let the continents drift apart until they are located where they are today . . . Return to the room on the magic carpet and open your eyes . . . Share your experience.

Ask the following questions as you discuss the students' experiences:

- Do you think the continents made any noise or sounds as they moved?
- What do you think happened to animals and plants when the continents started to separate?
- How fast do you think the continents separated?
- Do you think the continents are moving today?

2. Have students trace the six continents and cut them out. Then have them fit the pieces together like a jigsaw puzzle and glue them on a sheet of paper. There should be as little space between the continents as possible. Have pictures and drawings available from textbooks so that the students can compare their puzzle solution to geologists' solutions.

As a follow-up activity, have students make the flip book in the Side Path activity below.

Side Paths

Lesson 7. Continental Drift Flip Book[1] (Geography)

The theory of continental drift proposes that the geography of the earth has changed over the last 200 million years. Continents have moved to their present geographical position from very far off places. For example, India broke off of Antarctica and drifted north across the equator to its present position!

Students can make a flip book and use it to watch the continents change position. To do this, distribute one copy of page 194 to each student. Give each student 10 index cards and glue, and have a stapler on hand. Have students cut their cards in half (3 by 2½), glue the maps on the index cards, stack the cards in order of age, and then staple them together to make a flip book.

Lesson 8. Home Inventory (Social Studies)

Many earth materials are commonly found around the home. Have students use the Home Inventory Chart, page 195, to identify earth materials at home. They should identify as many items as they can and bring samples to class.

Lesson 9. Values and the Environment (Social Studies)

Discuss with students that people react to things in different ways: what seems beautiful to one may seem ugly to someone else; what seems serious to one may seem unimportant to someone else; what seems to be a solution to one may seem to be a problem to another.

Prepare a set of pictures that depict a variety of value laden scenes; such as a garbage dump, a national forest, a garden, a quarry, a bulldozer preparing a building site, a crowded freeway, an oil rig, an oil spill and so on.

Have pairs of students discuss the pictures using the following questions as a guide.

- What in each picture seems important to you?
- What in each picture seems to be a problem?
- What are some solutions to the problems you see in the pictures?
- What in each picture makes you feel good, happy, nice?
- What in each picture makes you feel bad, angry, or sad?

Lesson 10. Gravel Art (Art)

Students usually enjoy art activities. At a local pet store or nursery, obtain gravel in a variety of colors. The gravel used to form a base for a fishtank is recommended. Students will also need glue and construction paper.

To make gravel art, have students follow these instructions:

1. Draw a picture on the construction paper.
2. Cover those parts of the drawing that will be the same color with glue.
3. Sprinkle gravel on the glue and let it dry for a few minutes.
4. Shake off the excess gravel.
5. Put glue on all parts that will be a second color and sprinkle those parts with gravel.
6. Continue gluing and sprinkling gravel until the picture is complete.

Lesson 11. Clay Models and Sensory Observation (Art)

This activity is powerful, yet simple, and is an easy way to access the right hemisphere of the brain. Give each student a bag containing a piece of earth material, such as a crinoid stem, or a shark's tooth fossil. Instruct the students not to look at the object. They may, however, put their hand in the bag and observe the object through touch.

Give the students a small piece of clay; tell them to make a replica of the object that they feel inside the bag.

When the replicas are finished, have small groups compare their replicas and discuss how they are alike and how they are different. Have students guess what the object is before allowing them to look in the bag.

Lesson 12. Creating Stories (Language Arts)

Give students a copy of page 196 with the drawing of footprints on the sand dunes. Ask the following questions:

- What happened here?
- What kind of creatures made these tracks?
- In what direction were the animals moving?
- How fast were the animals moving? How do you know?

Have students write a brief story about what they think happened on the sand dune.

Lesson 13. Writing About Science (Language Arts)

In *A Celebration of Bees*, Barbara Esbensen suggests a variety of ways to help students write poetry. Here are a few suggestions related to this unit.

- Peer though a magnifying glass at grains of sand or chips of rocks and minerals. Describe what you see.
- Use a microscope to look at grains of sand or thin sections of rocks. What discoveries can you describe?
- Use a magnifying glass to look at a sidewalk or street. What do you see?
- Imagine earth sounds—earthquakes, avalanches, landslides. Write sentences to describe the sounds.
- Look at films about rocks, fossils, and prehistoric animals. Use what you learn to write stores, articles, or movie reviews.

Searches

Lesson 1. Locating Earthquakes

Most earthquakes occur in a belt around the Pacific known as the "ring of fire." There are other earthquake belts that your students can discover through a very simple project—plotting the location of earthquakes. Here's what you need to do:

- Display a large map of the world.
- Order earthquake location cards (epicenter cards) by writing to the director of the Coast and Geodetic Survey, Environmental Science Services Administration, Rockville, MD 20852.
- The cards will arrive monthly. Have students use the cards to mark the earthquakes epicenters on the map.

Lesson 2. Shells as Architects

Among earth's natural architects are the 100,000 species of organisms with shells. In this project encourage students to collect and organize shells using the following suggestions:

- Group shells by shape: conical, rectangular, circular, elongate, irregular.
- Describe the shells and mount them on cards.
- Write a poem about each shell, explaining what makes it unique.
- Using a shell identification book, name the shell and briefly describe the habitat of the creature who lives in it.

Lesson 3. Mineral Madness

Many people—perhaps even some of your students—are crazy about collecting, studying, and using minerals. Provide books and magazines on minerals and rocks, hand lenses, and mineral samples. Have students test mineral hardness using a fingernail (2.5), a penny (3.0), and a paper clip (5.5).

Students can label and describe each sample in their collection and present it on Mineral Madness Day. On this day everyone adopts a mineral in celebration of earth materials.

Additional activities for the day might include:

- Making mineral booster buttons.
- Singing rock songs.

- Making food that contains minerals.
- Seeing films on rocks and minerals.
- Displaying minerals and rocks students have collected.
- Presenting mineral and rock projects.
- Listening to guest speakers: geologist, gem store owner, miner.

Lesson 4. To the Field

Field trips to crusty areas offer an opportunity for geology to come alive. The illustration shows some of the equipment that students should have on a field trip, and the list provides some possible field activities.

- Identify the least common fossil at the site you have visited.
- Discover as many different fossils at a given site as you can. Describe each different one. Do the same with rocks and minerals.
- Map the location of fossils in the area that you have visited.
- Using field guides, identify the name of at least three different fossils, rocks, or minerals found at the site.

Evaluation

Evaluation of student progress in this unit can center on the student's ability to solve geological problems. Following are some suggestions. Refer to the Adventures and Side Paths for further problem-solving situations.

- Your little brother finds a rock and asks if you know what it is and how it was made. The rock has these characteristics: its color is red; the grains that make up the rock appear to be cemented together; nothing happens when acid is poured on the rock. How would you find out what kind of rock this is?
- The headline of a newspaper article reads: Africa and South American Once Were Joined—Split Began About 200 Million Years Ago! A friend of yours says this cannot be true. What information (evidence) would you use to help your friend understand that scientists do think Africa and South America were once joined together?

Books for Kids

Benton, Michael. *The Dinosaur Encyclopedia*. New York: Simon and Schuster, 1984.

Brasch, Kate. *Prehistoric Monsters*. Salem, N.H.: Salem House, 1985.

Gilbreath, Alice. *Ring of Fire: And the Hawaiian Islands and Iceland*. Minneapolis: Dillon, 1986.

Harrington, John. *Dance of the Continents: Adventures with Rocks and Time*. Los Angeles: J.P. Tarcher, 1983.

Knight, David. *"Dinosaurs" that Swam and Flew*. Englewood Cliffs, N.J.: Prentice-Hall, Inc. 1985.

Our Continent: A Natural History of North America. Washington, D.C.: National Geographic Society, 1976.

Raymo, Chet. *Biography of a Planet*. Englewood Cliffs, N.J.: Prentice-Hall, Inc. 1984.

THE ROCK

With your eyes closed, imagine that you are walking in a
forest along a trail . . . As you are walking along, you
notice a single rock lying on the trail . . . It is the same
rock you are holding . . . Imagine that you can make
yourself very tiny—so tiny that you become smaller than
the rock . . . Imagine yourself crawling around on the rock
just like an ant would do . . . Use your hands to grab onto
the rock as you crawl over it . . . Feel the rock . . . Is it
rough or smooth?

   Can you crawl around on it easily? . . . Put your face
down on the rock . . . Can you feel the warmth of the sun
in the rock? . . . Are there any creatures—plant or
animal—living on the rock? . . . What are they? . . .

   What colors do you see in your rock? . . . Can you dig
your fingernails into any of the colors in your rock or is it
too hard? . . . Smell the rock . . . What does it smell like?
. . . Lie on your back on the rock and look up at the sky
and the trees in the forest . . . How do you feel? . . . Now
carefully climb down off the rock, and when you reach
the ground, gradually make yourself larger and larger
until you are yourself again . . . When you are ready, open
your eyes, and share your experience.

Page reference: 178

EXPLORING MINERALS

Sample Number	Luster: M if metallic; N if nonmetallic	Hardness: H if harder than glass; S if softer than glass	Color of Streak	Response to acid (Does it fizz?) Yes/No
1				
2				
3				
4				
5				
6				

Page reference: 178

ROCK OBSERVATION CHART

Rock Sample	Observations	Type of rock: Igneous, Metamorphic, or Sedimentary
1		
2		
3		
4		
5		
6		

Page reference: 178

ROCK IDENTIFICATION KEY

DIRECTIONS: This key will help you determine whether a rock is igneous, metamorphic, or sedimentary. Start with item **1a** and identify one rock at a time.

1a. If the rock is made up of minerals that you can see, go to **2a**.

1b. If the rock is not made up of minerals you can see, go to **5a**.

2a. If the rock is made up of minerals that are melted together, go to **3a**.

2b. If the rock is made up of minerals that are stuck together, go to **6a**.

3a. If the sample has only one kind of mineral, the rock is **metamorphic**.

3b. If the sample has two or more different minerals, go to **4a**.

4a. If the minerals in the sample are distributed in a random pattern—not lined up—the rock is **igneous**.

4b. If the minerals in the sample are not distributed randomly but look banded or lined up, the rock is **metamorphic**.

5a. If the rock is either glassy or frothy—has small holes—it is **igneous**.

5b. If the rock is made up of strong, flat sheets that look as though they will split off into slatelike pieces, it is **metamorphic**.

6a. If the rock is made of silt, sand, fossils, or pebbles cemented together, it is **sedimentary**.

6b. If the rock is not made of sand, silt, or pebbles but fizzes when acid is pour on it, it is **sedimentary**.

Page reference: 179

HISTORY OF THE EARTH

Age	Event
11,000–1M	Pleistocene Ice Age
1–4M	Homo Sapiens
5M	First hominids
26M	First grasses
54M	Mammals diversify
65M	Extinction of Dinosaurs, flying reptiles, some marine reptiles
136M	First frogs
190M	First dinosaurs
225M	Extinction of Trilobites
280M	First conifers, insects Ice age, So. Hemisphere
280–345M	Uplift and folding of the Appalachian Mountains
395M	First land plants
570M	First trilobites First abundant fossils
700M	Sponges, jellyfish
1B	First advanced cells
2.5B	Blue-algae fossils
3.4B	First primitive cells
3.6–3.9B	Oldest rocks dated
4.55B	Formation of Earth

M = millions

B = billions

Page reference: 180

MAP OF THE CONTINENTS

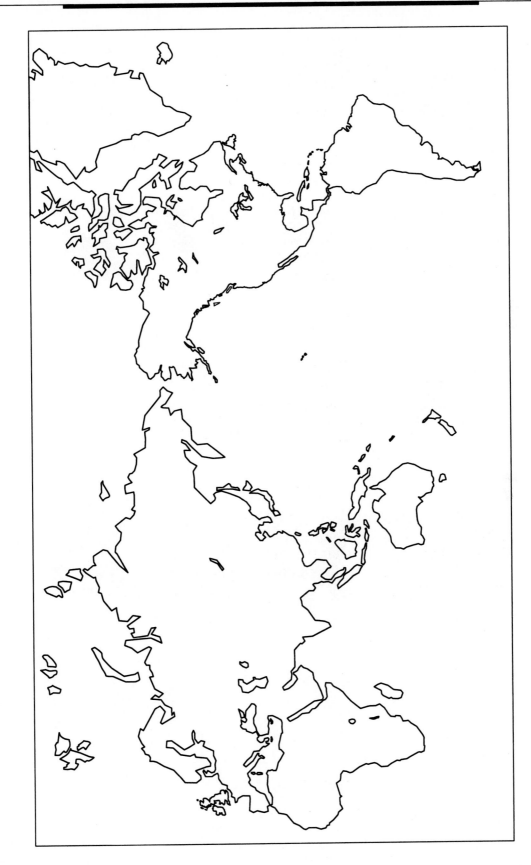

Page reference: 182

CONTINENTAL DRIFT FLIP BOOK [1]

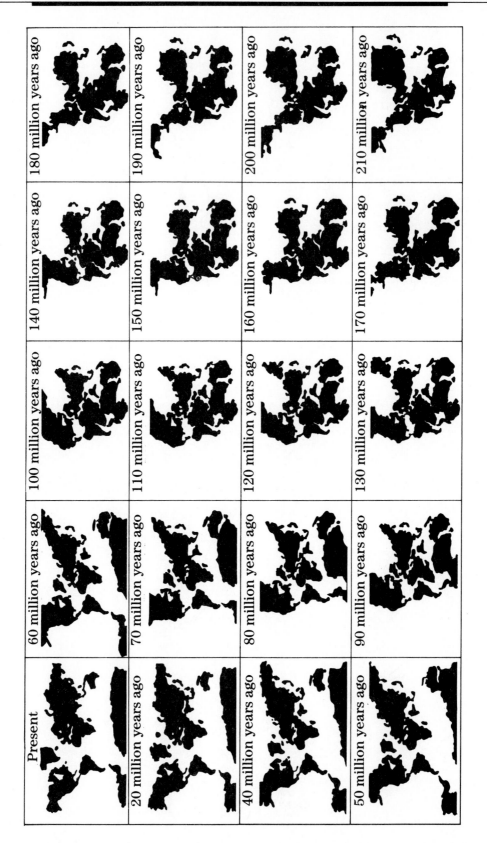

Page reference: 183

©1975 C. Scotese. Reprinted by permission of C. Scotese.

HOME INVENTORY CHART

Category 1: Building materials					
	Located in home	Not found in home		Located in home	Not found in home
Adobe brick	☐	☐	Marble	☐	☐
Asbestos	☐	☐	Pebbles	☐	☐
Cement brick	☐	☐	Putty	☐	☐
Ceramic tiles	☐	☐	Wooden shingles	☐	☐
Common brick	☐	☐	Sandpaper	☐	☐
Granite	☐	☐	Sandstone	☐	☐
Gypsum	☐	☐	Slate	☐	☐
Limestone	☐	☐			

Category 2: Gems and Collections					
Diamond	☐	☐	Rock	☐	☐
Emerald	☐	☐	Ruby	☐	☐
Fossil	☐	☐	Shell	☐	☐
Pearl	☐	☐	Topaz	☐	☐
Quartz	☐	☐	Tourmaline	☐	☐

Category 3: Kitchen Items					
Baking Soda	☐	☐	Glass containers	☐	☐
Chinaware	☐	☐	Rock salt	☐	☐
Enameled cookware	☐	☐	Salt	☐	☐
Iron cookware	☐	☐			

Page reference: 183

TRACKS ON THE SAND DUNES

What happened here?
What kind of creatures made these tracks?
In what direction were the animals moving?
How fast were the animals moving? How do you know?

Write a brief story about what you think happened on the
sand dune.

_____

_____

_____

_____

_____

_____

_____

_____

_____

_____

_____

Page reference: 184

IF YOU WERE A BOAT, HOW WOULD YOU FLOAT?

A Physical Science Experience

TEACHER INFORMATION

Background Information

When was the first time you became aware that objects in your world float and sink in liquids? It was probably very early in your life, since many psychologists believe that humans possess an intuitive knowledge of floating and sinking at birth. This is because all of us spent our pre-natal lives in the amniotic fluid in our mother's uterus. Psychologist Arthur Janov has, for example, developed therapy sessions in which individuals relive the birth experience through aquatic simulation.

As young children develop intellectually, they begin to understand the physical principles of buoyancy that explain the conditions under which objects float or sink. Under Piaget's system of intellectual development, this understanding occurs when the learner reaches the concrete operational level of thinking. This Experience is designed, therefore, to blend the earlier intuitive conceptions students have about buoyancy with concepts outlined below.

Overview and Planning

Take a few minutes to review the Overview and Planning Chart for If You Were a Boat, How Would You Float? There are six Adventures, two Side Paths, and one Search in the Experience.

Overview and Planning Chart: If You Were a Boat, How Would You Float?

Activity	Science Concept	Science Process	Modes of Learning	Attitude
Adventures				
1. Exploring Buoyancy	What makes objects float.	Inferring Identifying variables	Left Affective	Curiosity
2. Sink or Float	Objects can be classified according to their density.	Observing Classifying Predicting	Left Physical-sensory	Creativity
3. Clay boats	Density of an object can be modified by redesigning its shape.	Inferring Formulating hypotheses	Left Physical-sensory	Creativity
4. Testing Boats	Materials can be shaped into various functional designs.	Observing Identifying variables Predicting	Left Physical-sensory	Persistence
5. Upward versus Downward	Objects will float if the upward force of buoyancy is greater than the downward force of gravity.	Observing Inferring	Left Physical-sensory	Sensitivity to environment

Activity	Science Concept	Science Process	Modes of Learning	Attitude
6. Popcorn/ Alka-Seltzer® Problem	Buoyancy principles are applied to new situations.	Observing Predicting Inferring	Physical-sensory Left Affective	Creativity
Side Paths				
7. Fantasy Clay (Language Arts)	Materials can be shaped into various functional designs.	Formulating hypotheses	Left Right Affective	Creativity Curiosity
8. Boats that Fly (Language Arts)	Buoyancy principles are applied to new situations.	Observing Identifying variables	Left Right Affective	Creativity
Searches				
1. Experimenting and Finding out About Boats	Buoyancy principles are applied to new situations.	Experimenting	Left Affective	Creativity Self-reliance

Objectives

At the end of this Experience, students should be able to:

1. Demonstrate buoyancy principles using common materials.
2. Design boat-like objects that will float.
3. Describe situations in which objects will either sink or float.
4. Predict the necessary conditions for objects to sink or float.

Key Concepts

The following represent the major concepts that students will study:

Downward force Is due to the gravitational attraction all objects have towards the earth's surface. A characteristic of this force is that it is directly related to how much mass the object has. Heavier objects, i.e., boats, therefore, possess a greater downward force than lighter ones. Another feature about this force is that it is uniform and presses down in all directions. In buoyancy terms, this downward force is the force responsible for the tendency of an object to sink. Whether we are talking about a helium balloon, a boat in water, or vinegar layered over oil, there is always a downward force.

Upward force Is due to the tendency for any medium—liquid or gas—to change size and shape when objects are placed in them. When, for example, a boat is placed in water, it pushes the liquid away to make room for it. At the same time, the water pushes back on the boat to try to regain its space. This push is upward in direction and is also known as a displacement force. In buoyancy terms, the upward force is the force responsible for the tendency of an object to float.

Sinking Whenever the downward force is greater than the upward force, the object will sink into its medium—air or liquid.

Floating Whenever the upward force is greater than the downward force, the object floats on its medium—air or liquid.

Teaching Tips

Most of the activities in this Experience include class discussion times, and it is strongly suggested that you encourage students to share their conceptions about floating and sinking objects.

Use networking to help students explore the topic (see page 70). Write "Floating and Sinking" on the board and have students brainstorm ideas. You might repeat the networking process at the end of the unit to see how students' ideas have changed.

Teaching Phases

Following are three phases for implementing the activities in the Experience:

Phase I. Direct Instruction/Interactive Teaching

Most of the lessons will require direct instruction. It is recommended that you do most of the Adventures before doing the Side Paths.

Phase II. Cooperative Learning

The procedures for each lesson are designed to be carried out by pairs of small teams of students, although some of the activities may be done with the whole class.

Introduce the projects, which are designed for learning centers, and have teams work on them independently. The project results can be used as part of a culminating activity.

Phase III. Culminating Process

It is recommended that you have the learning teams report on the results of their projects. Since there are four different projects, you may have to allow a full period for reports and discussion.

The evaluation process is designed as a separate lesson in which the students use the concepts they learned to solve an interesting problem.

Evaluate and obtain feedback on the students' opinions and attitudes toward this unit. Use the form provided on page 111.

STUDENT INFORMATION

Adventures

Lesson 1. Exploring Buoyancy

In this lesson you will organize the unit by providing the students with an opportunity to share their conceptions about the principles of buoyancy.

Materials
Science log.

Action

1. Have students sit in a circle and begin the session by explaining that they are going to explore what makes objects float and sink. Ask when students first became aware that objects float and when they became aware that objects sink. Encourage the discussion by asking the following questions.

   • What are some of your favorite floating objects?
   • What are some of your favorite sinking objects?
   • What would you like to find out about floating and sinking objects?

      Use students' responses to help you plan the Experience. You might also conduct the networking exercise.

2. Have pairs of students discuss what they think causes objects to float or sink and then have them summarize the key ideas. Write the key ideas on the chalkboard for future reference.

3. Have students draw pictures in their science logs to show what happens when an object is put into a liquid.

Lesson 2. Sink or Float

In this Adventure, students will demonstrate buoyancy principles using common objects. Students will also be encouraged to make predictions about buoyancy.

Materials

Two clear containers—plastic shoe box, aquarium; several miscellaneous objects, half of which float in water and half which sink in water—crayon, pencil, paper clip, seed, rubber band, ball of clay; water; water with salt dissolved in it so that it is clear; science logs.

Action

1. Arrange the classroom so that each student can view the demonstration area and set up the container filled halfway with water. Display objects next to the container.

      Ask students to think about whether these objects will float or sink when placed in the container of water and have them write their predictions in their science logs.

      Hold up one object at a time and have students make their guesses. Test each object by gently placing it on the surface of the water. Record the buoyancy of each object. After the demonstration, have students discuss the accuracy of their predictions.

2. Repeat the process using the container of salt water and discuss students' predictions. Ask whether there was any difference in the behavior of any of the objects in this container of liquid and discuss what might have caused it. Explain that salt water is more dense than fresh water thereby creating greater buoyant force.

Lesson 3. Clay Boats

In this activity, students will design boat-like objects from pieces of clay and determine whether they float.

Materials

A 100-gram piece of oil-base clay for each student; 5 or 6 containers of water—plastic dishpans, buckets, and so on, plenty of paper towels; weights—marbles, paper clips, washers.

Action

1. Before beginning the activity, divide the clay into 100-gram portions. If you do not have a scale, estimate the quantity by making each piece equal to the weight of a D-cell flashlight battery. Place the containers in strategic locations around the room so that the teams can use the stations.

    Remind students of their predictions about whether objects would float or sink in water and in salt water.

    Challenge students to explore the properties of floating and sinking using a piece of clay. Remind them that the clay sank in both containers during the demonstration. Have students work the clay into a shape that will float.
2. Pass out the clay and form teams of 4–6 students. Allow time for students to design their boats and let them try out their designs.
3. Ask the students to draw their best design in their logs.

Lesson 4. Testing Boats

In this continuation of Lesson 3, students will test their boats to find out how much weight they can hold before they sink.

Materials
Same as Lesson 3.

Action

1. Arrange the class as you did in Lesson 3. Then explain that students are to test their clay boats to see how much weight they can carry before sinking. Suggest that students modify their designs to carry a maximum amount of weight.
2. Allow the students to test their designs by adding weights to their boats. Have them record the data in their science logs and draw a picture of their new designs.
3. Bring the class together to summarize their findings and discuss design differences. Then have them discuss reasons for why lumps of clay sink and clay boats float.

Lesson 5. Upward Vs. Downward

Now that the students have experimented with clay boats, they are ready to receive information on buoyancy principles and discuss their ideas as they relate to buoyancy principles.

Materials
Science logs.

Action

1. Arrange the class for a brief lecture and chalkboard presentation. Explain that two forces account for why the clay boats float. Draw the following diagram on the chalkboard, project it onto a screen, or distribute it on a handout. Explain that the force pushing down on the piece of clay when it is put in water is caused by gravity. The upward force pushing up on the piece of clay when it is put in water is caused by the movement of the water trying to regain or take back the space that the clay takes up. The two forces push against each other just as students' hands can push against each

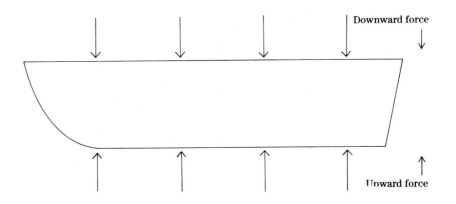

other. Ask students to place one hand on top of the other and have them push.

Explain that when the upward force is larger or greater, the boat will float; when the downward force is larger or greater, the boat will sink. Remind students that when the clay was in a ball, it didn't float; when it was shaped into a boat, it did float.

2. Discuss what happened to the upward and downward forces when the shape of the clay was changed. Elicit that when the clay is shaped into a boat, it occupies a bigger space in the water, so the upward force is greater then the downward force and the boat floats. Point out an important idea: The larger the object, the greater the upward force. Have students think about what happened when the weights were put into the clay boat and it finally sank.

   Be sure students use *upward* and *downward force* when they explain that when the weights were added, the downward force was greater and therefore the boat sank. Point out another important idea: The heavier the object the greater the downward force.

3. Conduct a brief review and allow time for students to record ideas and diagrams in their science logs.

4. If time remains, briefly discuss students interests in buoyancy.

Lesson 6. The Popcorn/Alka-Seltzer® Problem

In this activity, students apply concepts of buoyancy to a problem.

Materials
Science logs, a clear container filled halfway with water, several kernels of unpopped popcorn, an Alka-Seltzer tablet.

Action

1. Assign pairs of students to work stations around the room. Explain that this activity will help them think more about floating and sinking. Have each pair gather the items listed on the chalkboard and take them to their stations.

2. Before students place the popcorn in the water, have them predict whether it will float or sink. Record their votes on the chalkboard. Then have them place the popcorn into the water to check their predictions. Before they put the Alka-Seltzer in the water, have them discuss what they think will happen. Will there be a change in the popcorn? Make sure students watch carefully so that they can write their observations in their science logs.

Then have them put the Alka-Seltzer into the water and observe. Allow 5–7 minutes for students to complete this part. Circulate among the groups and keep in mind the questions students have.

3. Use the following questions to lead the summary discussion.

  • What is the most interesting observation you made?
  • What are some other observations?
  • What are some inferences you could make about these observations using the terms *upward* and *downward force*?

Lead students to make the following conclusions: The popcorn's weight created a larger downward force than upward force and it sank. After the Alka-Seltzer dissolved, bubbles attached to the popcorn's surface, making it larger and therefore creating a larger upward force. The larger upward force was more than the downward force and therefore it floated. When the bubbles popped, the popcorn became smaller again. The upward force decreased, and the popcorn sank.

Side Paths

Lesson 7. Fantasy Clay (Language Arts)

In this activity, imagery is used to further extend the students' knowledge and experience of buoyancy.

Materials
A 100-gram piece of clay for each student.

Action

1. Arrange the class into the small groups that made the clay boats. Have each student describe their best design and tell how it was created, how many tries it took to create it, and its best feature. Then discuss the designs as a group. Ask several students to share their drawings of their boats. Ask about the best features of each design.
2. Have students think about other ways to make a boat from clay. Before they decide on their new designs, guide them in an imaginary journey to help them think more creatively about boat designs.

    Ask students to remove any materials from their desk tops and to relax. Give each student a piece of clay.

Clay Boats

Roll up your clay into a ball and set it gently in front of you . . . Close your eyes, sit in a comfortable position, and relax . . . Think about your hands and fingers that have just been exploring the clay . . . Now keeping your eyes closed, I want you to picture the round ball of clay that is in front of you . . . Imagine that it will slowly change itself into the shape of the boat that you made earlier. This is the boat that held the most weight without sinking. . . .

Now I want you to become this boat . . . How do you feel as this floating piece of clay? . . . Notice how you feel in each part of your body . . . What is it about you that makes you float? . . . Where are the weights placed on you? How does it feel to have this weight on you? . . .

Now I want you to become yourself again . . . Think about what it was like to become a piece of clay . . . Now I want you to imagine that you are one of the best cargo boat builders in the world . . . How do you feel as this person? . . . What is your life like? . . . The kind of boats that you build are made to hold huge amounts of material and are not made to travel fast . . . You know what makes a boat float and how much of a load it can carry without sinking . . . What is the shape of the boats you make? . . . How great a load will they carry, and where is it placed? . . .

Now I want you as the boat builder to picture your very best boat, the one that holds the most cargo . . . How is this boat like or different from the clay boat you made earlier? . . . Now keeping your eyes closed, become yourself again . . . Try to picture the round ball of clay that is in front of you . . . Imagine that it will slowly change and shape itself into the very best boat you made when you were a boat builder. Remember that this is a boat made to carry cargo and not made to go very fast.

Now I want you to reach out to the real ball of clay that is in front of you . . . Hold it gently in your hands for a little while . . . Get to know your piece of clay again . . . Now with your eyes closed I want you to shape the very best cargo boat you made when you were a builder . . . Let the clay and your fingers lead you into this new creation.

Now slowly open your eyes and look at what you have made out of the clay . . . Continue to work on it if you wish so that you come closer to the picture of your cargo boat.

---

3. After the visualization, bring the class together to summarize the lesson. Discuss what it was like to be a boat builder and how it felt. Ask students how they liked the Clay Boats visualization.
4. Have students test their designs in water.

Lesson 8. Boats That Fly (Language Arts)

In this activity, metaphors (synectics), poetry, and drama are used to help the students explore the concepts of buoyancy.

Materials
Science logs, 3-by-5 inch cards

Action

1. Arrange the class in a semicircle. In order to encourage right-mode learning about buoyancy, introduce the lesson with several divergent questions to stimulate creativity.

    *   How was your clay boat like a flower?
    *   How would it feel to be an oil tanker? What would your life be like?
    *   How do you think fish respond to boats when they pass by?
    *   How would you fill in the blanks in this sentence: A boat is like a _____ but not like a _____.

2. Invite students to write in their science logs syntus about their clay boats. Remind students that in a syntu the first line of the poem names the object. The second line states an observation. The third line describes a feeling. The fourth states another observation. The fifth line is another name for a *boat*.
3. Form teams of four or five students for a drama activity. Write the following actions on 3-by-5-inch cards and give one card to each group: a hot air balloon lifting off, a bird learning to fly, astronauts floating in space, a hang glider in flight, a submarine going under water, an ice cube in a glass of water, an Alka-Seltzer tablet in a glass of water.

    Then have each group act out the action for the rest of the class and have the class guess what it is. Allow time for each group to decide how to present the action. Be sure each person in the groups participate.
4. After the enactments bring the class together for a summary discussion about what they discovered about floating and sinking.

Searches

Lesson 1. Experimenting and Finding out About Boats

This project is organized into four learning centers, each designed to help the students delve further into the study of sinking and floating.
Set up the centers as follows:

Center 1: 100-gram units of clay, water, paper towels, pieces of aluminum foil, and plastic containers of alcohol and salt water.

Center 2 and Center 3: Books about boats, magazines from the school library.

Center 4: Books about boat construction and drafting paper.

Action
You should set up the centers and introduce them early in the Experience so that students can work in them when they have time.

Following is the information for each center.

Center 1: Experiments with Boats

Present two problems to the students:

- How does the kind of liquid a clay boat floats in affect the amount of weight it can carry?
- If the boat were made of aluminum foil instead of clay, how much weight could it carry?

Experimenting with Boats

Kind of Liquid	Number of weights in Clay Boat	Number of weights in Foil Boat
water		
alcohol		
salt water		

Allow students time to copy the chart in their science logs, record their observations, and draw their conclusions.

In general, the salt water creates more upward force than water or alcohol and should be able to carry more weights. The aluminum foil boat will create less downward force than the clay boat and if constructed tightly should be able to carry more weight than the clay boat.

Center 2: Boats—Past, Present, Future

Place books and magazines around a poster that has these directions: Select a book or magazine. Find out how boats have changed throughout history. Find out how boats were made in different countries. Find out what boats were used for. Predict what boats will look like in the future.

Center 3: Naval Battles in American History

Place books and magazines around a poster that has these directions: Naval battles were fought in the wars of this country. Find out about how battleships are designed and what makes them good ships of war. What can battleships be used for during peacetime?

Center 4: How Is a Boat Constructed?

Place books and magazines around a poster that has these directions: Find out how boats are made. Look at many different drawings and designs. Use drawing paper to make several scale drawings of your favorite boat design, or use the information to make up your own design.

Evaluation

Evaluate this Experience by having students think creatively. The evaluation suggested here is actually a magic trick. It is not only fun to do but will enable the students to apply what they have learned.

Advance preparation: You will need two raw eggs and two glasses of water, one with sugar in it. Prepare the sugar water mixture by adding at least 5 tablespoons of sugar to warm water, or enough to make the raw egg float. (Make sure to test the mixture. If there is not enough buoyancy, add more sugar.)

Follow these procedures for the test:

1. Distribute copies of An "Eggzact" Test, page 209. Show the class the two eggs and the glasses of water. Tell them that you have two intelligent eggs.[1] On one egg write the word *Float*, on the other, write *Sink*.
2. Tell the students to answer question 1 on the handout: What do you think will happen when the eggs are placed in the glasses of water? Explain your answer.
3. Now tell the students that you have been keeping a secret from them. Tell them that you are a really a magician, and tell them the following story.

Did you hear about the two identical twins who once lived in our town? One was an eternal optimist who always saw a glass of water as being half full. Her name was Float. (Hold up the egg with *Float* written on it.) Float always looked on the bright side of things, unlike her sister, Sink. (Hold up the egg with *Sink* written on it.) Sink was an eternal pessimist who always saw the glass of water as being half empty. These two sisters had totally different outlooks on life. As a result, this is what happened to each of them. (Drop the eggs in the appropriate glasses). As you can see, Sink has sunk—her pessimism has led her to feel really low. On the other hand, Float goes through life with a buoyant attitude.

---

4. Now have the students answer the other questions on the handout: How do you think the trick worked? What is buoyancy? Do you know any buoyant people? What are they like?
5. Collect the papers. Have two students come to the demonstration table and ask them to use their common sense to see if they can figure out the trick. Tell students that usually is *not* a good idea to taste unknown substances, but in this case, they may use their sense of taste to solve the mystery if they wish.

Books for Kids

Cooper, Chris and Jane Insley. *How Does It Work?* New York: Facts on File, 1986.

Vowles, Andrew. *The EDC Book of Amazing Experiments You Can Do At Home.* Tulsa, Ok.: EDC Publishing, 1985.

Whyman, Kathryn. *Forces in Action.* New York: Gloucester, 1986.

AN EGGZACT TEST

1. What do you think will happen when the eggs are placed in the glasses of water? Explain your answer.

2. How do you think the trick worked? (You may collaborate with one other person.)

3. What is buoyancy? Do you know a buoyant person? What is she or he like?

Page reference: 208

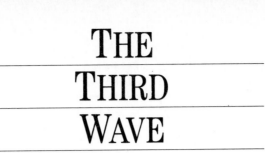

CHAPTER 9

THE
THIRD
WAVE

A Futuristic Experience

*A new civilization is emerging in our lives and blind men everywhere
are trying to suppress it. This new civilization brings with it new
family styles; changed ways of working, loving and living; a new
economy; new political conflicts; and beyond all this an altered consciousness as well. Pieces of this new civilization exist today. Millions
are already attuning their lives to the rhythms of tomorrow. Others,
terrified of the future, are engaged in a desperate, futile flight into
the past and are trying to restore the dying world that gave them
birth.*

ALVIN TOFFLER
The Third Wave

TEACHER INFORMATION

Background Information

Item.   October 17, 1957, Natick, Massachusetts.

The news bulletins flashed with the announcement that the Soviets had launched humanity's first satellite. It was called Sputnik. It changed everything. And this was my first experience with space science.

Item.   March 22, 1982, The John F. Kennedy Space Center.

Another experience with space science. This time I was more involved. Along with a thousand people in NASA's viewing stands three miles from the launch pad, I heard the familiar voice of mission control: "10, 9, 8, 7, 6, main engines ignited, 5, 4, 3, 2, 1, solid rocket booster fired, lift off—we have a lift off!"
As I stood there with my friend Ted Colton watching the Orbiter Columbia lift off its launch pad, I felt as if I was being lifted, too—not into space, but into the future. The event was truly astounding. Within two minutes the Space Shuttle was out of sight, and within 8 minutes it was in orbit! In that time I had not even left the field from where we witnessed the launch.
At lift off, a thundering beat rolled across the ground, causing my chest to vibrate and connecting me to the Columbia. It also did something else. The noise was like the sound produced by a distant drummer, signaling the advance of a new era— *the future*.

Item.   January 28, 1986, The John F. Kennedy Space Center.

Seven space explorers, the Challenger astronauts, lost their lives in America's worst space disaster. We all felt the anguish and the sense of terrible loss when the Challenger exploded 73 seconds into its flight. A part of each of us died with the astronauts, and it is up to us to see their dreams fulfilled.

Underlying the dreams of the astronauts was the vision of making a future in space a reality for all of us. In spite of the Challenger disaster, the exuberance of exploration pushes humans to go beyond terrible setbacks such as this. The exploration of space provides visible and tangible evidence of the importance of studying the future.

Rapid changes are taking place, not only in space exploration but in just about every aspect of our lives. The following events have been predicted to happen within the next 70 years:

- Regional weather control.
- Automated voting.
- Facsimile newspapers printed in the home.
- Biochemicals aid growth of new organs and limbs.
- Drugs raise levels of intelligence.
- Long-duration coma permits time travel.
- Aging process control extends life 50 years.
- Limited control of the force of gravity.
- Use of telepathy and ESP in communications.
- Two-way communication with extraterrestrials.
- Permanent space base established on the moon.
- Permanent space colonies orbiting earth.
- Mining of the moon and asteroids.[1]

The future has been ignored as a subject for study in the science curriculum. Although individual teachers have blazed trails, opening the future to their students, the majority of students do not think about the future or learn processes that will help them think about the future.

The purpose of this Experience is to help you prepare and develop your own units about the future. Students need to be prepared for a rapidly changing and increasingly technological world. Much of today's curriculum prepares students for life as it was in the 60s and 70s; very little preparation is made for the year 2000, when today's students will be young adults.

Another purpose of this unit is to provide some processes and activities about teaching the future that can be integrated into other units of science teaching. Many of the activities in this unit could be applied to an ongoing science curriculum.

Teaching the future does not mean teaching facts about the future; it means providing a psychological and knowledge base for thinking about the future. An important point to emphasize is that the future cannot be predicted, but it can be investigated. According to Alvin Toffler:

> *Even more important than any specific bits of advance information, however, is the habit of anticipation. This conditioned ability to look ahead plays a key role in adaptation. Indeed, one of the hidden clues to successful coping may well lie in the individual's sense of the future. The people among us who keep up with change, who manage to adapt well, seem to have a richer, better developed sense of what lies ahead than those who cope poorly. Anticipating the future has become a habit with them. The chess player who anticipates the moves of his opponent, the executive who thinks in long-range terms, the student who takes a quick glance at the table of contents before starting to read page one, all seem to fare better.[2]*

According to futurists such as Draper Kauffman, we should provide experiences for students in which they (1) have access to available information about important future possibilities; (2) develop the habit of looking ahead; and (3) develop the skill of anticipating effectively.[3]

The psychological set for this unit is *the third wave*, a term coined by Alvin Toffler. According to Toffler and many other futurists, humanity faces a quantum leap forward, a deep social upheaval and creative restructuring greater than anything witnessed by the human race. He says, "Without clearly recognizing it, we are engaged in building a remarkable new civilization from the ground up. This is the meaning of the third wave."[4]

In his analysis, Toffler identifies two great waves that humanity has passed through. *The first wave* was the agricultural revolution, and *the second wave* was the industrial revolution. The impact of the first wave took thousands of years; the impact of the second wave took 300 years. Toffler predicts that the impact of the third wave will take only a few decades.

It is predicted that a third wave society will be characterized by the following:

- A new way of life based on diversified energy sources.
- The creation of new, non-nuclear families.
- The new concept of the home, called the electronic cottage.
- Radically changed schools and corporations based on the principles of humanism and holism.
- Creation of new industries such as in-space manufacturing, gene industries and other molecular biology corporations, and homesteading the ocean floors.
- Establishment of interdisciplinary science areas such as: quantum electronics, information theory, molecular biology, oceanics, nucleonics, ecology, space sciences.
- The de-massification of the media.
- The creation of the so-called intelligent environment.

Many other predictions for the future could be listed. It is important to be aware of how quickly things will change in the future compared to the rate of change in the past. Students today need to be prepared to cope with accelerating changes. As has been mentioned, we cannot predict the future, but we can engage our imaginations and our intellect in learning how to think about the future.

Overview and Planning

Take a few minutes to review the Overview and Planning chart for the The Third Wave. There are six Adventures, seven Side Paths, and two Searches in the Experience.

Overview and Planning Chart: The Third Wave

Activity	Science Concept	Science Process	Modes of Learning	Attitude
Adventures				
1. Fives Walk on Thursday	A forecast is a scenario of the future based on trend data and interpretation.	Predicting Formulating hypotheses	Right Left	Sensitivity to environment
2. Imagining the Future	Understanding humans and their social relationships is important in imagining the future.	Inferring Predicting	Right Affective	Creativity Sensitivity to others
3. Thinking About the Future	A value is the result of a process involving choosing, prizing, and acting.	Classifying Interpreting data	Left Affective	Objectivity Curiosity
4. Polling the Future	Polling is a method of forecasting the future.	Predicting	Left	Objectivity
5. Connections	A futures wheel is used to forecast the future.	Predicting Classifying	Left	Creativity Persistence
6. Hard Choices	Decisions are based on information, beliefs, and attitudes.	Interpreting data	Left Affective	Concern for others
Side Paths				
7. A Model Future City (Art)	Science and technology have a fundamental role in shaping human environments.	Predicting	Left Right	Creativity
8. We've Come a Long Way (Art)	Science and technology interact with each other.	Classifying	Left	Creativity
9. Time Line (Social Studies)	The environment is constantly changing.	Classifying Predicting	Left	Curiosity
10. Analogies and Metaphors of the Future. (Social Studies)	Metaphors can be useful to analyze the future.	Interpreting data	Right	Sensitivity to environment
11. The Intelligent House (Social Studies)	Science and technology affect the home environment.	Predicting	Left Right	Curiosity
12. Trends (Mathematical)	A trend is a description of the way something is changing.	Predicting	Left	Objectivity Curiosity
13. Scenario Writing (Language Arts)	Scenarios are fictional forecasts of the future.	Interpreting data	Left Right	Curiosity Creativity

Activity	Science Concept	Science Process	Modes of Learning	Attitude
Searches				
1. Future Science Fair	Accessing information.	Observing Predicting Formulating hypotheses	Left Affective	Creativity Curiosity
2. The World's Future	Understanding the human environment.	Formulating hypotheses Experimenting	Left Affective	Creativity Curiosity

Objectives

At the end of this Experience students should be able to:

1. Develop hypotheses and images of the future.
2. Analyze pessimistic and optimistic forecasts of the future.
3. Identify strategies and and the means to influence their own futures.
4. Envision the world as a single, interacting system.
5. Evaluate their own values and beliefs and how they influence their attitudes about the future.
6. Evaluate the consequences of decisions on the future.
7. Make predictions and forecasts about the future.

Key Concepts

The following represent the major concepts that students will study:

Access to Information Through reading, listening, reference books, computerized retrieval systems, experts, and other means, information is available for problem solving.

Thinking Clearly Through values clarification, forecasting techniques, and problem-solving exercises, clear thinking is developed.

Communicating Effectively Interacting with others through informal speaking, public speaking, in multi-cultural settings, and by using communication tools such as graphs, flowcharts, computers, and so on.

Understanding the Human Environment Science and technology have a fundamental role in shaping the human environment.

Understanding Humans and Society Relationships and interdependencies are concepts that are important in making decisions about the future.

Personal Competence The development of skills, competencies, and higher-order thinking strategies are fundamental to futuristic thinking.

Teaching Tips

The nature of the activities in this unit will have an impact on you and your students. You will be, in Kauffman's terms, "futurizing your classroom." What does this mean?

First, many of the activities focus on having the students think personally about the future. You may want to provide discussion time to give students an opportunity to think about their futures and the possible futures of society.

The activities in The Third Wave emphasize interpersonal and communication skills. In many cases, students will have to research topics, making use of a variety of information sources. Stock your room with newspapers, magazines of all sorts, and reference books.

A third point to keep in mind is the social climate of the classroom. The success of the activities will depend upon the extent to which the classroom is democratized. Scientific thinking flourishes in a democratic environment, one in which open discussion, dissent, and free expression of ideas are encouraged.

Teaching Phases

Following are three phases for implementing the activities in the Experience:

Phase 1. Direct Instruction/Interactive Teaching

The first activity is a science fiction story that is sure to get your students thinking about the future. It is called Fives Walk on Thursday, and it immediately thrusts the students into the world of the future in the year 2431. It is a good place to begin the Experience. It is suggested that you work through the Adventures in order with the class, having small groups carry out the individual activities, so that students can concentrate on future-oriented thinking strategies.

Phase II. Cooperative Learning

Once you have the unit underway, help the learning teams choose which project they will work on: (1) Future Science Fair or (2) The World's Future. In both projects students explore topics from a futuristic perspective and have to do research and prepare a class presentation. The earlier you get the students started on the projects the better.

Phase III. Culminating Process

Using the project reports is one way to culminate the Experience. Since the topics students will investigate are very interesting, you might want to devote at least two days to the reports.

Evaluate and obtain feedback on the students' opinions and attitudes toward the unit. Use the form provided on page 111.

STUDENT INFORMATION

Adventures

Lesson 1. Fives Walk on Thursday

There are many ways to introduce your students to thinking about the future. It is possible to make a number of alternative forecasts about the future. In this unit, three general types are presented:

1. The extension forecast: Current trends continue.
2. The pessimistic forecast: Things go bad.
3. The optimistic forecast: The world lucks out.

This lesson thrusts the student immediately into the future. First, students listen to a story either on tape or read by you. They are then asked to think about the story as a forecast, decide what type of forecast they think it is, and create an image of the future that is different from the one depicted in the story.

Materials

Recording of Fives Walk on Thursday (pages 219–223 or tape), drawing paper, crayons, shoe box, aluminum foil, coathanger, knobs from an old radio.

Action

1. Tell the students that you are going to share a secret with them. For years you have been hiding a contraption that you invented but were afraid to announce to the world until today. The invention is a machine that is able to communicate with inhabitants of the future. To make this invention, place a tape recorder in a shoe box. Cover the box with aluminum foil. Make an antenna using a coathanger or a piece of wire. Push a couple of knobs from an old radio into the front of the box to make it look like a receiving station. Place the invention in front of the students; turn it on and listen to Fives Walk on Thursday.
2. You can record the story, use the commercial tape, or simply read it to your class.

Fives Walk on Thursday[5]

[Sound of static.] Hello. Hello. Are you there? My instruments tell me that you are able to hear my voice but unable to talk back to me. My computations tell me it is impossible for your voice to carry forward to my time. But I have been able to make changes in the wiring and communications systems of my room so that I can traverse time and talk to you. If my calculations are correct and you are hearing my voice on some type of electrical apparatus, then this is quite a significant day in history—the first trans-time electro-wave communication!

Imagine, you're hearing my voice all the way from the year 2431 back to your time, which I have computed to be in the late 1980s. However, if I am wrong and you are not listening to this transmission, there's no way for me to know it. I suppose there is nothing for me to do but assume that you're hearing my voice.

Well, let me introduce myself. My name is Trinum and my number is 60050960215. I live on the planet Earth in approximately the same place that you are now sitting. My studies have shown that I can most easily communicate through time if I beam my radio

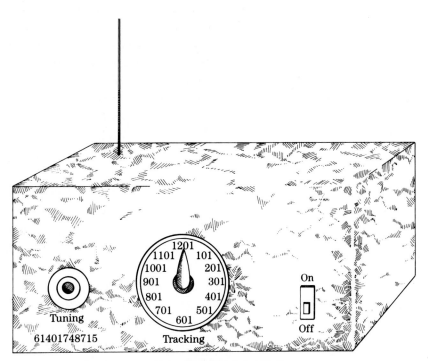

Trans-Time Receiving Station

waves in this same location. That is to say, in the year 2431 my room will be sitting on the spot where you are now. I wish it were possible for me to re-wire the viewing screen in my room so that I could see this place in your time.

My studies of history and geography tell me that in all likelihood you are familiar with such primitive things as trees, dirt, and running water. These are things which I've only read about or seen in pictures on my viewing screen. I'm also told by history, although I find it hard to believe, that the air in your world is not poisonous and that you don't fear leaving your room without your breathing apparatus.

Today very little space on earth can be devoted to the green trees and plants that in your century replenished the oxygen supply in the air. That you should so thoughtlessly breathe the earth's air is one surprise, but even more amazing is the practice that I observed in history lesson 706159, the lesson that made the fantastic assertion that the substance called water was so plentiful and pure in your time that you were able to move about in it, instead of receiving only enough to maintain your life. It is hard for me to imagine such a time when pure water—that life-giving commodity—was splashed about so carelessly, as though its supply would never end. If this description is true, I regard you as wasteful and thoughtless. You see, your generation added mercury, lead, and DDT to the soil and oceans. These toxic substances polluted the water for centuries to come.

Oh, well. I suppose that there's little value in expressing anger from my time to yours. For all I know, you're not even there listening.

Let me change the subject now, as it won't accomplish anything to blame you for the depleted condition of my world.

I will describe for you my room—the environment in which I am fortunate enough to spend almost all of my time. I have heard myths about times when men and women used to live and pass their time outside of their rooms. Such tales are difficult to believe because of our population density. We have a thousand times as many people on earth now as in your era, so there's little free space. Every square foot that is not used for living units is needed for the production of food. Factories make food from chemicals, since farms are much too wasteful and were abandoned centuries ago. My room is a marvel of the human ability to build and supply his or her needs. It's six feet long and approximately two feet wide. My whole room is about the same size as your furniture piece for sleeping, which I believe you called a bed.

The viewing screen and other communication systems are located in the ceiling directly above my face. Oxygen, water, and nutritional elements are supplied through tubes attached to the left wall of my room. Waste materials are carried out through tubes attached to the right wall of my room. The temperature of my room is controlled automatically, as is my schedule of waking and sleeping.

My room takes care of me. It provides all the things I could possibly want. On the viewing screen I can dial any lesson on any topic I choose. I can also dial the rooms of my friends. We can talk together about the interesting things we are learning from our viewer screens. Of course, we don't have much time for such social communication because we are awake only four hours a day. You see, when awake a person consumes more energy for life support and for the viewer screen. Energy must be strictly rationed so that there will be enough for all of us. Ah, yes. It is a good life that I have here in my room. Everything is provided for me. I don't need to move at all. I suppose I shouldn't really tell you so much about my room; I know you'll start wishing for such a perfect environment for yourself. No need to go from place to place or do things with other people or worry about the details of life.

My favorite kinds of lessons on the viewing screen are the ones about science and history. It was through the study of science that I was able to discover the principle involved in sending electro-waves through time.

From history lesson number 706159 I have heard about life in your time. Here, I'll dial that lesson and let you hear parts of it for yourself. . . .

This is history program number 706-159, which tells of the exploitation of the planet earth by the carelessness of the humans of the twentieth century . . .

Well you don't want to hear the introduction to the lesson. Let me move to the part about the depletion of natural resources. . . . Ah, yes. Here it is. . . .

> *Coal and petroleum reserves were consumed at a rapid rate. Automobiles, power plants, and factories all used ever increasing quantities because of the surging population. Finally the supply of coal and oil ran out in the year 2250, and we've had to rely on nuclear power ever since. Most objections . . .*

The lack of fuel doesn't matter so much, though. We have no need for gasoline, since we have no automobiles. We certainly can't waste space on roads as was done in your day. Besides, our lives are planned so that we seldom need to go anywhere.

Of course sometimes I dream about how the earth used to be before it became so crowded. Here let me play the part for you about the rapid growth of people on the earth—the population explosion as they used to call it. Ah. Here it is. Let's see how you like it.

> *Medical science discovered the cure for plague and sickness and this prolonged the lifespan. Even though some efforts were made to reduce the birth rate, they were not effective. As a result, more people were born than died, and the population grew at the rate of 130 thousand each day in the 1970s. Thus, the 3 billion people of the 1970s grew to 6 billion by the year 2000 and 12 billion people were alive on the earth just 30 years later. Finally no more space could be found for the people, power plants, oxygen processors, and food factories. By the year 2271 . . .*

Well, that's what happened. With the population doubling every 30 years, any child could figure out that it wouldn't take long for the earth to become a thousand times more crowded than it was in your time. Oh, well. I suppose I should be glad I have my room to feed me, keep me warm, and clean my air for me. If it weren't for our rooms, we all would have died years ago.

But as it is, we live a good life—enough food and water to maintain life, the viewing screen to occupy our minds four hours each day, and on Thursday we Fives go for a walk! That's right. Every Thursday those of us whose numbers end in 5 get to walk for an hour. Of course it would be impossible for everyone on earth to go walking at the same time—there's just not that much space.

Things are organized so that each group is allowed one hour each week in which they may leave their rooms and, with the help of the strong ones, walk about on the footpaths between the rooms. And what an experience it is. As Thursday draws near, I get more and more excited. I eagerly strap on my breathing apparatus and my life support system and wait for the strong ones to come. . . .

And when they come and open my room and help me out, I drink in every golden minute of the walk. The memory must last for a whole week. As I walk along the concrete footpaths I look at the beautiful towers thousands of feet high, each filled with survival rooms. Just think of it, miles and miles of survival rooms, each containing a person just like me, waiting for his or her day to walk.

I can hardly wait until tomorrow, because tomorrow is Thursday, and we Fives walk on Thursday. . . .

---

3. Thinking Ahead

   a. Ask students questions about the story:

      • Would you like to live during Trinum's time? Why?
      • Is such a future possible? Why?
      • Is such a future probable? Why?
      • How could such a future happen?
      • How could such a future be prevented?

   b. Which of the following forecasts does the story "Fives Walk on Thursday" fit? Ask the students to give reasons for their choices.

      • Extension forecast: The future is simply the same as today; current trends will continue.
      • Pessismistic forecast: The future is bleak; things will not turn out well for humankind.
      • Optimistic forecast: The future is bright; things will turn out well for humankind.

   c. Trinum's world is the result of events that happened and decisions that were made in the twentieth century. Ask the students to identify the trends that may have resulted in a world such as his. They should consider the following:

      • Population
      • Usage and distribution of natural resources
      • Energy usage
      • Food consumption
      • Food production
      • Housing
      • Transportation
      • Political ideologies

    d. What did Trinum's world look like? Have students draw pictures of Trinum; Trinum's room; Trinum's city; a day in the life of Trinum, especially Thursday.

Lesson 2. Imagining the Future[6]

Time travel has always been a fascination and a dream of humankind. Much of science fiction is based on images of the future. In this activity, you will take your students on a guided trip into the future. They will use their imaginations and your guiding questions to visualize the future, think about how they feel about the future, and evaluate their impressions of the future.

Materials
Record player, classical music to stimulate imagery and to help relax the students.

Action

1. First set the stage for the trip by establishing an environment of relaxation, as well as one of anticipation. To help the students relax, play classical music throughout the imagery experience. To create anticipation, have the students imagine that they are able to travel to the future in time machines. To create this illusion, arrange the chairs in the classroom in pairs. Tell students that their time machines each have two seats—one for them and one for a guide who will go along on the trip to answer questions and point out things of interests. You could also use a large cardboard box as the time machine. Students could enter the box in pairs and listen to the imagery experience, which may be read by you or recorded on tape.
2. Read the Time Travel imagery experience to the students while the music is playing.

Time Travel

Relax your bodies and be comfortable. Let your arms fall to your sides. Make sure you are securely within your time machine . . . Close your eyes and let your breathing deepen and relax you . . . You are going to go on a trip into the future in this safe machine that will carry you there and bring you back . . . Are you ready? OK. Here we go . . . 5 . . . 4 . . . 3 . . . 2 . . . 1 . . .

    You are now moving forward through time . . . 1995 . . . Observe the events you see . . . A future history you will remember on the way back . . . Make mental notes of what you see . . . Sitting next to you is your guide . . . Your guide will answer any questions you may have and may even make suggestions

and point things out to you . . . Use your guide wisely
. . . You and your guide continue forward in time . . .
1997 . . . 2010 . . . 2040 . . . 2080.

You are at your destination . . . What is the first
thing you see? It's very important, so try to remember
it . . . What are you feeling now that you have arrived
in the year 2080? Are you happy? Sad? Scared? Undecided? . . . How do the people look? . . . What clothes
are they wearing? . . . What kind of food do they eat?
. . . Does it appeal to you? . . . What types of work are
people in the future world doing? . . . What kinds of
entertainment and recreation do you see? . . . How do
people communicate with each other? . . . Do they
seem happy? . . . Sad? . . . How do people you see
seem to travel? . . . Do they travel in ways you've
never seen before? . . . What is the strangest thing
you see in this place you are visiting? . . .

Imagine that someone sees you . . . The person
seems friendly so you welcome this person . . . This
person asks you who you are and what you are doing
here . . . What do you say? . . . The stranger seems
interested in you and what you say. The person
reaches into a bag and gives you something and tells
you to keep it . . . What is it? . . . What does it tell you
about this person's world? . . .

It's time for you to return, so you must say good-
bye to the stranger . . . As you do, the stranger tells
you something very important . . . It is something
about the stranger's world, and the stranger wants
you to know about it . . . What is it that the stranger
tells you? . . . Take a last look around and return to
your time machine to get ready for your trip back to
the present . . . Are you ready? . . . OK. Here we go . . .
5 . . . 4 . . . 3 . . . 2 . . . 1 . . . You're beginning your
return to the present . . . 2080 . . . 2040 . . . 2001 . . .
1997 . . . 1995 . . . the present. Now slowly come back
to this room and when you are ready, open your eyes
and get out of your time machine . . .

---

3. Give the students the list of questions and activities for the guided
   imagery experience (pages 239 and 240). Let them use these
   questions to help recall the Experience.

Lesson 3. Thinking About the Future

Personal values are guides that carry us through life and thus into the future. Throughout our lives, our values change, yet at any one time, they are the guideposts that influence the way we interpret and see the world.

In our work with students, we should respect their values while providing opportunities for them to test and clarify those values. Furthermore, they should learn to respect the values of others. Science lessons can provide opportunities to gain knowledge about values. Simon, Kirchenbaum, and Howe have developed a strategy in which students explore and clarify values through experiential activities, not indoctrination.[7] In this process, known as values clarification, three qualifications must be met in order for one's beliefs to be considered values.

1. The belief must be freely chosen from among alternatives, without coercion and with consideration for the consequences.
2. The belief must be happily and positively prized and be willingly affirmed and shared with others.
3. The belief must be acted upon, regardless of the consequences.

In this activity students vote on various issues and statements about the future to encourage active thinking about issues and ideas.

Action

1. Have students sit in a circle. Explain that they will be voting on how they feel about certain statements. If they have a strong positive response, they should raise a hand and wave it in the air; if they have a positive response, they should raise a hand; if they have no opinion or do not wish to respond, they should hold a hand out straight; if they have a negative response, they should lower a hand; if they have a strong negative response, they should lower a hand and shake it.
2. Read the questions on page 241 to the group, giving students time to respond. If you wish to participate, wait until everyone has voted before revealing your opinion.
3. Have students pay attention to how their vote compares to others'. Ask the questions at a fairly rapid pace. Unless students feel an urgent need to discuss the question for the sake of clarification, avoid discussion at this point, so that students can find out how others feel about issues without the ideas of any one person dominating the discussion.
4. Thinking Ahead

   a. Give the list of questions to the students and have them ask their parents how they feel about the future. Discuss how the ideas and opinions of the adults differ from those of the students.
   b. Ask students to select the statements they feel the most positive about and the most negative. Have them write about why they feel the way they do and share their ideas with their learning teams.

Lesson 4. Polling the Future

Polling is a method futurists use to forecast the future. It is important to note that futurists do not predict the future but rather make the most informed statement of probability that is possible. There are many methods for doing this. Polling experts as well as ordinary people to gather opinions about issues and problems is one method of compiling data from which to make a forecast.

Materials

Chart paper with a time line showing five-year increments from 1995 to 2025.

Action

1. Have students work in learning teams for this activity. Their first task is to select an area of interest about which to make forecasts. Here are some ideas:

   Bioethics   Health care
   Behavior control   Life styles
   Cities   Occupations, careers
   Education   Population
   Energy   Privacy
   Environmental protection   Space travel
   Food production   Transportation
   Genetic engineering

2. After each learning team has selected an area of interest, help them identify specific topics related to the area to use as guidelines for writing poll questions. For example, the list below shows topics related to the area of space travel.

   Space Travel

   Temporary lunar base
   Manned Mars and Venus fly-by
   Permanent base established on moon
   Manufacturing plants on moon
   Commercial travel to earth—orbiting hotels/space stations
   Communication with extraterrestrials
   Extraterrestrial farming

3. Introduce Space Travel and list the related topics on the chalkboard. Encourage students to add to the list, perhaps using one of the brainstorming techniques.

4. Explain that students will use the topics to write questions. Once the poll is taken, students will use responses to make a forecast. Help students use the list to write questions such as the following:

   • Do you think there will be a factory on the moon by the year 2010?
   • Do you think there will be one by the year 2020?
   • Do you think there will be one by the year 2025?

5. Use the questions above to poll the class and then show them how to record the data on a time line. Display the time line and use it to

record students' responses to the question; a sample is shown below.

Poll showing when people think there will be a factory on the moon.

					X		
					X	X	
			X		X	X	
			X		X	X	
			X		X	X	
1995	2000	2005	2010	2015	2020	2025	2030

X = 2 students

Forecasts may be based on the average response or on the most frequent response. Discuss the implications of the responses with the group.

6. Thinking ahead

   a. When students feel confident about the polling process, have them get together with their teams and write up questions for the area of interest they chose. Then have them poll other class members and use time lines to record the responses. Have students use the responses to forecast the future.
   b. Discuss the results of the polls and the forecasts that teams made. How bright does the future look, according to the forecasts?

Lesson 5. Connections

This lesson uses another forecasting technique known as the Future Wheel. It is a device to show the possible results, effects, or associations of a trend, an idea, or an event.

Materials
Copy of the Future Wheel (page 242)

Action

1. Give students a copy of the Future Wheel. Tell them that it is used to show the effects of a trend, event, or idea. In this case the event is Control of the Aging Process. Ask students to add effects to the wheel. Can they think of other things that will happen if the aging process is controlled? Discuss the wheel before moving on.
2. Introduce cause and effect using *if, then*: *If* something happens, *then* something else will happen. Point out some examples on the Future Wheel.

   a. If aging is controlled, then more people will exist.
   b. If more people exist, then more housing will be needed.
   c. If more housing is needed, then the use of natural resources will increase.

3. Have students continue making up *if, then* statements.

4. Have students work in learning teams and create a Future Wheel for one of the trends, events, or ideas listed below.

Trends	**Events**
More people living in cities	Manned landing on Mars
Decline of birth rate	World disarmament
More leisure time	Communication with
More homes with	extraterrestrials
microcomputers	Elimination of all genetic
Increased spending for	disorders
space travel	Perfection of mind reading
Decreased spending for	
space travel	
Decreased spending for	
military budget	
More genetic diseases	
eliminated	
More windmills	
Increased unemployment	
Increased depletion of	
natural resources	
Increased commercial use	
of national parks	

5. Thinking Ahead

    a. Have students use the Future Wheel that they produce to write a story about the future.
    b. Have the class choose one topic and then have each team make a Future Wheel. When the wheels are complete, have students compare them. Did students identify similar effects or consequences for the initial topic in the wheel? How are the wheels similar? How are they different?

Lesson 6. Hard Choices[8]

Problem solving is one of the most important skills we can teach students to prepare them for the future. Futuristic thinking thrusts us into situations where hard choices have to be made. In this lesson, students will use role playing to solve future problems.

Materials
Copies of the role-playing dilemmas (pages 243–244)

Action

1. This activity can be done in one of several ways:

    a. The fishbowl method: Arrange the class in a circle with seven chairs in the fishbowl. Have four to six students in the fishbowl with you. Select one of the dilemmas and have students in the fishbowl role-play the situation.
    b. The small group method: Give each learning team one of the dilemmas, and have them act it out. Tell each group to be prepared to report to the entire class at the end of the designated time period.

c. The center stage method: Ask a volunteer to direct a dilemma by selecting one of the dilemmas and choosing a cast to role play the situation. The director indicates the roles each person will play, arranges the stage, and decides what props are needed.

In all cases, keep the role-playing time to about 10 minutes. Provide time for feedback and discussion before going on to another dilemma.

Side Paths

Lesson 7. A Model Future City (Art)

Teams of students can design a self-contained model city that will house about 50,000 people. All basic services—police, health care, shopping, waste disposal, water, power, recreation—are provided. Give students felt tip pens and large sheets of chart paper.

Introduce the requirements and constraints for the model future city. If you wish, give different teams different parameters.

The city must

- Recycle all its waste.
- Supply all its power.
- Be completely safe.
- Have a mass transportation system.
- Take up no more than two square miles of land area.
- Be pollution free.

Students can consult reference books and magazines. Their drawing of the model future city should be detailed and labeled. When all are finished, have each team report their final "blueprints" to the class.

Lesson 8. We've Come A Long Way (Art)

Have students make posters to show how things have changed technologically in the past 20 years. Begin by having them brainstorm a list of things that did not exist 20 years ago. They might ask their parents and grandparents what the most important technological innovation has been. Have students find pictures of the things and arrange them on poster board to show how things have changed in a relatively short time.

Lesson 9. Time Line (Social Studies)

Have students make two time lines representing the time span from their birth through the year 2050. Explain that one time line should show personal events that they have experienced or expect to experience; the other should show social, political, historical, and scientific events and forecasts.

Provide adding machine tape or long sheets of butcher paper. Help students set up the time lines before filling in the events. You might draw a version of the time line on the chalkboard as shown below.

| 1970 | 1975 | 1980 | 1985 | 1990 | 1995 | 2000 | 2005 | 2010 | 2020 |

To get students started, provide them with copies of the Time Line Data Sheet (page 245).

When students have finished the data sheet, have them fill in the two time lines. Make sure they draw their time lines to the same scale so that they can easily compare them.

Lesson 10. Metaphors of the Future (Social Studies)

In *Teaching the Future*, Draper Kauffman identified four metaphors for the future. Present these metaphors to students, either by reading them or by providing copies. Have students choose the metaphor that they think is closest to how they perceive the future. When they have made a choice, have them draw pictures of the metaphors, adding whatever they wish to it to convey the meaning of the future. When they are finished, share the drawings. You might also consider one of the follow-up activities below.

1. Select one metaphor at a time, and have the entire class decide how to act it out.
2. Have students think of other metaphors of the future. Make suggestions such as a train, bus, airplane; library; computer terminal; school.
3. Ask students how metaphors are helpful in planning for the future.

The Metaphors of the Future[9]

Roller Coaster. The future is a great roller coaster on a moonless night. It exists, twisting ahead of us in the dark, although we can only see each part as we come to it. We can make estimates about where we are headed and sometimes see around a bend to another section of track, but it doesn't do us any real good because the future is fixed and determined. We are locked in our seats, and nothing we may know or do will change the course that is laid out for us.

Mighty River. The future is a mighty river. The great force of history flows along, carrying us with it. Most of our attempts to change its course are like mere pebbles thrown into the river; they cause a momentary splash and a few ripples, but they make no difference. The river's course can be changed, but only by natural disasters such as earthquakes or landslides, or by massive concerted human efforts on a similar scale. On the other hand, we are free as individuals to adapt to the course of history either well or poorly. By looking ahead, we can avoid sandbars and whirlpools and pick the best path through any rapids.

Great Ocean. The future is a great ocean. There are many possible destinations, and many different courses to each destination. A good navigator takes advantage of the main currents of change, adapts the course to anticipate the capricious winds of chance, keeps a sharp lookout posted, and moves carefully in fog or uncharted waters. Doing these things ensures a safe arrival at the destination (barring a typhoon or other disaster which can neither be predicted nor avoided.)

Game of Chance. The future is a colossal game of chance. It is entirely random. Every second, millions of things happen that could have happened another way and produced a different future. A scientist checks a spoiled culture and throws it away or looks more closely at it and makes a radical breakthrough. A citizen grows up in a slum, deprived of education or grows up to be president and changes the political course of America and the world. Since everything is left up to chance all we can do is play the game, hope for the best, and seize what good luck comes our way.

Lesson 11. The Intelligent House (Social Studies)

One of the forecasts that futurists have made is that someday homes will be entirely computerized. The addition of a computer to the home will give it a "brain," thereby providing it with a form of intelligence. In the house of the future, integrated sub-systems will be computer controlled, with control centers, home entertainment centers, computerized kitchens, and many other electronic features.

Students may want to investigate some of the future models for houses. They should collect pictures and diagrams of futuristic homes, organize them for a bulletin board or a portfolio, and then share them with the class. A good source of ideas on futuristic homes is the February 1982 issue of the *Futurist Magazine*.

1. Have students report on futurist's ideas about an "intelligent house." They should consider the following:

   - Is this innovation possible? Is it probable?
   - Is this innovation desirable?
   - What are the dangers of a computerized generation of homes?

2. Students might interview engineers and architects to find out their ideas about future home designs.

Lesson 12. Trends (Mathematics)

A trend is a description of the way something is changing. Things can increase, decrease, change irregularly, not change, change evenly (linearly), or change unevenly (exponentially.)

Materials
Graph paper, vials or baby food jars, popcorn kernels

Action

1. Show students samples of graphs that show trends. You should include graphs that show no growth, linear growth, and exponential growth. Here are some examples:

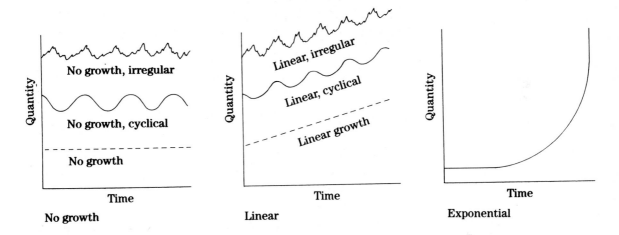

2. Ask students to describe what is changing in each graph and to explain how it is changing.
3. Tell the students that they are to simulate a trend and then determine what kind of change or trend it is by graphing their results.
4. Tell students that the kernels of corn represent money and that you are going to distribute amounts of money to them in successive time intervals. Set up the distribution in the following way.

Time (in months)	For Graph 1	For Graph 2
1	2 kernels	2 kernels
2	4	4
3	6	8
4	8	16
5	10	32
6	12	64

(Stop distributing corn at this point and have students calculate the rest.)

Time (in months)	For Graph 1	For Graph 2
7	14	128
8	16	256
9	18	512
10	20	1024

5. Have the students make separate graphs for each set of data. The time should be plotted on the *(x)* axis (horizontal), and the number of kernels on the *(y)* axis (vertical). The students' results should look like the following graphs:

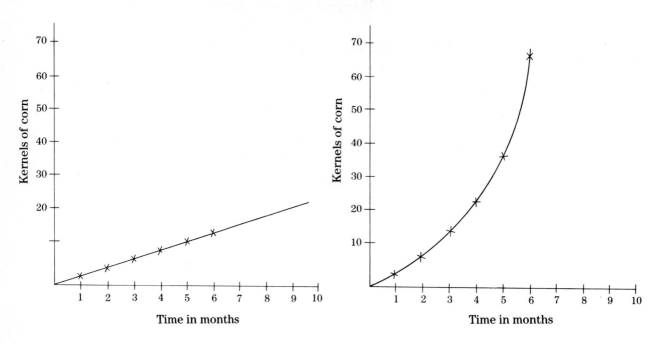

6. Show the students a graph of how the human population has changed since about 1500 A.D. Which type of graph does the human population graph resemble? (exponential, Graph 2) Ask what might have caused such a change in the human population and what effect it has on the environment of earth.

World Population
8,000 B.C. to A.D. 2,000

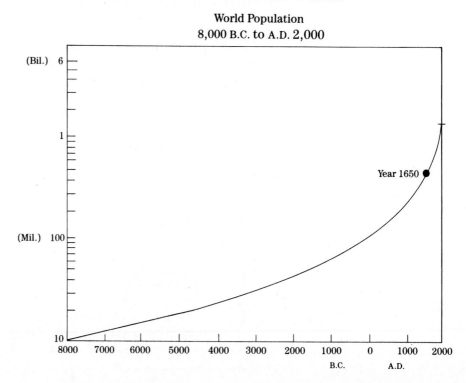

7. Introduce the concept of zero population growth (ZPG). ZPG means that each person is replaced with just one offspring: married couples would have an average of two children according to ZPG standards. If this happened worldwide, how would it affect the population graph?

Lesson 13. Scenario Writing (Language Arts)

Have students write a scenario that forecasts the future. You might combine this activity with the science fiction activity that follows. The following procedure has been adapted from Kauffman.[10]

Action

1. Organize the class into learning teams. In the first step, work with all the teams as one large group. Tell the class that they are going to create several alternative futures for the United States and the world. Have students brainstorm the following categories. Write their ideas on the chalkboard or on separate sheets of chart paper:

Category	Local-National Perspective	World Perspective
Biology		
Education		
Politics		
Life style		
Transportation		
Environment		
Space		
Housing		
Games		
Energy		
Population		
Natural Resources		

For each category, have students brainstorm possible events that they think might occur within the next 50 years. Have them consider both national and world perspectives for each category. When the group slows down on a category, quickly move to a new one. You may find it helpful to have an open category for items that do not seem to fit in any other category.

2. Have the learning teams assemble in various sections of the room and give each one a large sheet of chart paper. Assign an item from one of the categories to each team. For example, teams might be assigned moving sidewalks, teleports, automatic highways, and hover cars from the transportation category. Continue assigning items from each category until all of them are used.

3. Have each team create a scenario using the items they have been assigned. Here are some basic rules that should help the teams in their work:

    a. All scenarios should be written from the perspective of the same future year that you designate.

    b. Groups can agree to exchange items from the same category or from different categories on a one-for-one swap.

    c. At least half of the items assigned to a team must be woven into the scenario in some fashion.

    d. A team may introduce completely new items if they are approved in advance.

4. Post the scenarios where all students can read them. When this step is completed, assemble the groups. Give each group five minutes to describe their scenario and five minutes for group discussion.

Searches

Lesson 1. Future Science Project Fair

Announce that the class is going to participate in a future science Fair. The fair will be held in the classroom, parents and other students from the school will be invited to attend. Projects can include inventions, creations, models, or ideas that reflect the world in the year 2020. They can choose a project from one of a variety of areas:

    Communication
    Energy
    Family
    Food
    Health/Bio-engineering
    Housing
    International Relations
    Learning
    Computers
    Nuclear weapons
    Natural resources
    Population
    Space
    Transportation

Lesson 2. The World's Future

In this project, students explore their ideas and visions of the future through a problem-solving situation or task. The problem encourages them to think about how they would go about building a future world as they investigate areas such as:

    Energy forms
    New forms of communication
    Alternative forms of transportation
    Architecture
    Community planning
    Environmental planning
    Genetics
    Social organizations

The final product can be shared by using films or slides; models or maps; audio or video tapes; games or simulations; or drawings, cartoons, and animation. Give students the following problem to solve.

Your team has been assigned the task of planning and designing a futuristic colony. You can decide where the colony is to be located: in orbit, on another planet, under the ocean, underground, floating in the air. The solution to the problem should include a holistic plan in which your team integrates all aspects of the colony: its communication system, architecture, social organization, sources of energy, and forms of transportation.

Evaluation

Organize the class into learning teams. Have each team discuss a problem selected from the list below, and then report the results of their discussions to the class.

1. What effect would making contact with intelligent life elsewhere in the universe have on people here on earth?
2. Some people believe that if extraterrestrial life contacted us first they would be more advanced than we are and would probably know how to avoid a nuclear war. Write a fantasy story about what such an advanced society could teach us. What values and beliefs would these extraterrestrials hold?
3. How do you think most people regard the idea of sending signals to communicate with life elsewhere in the universe? What is your opinion?
4. Suppose scientists discovered that an ordinary liquid, such as water, could be used to power cars, trains, airplanes, and power plants. How would this affect civilization as we know it? What would be the impact on natural resources, the atmosphere, and the quality of life?

Use the following criteria to judge the effectiveness of the reports.

Criteria	Effectiveness: 1 (low) 2 3 4 5 (high)
1. Uniqueness of the report.	
2. Knowledge and understanding of the problem.	
3. Clarity of thinking.	
4. Use of information.	
5. Effectiveness of communication.	
6. Identified relationships that affected the problem.	

Books for Kids

Asimov, Isaac, Martin H. Greenberg, and David Clark. *Fantastic Reading: Stories and Activities for Grade 5–8.* Glenview, Illinois: Scott, Foresman and Company, 1984.

Billings, Henry and Melissa Billings. *Phenomena: 21 Extraordinary Stories.* Providence, R.I.: Jamestown Publishers, 1984.

Bradbury, Ray. *The Martian Chronicles.* New York: Bantam, 1958.

Foster, John. *Space Ways: An Anthology of Space Poems.* Oxford, England: Oxford University Press, 1986.

Heinlein, Robert A. *Space Cadet.* New York: Ace 1948.

_____. *Stranger in a Strange Land.* New York: Berkley, 1961.

McKie, Robin. *Robots.* New York: Watts, 1986.

_____. *Solar Power.* New York: Gloucester, 1985.

Naiman, Arthur. *What Every Kid and Adult Should Know about Computers.* Hasbrouck Heights, N.J.: Hayden, 1985.

Olney, Ross R. *Car of the Future.* Hillside: N.J.: Enslow, 1986.

Strachan, James. *Future Sources.* New York: Gloucester, 1985.

TIME TRAVEL QUESTIONS

1. What was the first thing you saw?

2. What did you feel when you arrived in the year 2080?

3. Were you happy? Were you sad? Were you scared? Were you confused?

4. How did people look?

5. What clothes were they wearing?

6. What kind of food did they eat?

7. Did the food appeal to you?

8. What types of work were people in the future world doing?

9. What kinds of entertainment and recreation did you observe?

10. How did people communicate with each other?

11. Did they seem happy? Did they seem sad?

12. How did people seem to travel?

13. Did they travel in ways you've never seen before?

14. What was the strangest thing you saw in the place you visited?

15. What did you say to the stranger?

16. What did the stranger give you?

17. What does it tell you about this person's world?

18. What did the stranger tell you?

Page reference: 226

TIME TRAVEL ACTIVITIES

1. Look over your answers to the Time Travel questions
   and the things you remember from your Time Travel
   trip. Use your answers to evaluate your feelings about
   the future. Mark each question as follows:

   + If it was positive or desirable.
   – If it was negative or
     undesirable.
   0 If you are undecided.

2. Draw a picture of the stranger you met and the object
   you received.

3. Write a brief description of what was happening on the
   day you traveled to the year 2080, and how you felt about
   the trip.

Page reference: 225

THINKING ABOUT THE FUTURE

1. Do you feel that the human race is moving toward a more desirable future?

2. Do you feel that people are swept along into the future by forces over which they have little control?

3. Do you feel that there are many possible futures, both desirable and undesirable, open to humankind?

4. Do you feel that a prediction is not basically different from a forecast?

5. Do you feel that if you could fully understand all the forces affecting the present you could accurately predict the future?

6. Do you feel that it is possible to have knowledge of the future?

7. Do you feel that it is unreasonable to expect a future in which there are no surprises?

8. Do you feel that social outcomes such as the future of marriage and the family can be predicted as well as natural outcomes such as the weather.

9. Do you feel that the future was more predictable for cave dwellers than it is for us?

10. Do you feel that the purpose of forecasting the future is to help us make better decisions in the present?

11. Do you feel that a side effect of forecasting the future is that it helps us better understand the present?

12. Do you feel that forecasting the future takes away freedom of choice?

13. Do you feel that how one thinks about the future is strongly related to how one deals with society and other people?

14. Do you feel that the future 20 years from now will be completely different from the present?

Page reference: 226

FUTURE WHEEL

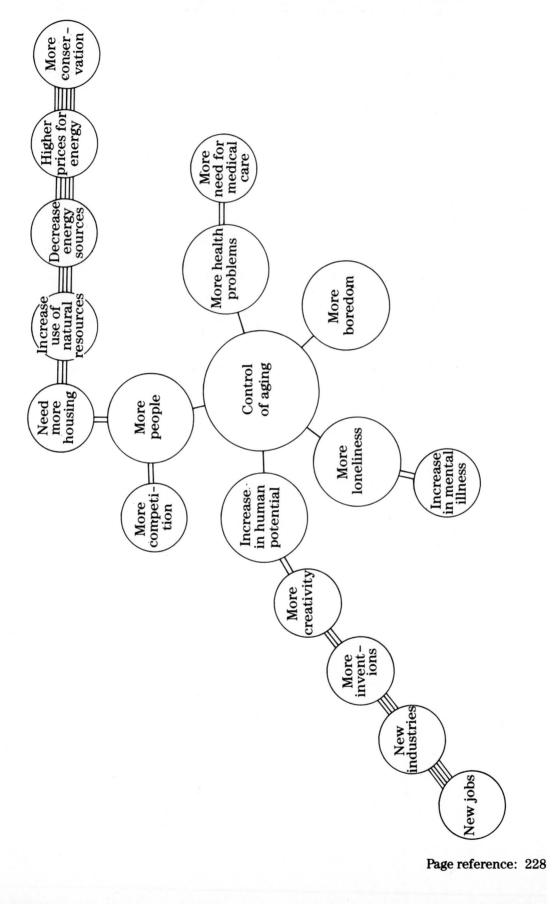

Page reference: 228

DILEMMA 1:
THE MAN WHO WANTED TO DIE[8]

A young man is badly injured when a leaking propane gas line explodes, an accident in which his father is killed. He has second and third degree burns over 68 percent of his body; his eyes, ears, and most of his face are severely burned. After many months of skin grafts, his hands have been amputated, he is susceptible to infections, and he has to be bathed daily in a special tank. Although he accepts treatment, he says he wants to die. Eventually he refuses further treatment and insists on going home—a move that would mean sure and early death. His mother opposes his decision, and a psychiatrist agrees to see the boy to determine his state of mind. Perhaps the boy should be declared incompetent so that a legal guardian can authorize treatment. But in examining the young man, the psychiatrist finds him to be bright, coherent, logical, and articulate—anything but incompetent. He says that he does not want to go on as a blind and crippled person and asks to be released from the hospital, by court order if necessary.

Questions for Discussion

1. What do you think should happen? Does the young man have the right to go home?
2. Under what circumstances does a person have the right to refuse treatment?
3. If you were the young man's mother, what would you do?
4. If you were the young man, what course of action would you take in this situation?

[8] Adapted from material in *Hard Choices: A Magazine on the Ethics of Sickness and Health.* © 1980 by KCTS/9. The Regents of the University of California.

Page reference: 229

DILEMMA 2:
THE FORBIDDEN EXPERIMENT[8]

The city council of a large city votes 5 to 4 for a three-month moratorium on research being conducted at a distinguished university there. At public hearings, the opposition, led by the mayor, charges that the research could endanger the public by polluting the water with disease-carrying microbes. Defenders of the research say that any dangers can be contained and condemn talk about pollution and diseases as being the result of hysteria. Prohibitionists insist that it is better to be safe than sorry and that by definition the results in any true experiment cannot be predicted. Scientists accept the three-month ban with good grace, but it is clear that they intend to reopen the issue at the end of that period.

Questions for Discussion

1. Do you think certain experiments should be forbidden altogether?
2. On what grounds should experiments be forbidden?
3. Which side would you take in this dilemma? Give reasons for your decision.

[8] Adapted from material in *Hard Choices: A Magazine on the Ethics of Sickness and Health.* © 1980 by KCTS/9. The Regents of the University of California.

Page reference: 229

TIME LINE DATA SHEET

Personal Event	Date	Social, Historical, Political, or Scientific Event (List here things that happened on the significant dates on your personal time line.)
Birth		
First year in school		
Graduation from elementary school		
First time in an airplane		
First date		
First year in high school		
Graduation from high school		
Graduation from college, degree and year earned		
First job		
Date of marriage		
Purchase of first car		
Travel to a foreign country		
First child born		
Retirement		
Death		

Page reference: 231

POWERING THE EARTH

An Energy and Ecological Experience

There is a source of energy that produces no radioactive waste, nothing in the way of petrodollars, and very little pollution. Moreover, the source can provide the energy that conventional sources may not be able to furnish. Unhappily, however, it does not receive the emphasis and attention that it deserves to receive.

The source might be called energy efficiency, for Americans like to think of themselves as an efficient people. But the energy source is generally known by the more prosaic term conservation. *To be semantically accurate, the source should be called conservation energy, to remind us of the reality—that conservation is no less an energy alternative than oil, gas, or nuclear. Indeed, in the near term, conservation could do more than any of the conventional sources to help the country deal with the energy problem it has.*

ROBERT STOBAUGH AND DANIEL YERGIN
Energy Future

TEACHER INFORMATION

Background Information

Powering the Earth is a science Experience dealing with the earth's energy resources. It is also an ecological Experience in which the impact of our increased energy use on our planet's natural resouces— air, water, land, minerals, plants, and animals—is explored.

One might assume that the master power source for the earth is the sun. The sun is responsible—either directly or indirectly—for most of the forms of energy that power the planet. Although we have to stretch things to show connections, the relationships are there and can be thought of as an energy chain.

For example, a student asks, "Where does the light in that light bulb come from?" One could say, "From the fossil remains of plants that lived over 200 million years ago." But a better answer is a long series of connections—an energy chain.

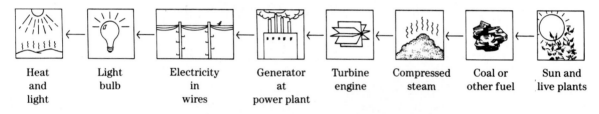

| Heat and light | Light bulb | Electricity in wires | Generator at power plant | Turbine engine | Compressed steam | Coal or other fuel | Sun and live plants |

The connections depicted in the above energy chain are symbolic of all energy conversions. In this Experience the energy chain idea should be reinforced as often as possible.

Our development as an advanced civilization has been coordinated with our technical knowledge of energy and our ability to extract sources of energy from the earth. Our progress—some might say our greed for more—has resulted in a series of eco-crises. These crises that we have experienced in the recent past, and the resulting detriment to the air, water, and land, are not new to humankind. Greek and Roman civilizations had ecological and energy problems; the Chinese completely deforested their land to use the wood for fuel.

In the twentieth century we face problems that earlier civilizations did not have, including the size of the population. Overpopulation has created an enormous rate of change in the use of energy and natural resources. Another problem is the concept of the earth as a global village, which runs in direct opposition to the nation-state mentality. Today all nations must be interdependent because our planet has shrunk in its proportions. We travel at speeds exceeding that of sound, and we communicate at the speed of light.

This Experience presents concepts that support the need for a world view in which our resources are synergically used for the betterment of humankind. As citizens of planet earth in the late twentieth century, we have a responsibility to the generations that follow. We are temporary inhabitants of spaceship earth, and in that role we must care for and nurture the earth. Our caring will be evident in the knowledge we have about the earth's resources and how we utilize and conserve what we have.

Overview and Planning

Take a few minutes to review the Overview and Planning Chart for Powering the Earth. There are six Adventures, four Side Paths, and three Search projects.

Overview and Planning Chart: Powering the Earth

Activity	Science Concept	Science Process	Modes of Learning	Attitude
Adventures				
1. Where Does the Energy Go?	Energy is transferred in an energy chain.	Observing Inferring	Physical-sensory Left	Curiosity
Note: Teacher's close supervision is necessary for Activity A in this lesson.				
2. When You're Hot, You're Hot!	Energy changes can be measured by observing temperature changes.	Observing Measuring Interpreting data	Physical-sensory Left	Self-reliance
3. Don't Fuel Me!	Energy exists in two forms: potential or kinetic.	Observing Interpreting data	Left Physical-sensory	Sensitivity to environment
4. Problems, Problems, Problems	Energy problems have resulted from the increasing use of different kinds of fuel.	Observing Interpreting data	Left Affective	Sensitivity to environment
5. The Marine Biologist and the Oil Tanker	Ecosystems can change if pollutants are introduced into the environment.	Interpreting data	Physical-sensory Left	Sensitivity to environment
6. Once Upon a Time	Humans' impact on the environment sometimes results in permanent change.	Interpreting data	Physical-sensory Left	Sensitivity to environment
Side Paths				
7. Noise Pollution	Noise pollution has an impact on the environment.	Observing Interpreting data	Physical-sensory Left Affective	Sensitivity to environment
8. Litter Pollution	Solid objects create litter that has an impact on the environment.	Observing Classifying	Physical-sensory Cognitive	Sensitivity to environment
9. Water Pollution	Air pollutants contaminate the water supply.	Observing Inferring	Physical-sensory Left	Sensitivity to environment
10. Air Pollution	Gases released by cars and factories are a major cause of air pollution.	Observing Inferring	Physical-sensory Left	Sensitivity to environment

Activity	Science Concept	Science Process	Modes of Learning	Attitude
Searches				
1. Blow the Whistle on Water Pollution	Ordinances help regulate uses of natural resources.	Identifying variables	Left	Sensitivity to environment Concern for others
2. The Opinionnaire	An opinionnaire is a way of gathering people's ideas about important issues.	Classifying Interpreting data	Left Affective	Concern for environment
3. The Foxfire Project	Interviewing older people gives historical perspectives on issues.	Observing Interpreting data	Left Affective	Concern for others Sensitivity to environment

Objectives

At the end of this Experience, students should be able to:

1. Describe how energy is transferred in an energy chain.
2. Measure energy.
3. Investigate the impact of energy problems on society.
4. Inquire into the variety of energy sources available to humankind.
5. Investigate energy and environmental problems in the local community and carry out the motto: Think globally, act locally.
6. Evaluate the impact of pollutants on the environment.
7. Express feelings and attitudes about environmental issues.

Key Concepts

The following represent the major concepts that students will study:

Conservation The protecton and careful use of forests, rivers, countryside, and the seas, and the careful use of natural products such as coal and oil.

Ecosystem A balanced community of living organisms and micro-organisms that exist together.

Energy The ability to do work. There are different forms of energy: potential (stored) and kinetic (motion), and different kinds of energy: light, sound, electrical, chemical, heat, and nuclear.

Fuel A material, such as coal, gas, wood, oil, that is burned to supply heat or power. Fissionable material (uranium, plutonium) used in nuclear reactors is also fuel.

Pollution The result of the introduction of harmful chemical or waste materials into the environment.

Teaching Tips

The instruction in this unit is intended to be self-paced. A self-paced approach individualizes the learning environment, allowing and encouraging students to move through the activities at a variable rate. A self-paced approach is suitable to use for learning teams.

In addition to adjusting the rate of learning, students have the opportunity to choose learning activities presented in the Side Paths and the Search projects.

The self-paced approach used in this chapter is based on the learning model in the *Intermediate Science Curriculm Study* (ISCS), a science program for students in grades 7, 8, and 9, developed at Florida State University. The figure shown below is a schematic showing the three major elements in the ISCS program: Core Chapters for all students; Excursions for interested students; and Techniques for students needing additional practice.

Techniques
Required activities for students
needing additional practice

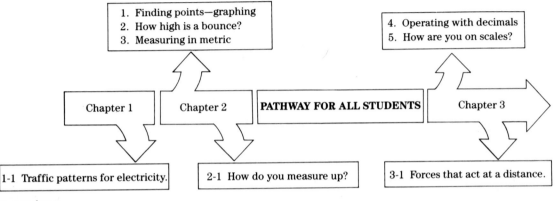

1. Finding points—graphing
2. How high is a bounce?
3. Measuring in metric

4. Operating with decimals
5. How are you on scales?

Chapter 1   Chapter 2   **PATHWAY FOR ALL STUDENTS**   Chapter 3

1-1 Traffic patterns for electricity.   2-1 How do you measure up?   3-1 Forces that act at a distance.

Excursions
Optional activities
for interested students.

In the ISCS program, students are expected to do all of the core activities in order and to do only those Excursions and Techniques that provide content they need or would like to study. In addition, teachers sometimes encourage students to do an Excursion or Technique that seems particularly appropriate. No one is expected to carry out all or even most of the available Excursions and Techniques. Students pass through a judicious selection of extension and review materials, so that the instruction is in effect designed especially for each individual.

The organization of this Experience is similar to that of the ISCS program and is shown in the figure below.

Searches
Required of students
working triads, with
choices

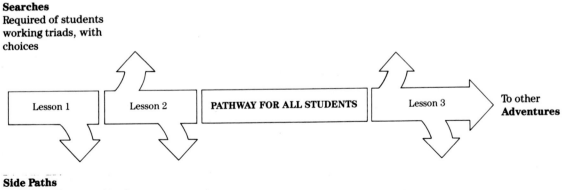

Lesson 1   Lesson 2   **PATHWAY FOR ALL STUDENTS**   Lesson 3   To other **Adventures**

Side Paths
Interdisciplinary optional
acitivites for interested
students.

All of the activities are written in student language. It is suggested that you do the following in preparation for the Experience:

1. Copy the Adventures and put them in Core booklets for each team of students. Establish an area where the materials for the Core activities are available to the students as they need them. Organize the materials in labeled shoe boxes.

2. Establish two learning centers as follows:

    Side Path Excursion Center: Copy all the Side Paths and glue them onto cards. Use them as the basis for the Excursion center. Give each student a list of the Side Paths and include it with the Core booklet. Display all the materials needed to do the Excursions and provide a collection of books to supplement the activities.

    Search Project Center: Copy the Searches and place each in a folder. Provide additional books and reference materials that will help students complete them.

Teaching Phases

Following are three phases for implementing the activities in the Experience:

Phase I. Direct Instruction/Interactive Teaching

Although this Experience is designed to be a self-paced unit for teams of students, the importance of direct instruction cannot be overemphasized. First, introduce the process of team-pacing to the students: explain that they will be working their way through the unit at a pace established by the team. Give a copy of the Core booklet to each team and explain that teams should do the activities in the order shown. Point out the areas in the classroom that have been established as learning centers for the Side Paths and the Projects.

Although teams will be working at their own pace, bring the students together as a whole class to discuss progress and to get feedback on the various activities.

Phase II. Cooperative Learning

This Experience can be totally accomplished by cooperative teams. You might want to design a learning contract for the teams, identifying how many Adventures (all), Side Paths (two), and Searches (one) each team must do. The learning contract will help the teams pace their work and help them manage their time.

Phase III. Culminating Process

In order to maintain a high level of communication in the class, various culminating points could be established during the Experience. The first culminating point should be at the end of the work on the Adventures. Mark a date when the teams are expected to complete the Adventures. On this day have each team report on a different Adventure. Review work on the Side Paths at a second culminating point, and have students present work on their projects at the end of the Experience.

STUDENT INFORMATION

Adventures

Lesson 1. Where Does the Energy Go?[1]

In this lesson you are going to discover some interesting things about energy. To do the activities you will need the following materials:

   1 paper clip
   1 pin wheel
   1 match
   1 birthday candle

Activity A must be done with the whole class and your teacher's close supervision and guidance.

Activity A. Light my fire

Press the candle into a piece of clay and place it on a table. VERY CAREFULLY, light the candle with the match. Energy is transferred from one system to another. The transfer of energy is called an energy chain. Complete the following energy chain chart to show what you just did.

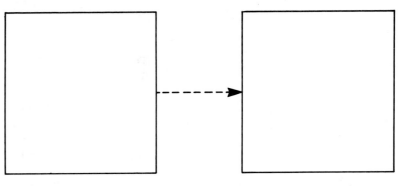

Energy source   Energy receiver

• How do you know that energy was transferred from the match to the candle?

Now go on to the following activities. Answer each question before going on to the next activity.

Activity B. The hand clapper
Clap your hands ten times.

- • How do your hands feel?
- • How do you know there has been an interaction?

Now rub your hands together ten times.

- • How do you know there has been an interaction?
- • When you rub your hands together, what is receiving the energy?
- • When you rub your hands together, what is giving the energy?

Activity C. Hot Lips
Bend a paper clip into the shape shown below

Touch the curve of the *V* to your upper lip. What do you observe?

Now bend the paper clip back and forth nine or ten times very rapidly.

Touch it to your upper lip. What do you observe?

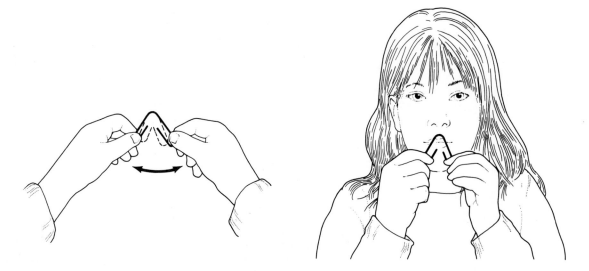

Look at the chart below to review what you have learned about energy.

Energy Chart

Event	Energy Source	Energy Receiver	Evidence of Energy Transfer
Bending the paper clip	Hands	Paper clip	Change in shape and temperature
Touching clip to lips	Paper clip	Lips	Feeling of heat on lips

Activity D. Guess Who?

Suppose you blow on a pinwheel. Complete the following energy chain chart.

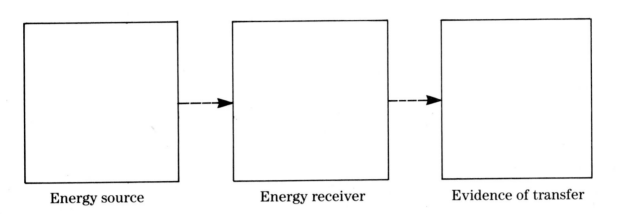

Energy source   Energy receiver   Evidence of transfer

Now blow on a pinwheel and watch the result.

Lesson 2. When You're Hot, You're Hot!

In this lesson you are going to learn how to measure energy changes. To do the activities, you will need the following materials:

4 thermometers	torn up paper
4 metal cans	cardboard box painted
1 styrofoam cup	black
warm and cold water	sand
salt water	

Activity A. Mix and Measure

- Do you think energy will be transferred when warm water is mixed with cold water? To find out, you are going to mix a can of warm water and a can of cold water.

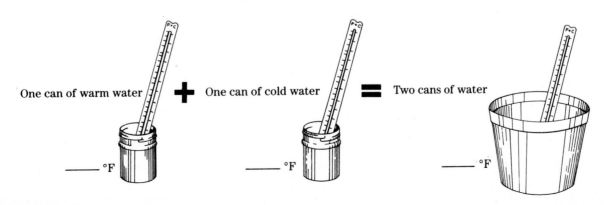

One can of warm water   +   One can of cold water   =   Two cans of water

_____ °F   _____ °F   _____ °F

Measure the temperature of the warm water and the cold water before you mix them. Record your observations in diagram above. Pour both samples of water into a styrofoam cup and measure the temperature of the mixture. Record the temperatures of cold, hot, and mixed water in the chart below. Have your team members record their temperature readings, too.

Data Chart

Student	Cold °F	Hot °F	Mixed °F
1			
2			
3			

Notice that the temperature of the mixed water always falls between the cold and the hot temperatures. Can you use your data chart to predict mixed temperatures? Try it here.

	Cold	Hot	Mixed
1	40°F	80°F	_____
2	50°F	100°F	_____
3	100°F	160°F	_____

Activity B. Cover and Measure[4]

Which material do you think stores solar energy the best: sand, water, salt, or paper? Fill each can with one of these materials and place a thermometer in each one. Put the cans in the black box. Place the closed box in the sun for one-half hour.

Now remove the cans and record the temperatures every two minutes for the next ten minutes. Record your observations in your Data Chart.

• Which temperature fell the slowest?
• Which material stores heat the best?
• Which material would you use to store heat in a solar-heated house?

Data Chart Temperature in °F

Material	Time box was opened	°F after 2 min.	°F after 4 min.	°F after 6 min.	°F after 8 min.	°F after 10 min.
Sand						
Salt						
Water						
Paper						

Lesson 3. Don't Fuel Me!

Energy has always been needed in order to do things. Early humans never would have survived during the Ice Age if they hadn't discovered how to heat their cave homes with wood-burning fires. In this lesson you are going to find out about the kinds of energy sources that are available. To do the activities, you will need the following materials:

1 piece of coal
photograph of a waterfall

Activity A. An Energy Hunt

Energy is what gets things done. Although you cannot see energy, you can see the results of energy. Look at the piece of coal and the picture of a waterfall and answer the questions.

- Which thing stores energy, the coal or the waterfall?
- Which thing has energy in motion, the coal or the waterfall?

You have probably guessed that energy is stored in the piece of coal. The energy in coal is an an example of *potential energy*. Other examples of potential energy are the energy stored in food, oil, gas, and wood.

A waterfall is an example of energy in motion. This kind of energy is called *kinetic energy*. Other examples of kinetic energy are moving cars, fire, and the wind. You will need to know these two terms to go on the energy hunt.

Before starting the hunt, make a chart like the one on page 258. Then find at least ten examples of energy.

When you complete the energy hunt, group the types of energy under headings such as electrical, chemical, mechanical, solar, sound, heat, light.

Energy Hunt Chart

Action, Event, or Material	Example of Kinetic Energy	Example of Potential Energy
1.		
2.		
3.		
4.		
5.		
6.		
7.		
8.		
9.		
10.		

Activity B. A Fuelish Survey

Now that you know something about energy types, you can conduct a survey of your neighborhood. A survey is a way of gathering information about something. In this case you will gather information about the types of energy sources your neighbors use in their homes. People may use more than one, so be sure to record each type.

Energy Source Survey

Type of Fuel	Number of Homes	Total	% of Total
Coal			
Gas			
Nuclear			
Oil			
Solar			
Wood			
Wind			

Lesson 4. Problems, Problems, Problems[2]

The types of fuels we use and the increasing use of energy in our environment has created many problems. In this activity you will be a reporter and interview at least one adult in your community.

Make an appointment to interview someone in the community. Explain that you are going to ask several questions about energy. Then make up three questions to add to the survey below. Note that you are to answer the questions as well.

Energy Survey

Directions: First think of three questions to add to the survey for items 3, 7, and 9. Write your answers to all the questions before you begin the survey. At the interview, ask the questions one at a time, allowing time for each response. At the end of each answer, you might share your response with the person you are interviewing. Be sure to record the answers on the survey sheet.

	Your Answer	**Adult's Answer**
Questions about the Environment 1. Have you ever had a cough or stinging eyes because of air pollution? How did it make you feel? 2. Do you know if anything is being done in your community to make the air cleaner? 3. _____ _____		
Questions about Limited Supply 4. Do you know where in the world the greatest deposits of fossil fuels are found? 5. Do you know what country in the world uses the most coal and petroleum? 6. Is it possible to make more oil when it's gone? 7. _____ _____		

	Your Answer	**Adult's Answer**
Questions about Cost 8. Can you name three fossil fuel products that have increased in price this year? 9. _____ _____		
Questions about Conservation 10. How can the supply of fossil fuel be made to last longer?		

Now that you are aware of some of the problems, consider some solutions. On page 277 is a chart showing conservation practices that could save energy. Examine the list, then do one of the following activities:

- Make a poster using some of the information and display it in the city or in the school.
- Take the list home and discuss it with your parents. What is your family doing now to conserve energy?
- Write a conservation commercial for a TV or radio station. If you have access to video tape equipment, you might work with some classmates to produce a commercial.
- How could governments use the information in the list of conservation practices to reduce energy loss?
- Think of things that groups of people can do to improve the energy situation.

Lesson 5. The Marine Biologist and the Oil Tanker[3]

What do you think a marine biologist—a scientist who studies the biology of the ocean—and an oil tanker have in common? Sadly, it is not a pleasant relationship. The two became involved when the oil tanker spilled millions of gallons of oil into the ocean. The oil spread over the surface of the water and smeared everything in its path with oil—including the birds who floated on the surface of the ocean hunting for food.

In this lesson you will read a true story about the wreck of an oil tanker and the effects the oil spill had on the coastal area near the accident. Read the story, stopping to do the experiments as indicated. You will need to collect the following materials before you start reading:

mineral oil
motor oil
screw top jar
sand
paper towels
newspaper
bird feather

Before starting to read, answer these questions and discuss them with your team mates:

- What effect do you think an oil spill would have on the ocean?
- Do you think animals that are trapped in an oil spill can be rescued?
- Have you read anything about oil spills on the ocean? If so, what information can you share with your team?

Supertanker Breaks Apart off Coast of Northern France

March 17, 1978

"The people of France are cleaning up after the fourth major tanker wreck off the coast of Brittany in eleven years.

On March 16, 1978, the *Amoco Cadiz*, carrying 230,000 tons (over 70 million gallons) of light crude oil from the Middle East ran aground when the captain ordered the engines stopped after the ship's steering mechanism jammed.

Rough seas prevented other ships in the area from unloading the oil before the *Amoco Cadiz* broke in two in the shallow waters off the French coast.

French government officials are meeting to decide how to prevent further shoreline damages. The French Navy has been instructed to enforce an order preventing tankers from passing within seven miles off the coast."

A Short Story: The Oil Tanker and the Marine Biologist

I think I noticed him standing there on the beach simply because he was the only person not moving around quickly. Everyone else seemed to be lifting something or brushing something or hauling buckets of things to some place away from the edge of the sea. He stood, still and quiet, his feet buried in hundreds of thousands of dead sea snails, his right hand touching clusters of periwinkles dying on nearby rocks. I saw him reach down to lift one tiny snail out of the blackened pile and watched him try to brush away the oil with the sleeve of his sweater. Then I saw him drop the snail on the pile and turn away, looking with angry eyes toward the sea.

There in the mist, looking like some broken-backed sea monster, lay the supertanker, *Amoco Cadiz*, dead among the restless waves. Its cargo of oil spread mile upon mile across the waves. Here on the shoreline, the oil coated everything it touched with a thick, black ooze.

> **Experiment:** Add a small amount of salad oil to a jar of water. Do they mix? Shake the jar vigorously. Hold it up to the light and examine it. Record your observations: _____
>
> _____
>
> Let the sample sit for a short time then examine it for possible settling action. Which material sinks? _____

The man was a marine biologist. It is his job to help assess the damage to sea life in the region and to keep a record of its recovery from the spillage of 66 million gallons of crude oil. He knows the effects will be major and varied. To his relief, no gigantic fish kill has been reported. But oyster and other shellfish will have to be measured carefully to find out when the levels of petroleum hydrocarbons are low enough to make them edible again.

The biologist saw beaches as far away as 65 miles from the spill paved with dead sea urchins, dead razor clams, and dead snails. Now he is especially interested in finding out what damage has been done to seaweed and kelp.

The people of Brittany in Northern France farm the sea as they do the land. They raise and harvest seaweed and use it in medicine, food, and fertilizer. The biologist is sure that this year's crop is ruined. How can new colonies of these important seaweeds get started again?

Early scientific data tend to show that sea birds have been harmed by the oil. Over 5,000 dead birds were found along the shore, and hundreds more are struggling for life in makeshift bird hospitals. But the outlook for these oil-soaked birds is grim. Oil and sea birds simply don't mix.

Experiment: Investigate the effects of an oil spill on bird feathers and sand. First, observe the bird feather. Notice its appearance and weight. Coat the feather with motor oil. Now using water, mineral oil, and a brush, find a way to clean the oil off the feather. How successful were you? _____

Next, coat some sand with oil. Find a method for cleaning the sand. What method did you use and how successful were you? _____

Sea birds have thick feathers, which provide almost perfect insulation from cold water. Oil destroys the structure of the feathers and exposes the bird's skin to freezing water. In addition, the bird loses much of its ability to float as the layer of air trapped between body and feathers disappears. As a result the bird rides lower in the water and most likely can no longer feed itself.

If the bird does not die of starvation, it will die from exposure. But the creature may float around for days, its heart beating in double time to compensate for the heat loss. Perhaps the end will be hastened by swallowing some of the oil, which acts like a poison.

If a bird is rescued, what are its chances? The biologist has to shake his head. Bird rescues have not had much success in the past, and most rescue operations have very poor results. First the bird is cleaned with mineral oil, and then the feathers are dried. However, the bird's delicate system does not recover quickly enough, and very few birds survive the cleaning and stress from captivity.

The biologist began to worry that clean-up techniques for beaches as well as for the birds might be doing more damage to the ecosystem than the oil spill itself. For example, will steam hosing and brush cleaning rocks and sand cause a whole new set of biological problems?

It will be a long time before the shore returns to normal. For the present and for the near future, the cost to the people and to plant and animal life of Brittany has been immense.

Now that you have read the story and completed both experiments, answer the following questions.

- What sentence in the story describes the marine biologist's job? Circle it.
- What plants and animals have been damaged or killed by the oil spill? Underline their names.
- What sentences describe the possible long-term damage to important seaweeds? Circle them twice.
- How are sea birds harmed by oil?
- What was the reason for the ship running aground?
- How might more problems arise from clean-up operations after the oil spill?
- What do you think people were lifting, brushing, or hauling to safer places on the beach?
- How do you feel about this story and what have you learned? Write a five-line poem to express your feelings.

Lesson 6. Once Upon a Time[4]

In the United States and in other countries like it, environments have changed due to the way humans use the land. In this lesson you will find out what happened to Peaceful Lake over a period of 200 years.
Before you read the story, look at the drawings of Peaceful Lake at the three different times shown. Notice the following things:

1. The type and number of boats in the lake.
2. The type and number of buildings around the lake.
3. The number of people living around the lake.

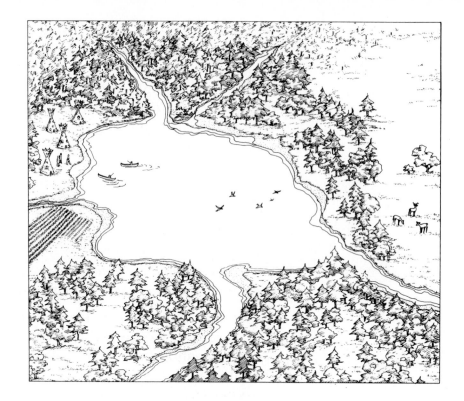

The Saga of Peaceful Lake

A large community of organisms lives beneath the surface of Peaceful Lake. Light that penetrates the surface and minerals suspended in the water support plants, which are the basis of the lake's food web. All the plants and animals in the lake are part of this food web. Some of the organisms in the food web are algae, Daphnia, minnows, bass, trout, perch, frogs, snails, crayfish, clams, turtles, and beaver.

The first Europeans to find the lake were fur trappers, who reported that several Indian tribes lived near the shore. The Indians apparently had been there a long time because their villages and fields were well established. Like the Indians, European settlers were attracted to the lake. The land was fertile and moist, and crops grown there could provide food for many families. Moose and deer from the forest, fish from the lake, and ducks and geese added meat to the settlers' diet. There was a great deal of fur trading because of the many mink, beaver, fox, and ermine living nearby. All in all, life was ideal.

As word about the lake's productivity spread, more and more people were attracted to the area. Soon the lakeside human population was too large to be supported by the existing fields. Forests were cleared to develop more and more farmland. As the forests diminished, the game that had been the settler's meat supply also disappeared. Cattle and sheep were raised to provide homegrown meat, and more forests were cleared to make grazing land for these animals.

Fur-bearing animals disappeared when the forests were cut down. The settlers originally traded furs for items such as cloth, firearms, plows, and luxuries they could not manufacture. They tried to solve this problem by producing some of the things formerly obtained through trade. Then the settlers expanded their workshops into small factories, producing items to take the place of furs in order to reestablish trade with other areas.

Many factories were successful, and people were attracted from other areas to work in them. As a result, population increased, additional food was required, and the remaining forests were converted into crop-land. Slowly but surely, the lake area evolved into the massive industrial and agricultural center it is today.

Soon after lakeshore industry was firmly established, there were no more forests that could be cleared for farming. In order to produce enough food to feed the rapidly growing population, the lakeside farmers stopped rotating crops and planted food crops on all available land. Within a few years they discovered they had made a mistake, because their yields decreased until finally farms could produce no crops at all.

About that time, commercial fertilizers were developed. By using fertilizers farmers could plant all their fields every year without worrying about using up the minerals in the soil.

When a large group of people lives in one area, there is a huge amount of waste material produced. Tons of garbage and sewage must be disposed of each day. The presence of the lake made this job easy, for it was a simple matter to run sewage lines to the water's edge, dump garbage from piers, and let the city's waste float away. Before long, people stopped dumping garbage into the lake because much of it floated and was ugly. The sewage was not visible, however, so there seemed no harm in continuing to dispose of it in the lake.

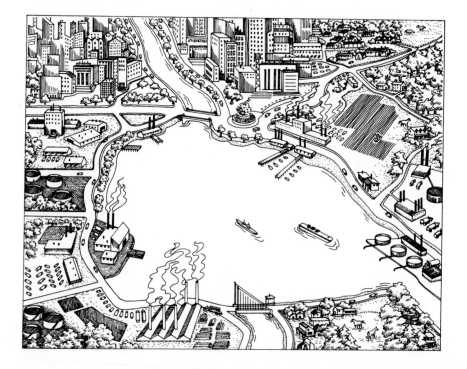

A few years later, people noticed more algae in the lake than before. At first this increase was apparent only as occasional, small clumps that had been washed ashore, or as a green film on offshore rocks. Then swimmers complained about the slime that clung to their bodies when they came out of the water, and boaters described large, propeller-snagging masses of algae floating in the lake. Soon, the mayor's office was swamped with many angry descriptions of the foul odor encountered everywhere near the water. By this time no more people who fished lived near the lake. They had moved elsewhere in order to catch enough fish to support their families. A reporter for the local newspaper wrote that the crowds of Sunday afternoon swimmers and picnickers on the beaches had been replaced by dead fish and masses of rotting algae.

Now that you have read the story, answer the following questions.

- What do you think caused the increase in the lake's algae population?
- How is the disappearance of the fish related to the foul odor and the increase in algae?
- Why were the lake's problems evident only in recent years?
- If you could rewrite the story, what events would you change to keep the lake from becoming polluted?

Side Paths

The Side Paths should be set up in a learning center. After students have worked through the Adventures, they can select from the Side Paths, which have been organized into four areas that are all related to pollution.[5]

Lesson 7. Noise Pollution Side Paths

Activity A. Shhh! Too Much Noise!
Make a list of different types of noise. Take a tape recorder to at least six different places to record the noises you have listed. Following are some suggested locations for noise testing: home, shopping center, construction site, busy street, sporting event.

Categorize each of the sounds according to one or more of the following characteristics: human made, natural, pleasant, unpleasant, low, high, soft, loud, near, far.

- Which noises that you recorded could be called noise pollution?
- What generalizations can you make about sources of noise pollution?
- How do human-made noises compare to natural noises?
- How much does noise pollution depend on the listener?

Activity B. Tune In

What effect do you think location has on noise levels? In the first column of the chart below, estimate by guessing which location has the highest noise levels. Test your estimates by recording a radio played in each location. Be sure to keep the radio volume and type of radio program the same in each location. Then play back the tape. How accurate were your estimates?

Noise Level Chart

	Estimate	Actual
Large room vs Small room		
Room with tile vs Room with carpet		
Empty room vs Room with furniture		
Acoustical tile ceiling vs Regular ceiling		

Activity C. In Other Words

Use a thesaurus to help you make a list of words that describe traffic sounds. Then combine words on your list to make new words. For example, *squeak* and *crunch* might become *squrunch*.

Use your noise pollution word list to compose a poem about traffic.

Lesson 8. Litter Pollution

Activity A. Scavenger Hunt

Conduct a scavenger hunt for litter on the school grounds or around the neighborhood. List the items of litter that you see. After each item, record the following information about it. After you have recorded the information, put the litter in a trash bag. Be sure to wear gloves when you pick up stuff.

1. Specify its size.
2. Specify its location. Draw a map of the area and mark where the item was found.
3. Indicate whether it is natural or human made.
4. Specify what it is made of: paper, metal, plastic, wood, glass, plant or animal matter, other.
5. Specify whether or not it is biodegradable.

How did each item get where you found it? What was the most common item found? Predict how quickly each item will break down—slow, medium, or fast.

Activity B. ''L'' is for Litter

Contribute three pages to a class booklet called ''The ABC Fact Book on Litter.'' Pick three letters from a container. Illustrate and write a description of a type of litter that begins with each letter. For example, if you choose B, you might write a page about soft drink bottles thrown from car windows and illustrate the description with a picture of a littered roadside.

Activity C. Waste Not, Want Not

We can reuse many materials by recycling. Glass can be returned to glass kilns, metal can be returned to foundries, and paper can be returned to pulp mills.

Think of new and worthwhile uses for items that often are thrown away, such as large grocery bags, egg cartons, large plastic containers with handles, jelly jars, baby food jars. Describe and illustrate your ideas in your science log. What materials could be reused in the same way they were originally used? What effects does recycling these items have on our natural resources, energy, and the environment?

Conduct a survey to get consumers' reactions about recycling. Ask people whether or not they recycle their newspapers or their aluminum cans and the reason for their actions. Pool your team findings and make a chart. Include your conclusions about the reasons that people give to support their preferences.

Lesson 9. Water Pollution

Activity A. The Heat is On

Just how pure is our drinking water? Have all particles
and impurities been removed? In this activity you'll do an
experiment to find out.

Put a small amount of tap water in an evaporation
dish.

Have your teacher help you heat it over a burner until
all the water evaporates.

Check the dish when all the water is gone to see if
there is any residue.

If there is residue, describe it by noting color, feel,
texture, size, and any other property.

What do you think this residue could be? Record your
ideas and observations.

Activity B. All-the All-the Alum in Free!

In order to make our water clean enough to drink, there
are several steps to be completed. The first of these steps
is called *settling.*

Water is pumped into large tanks where it stands so
that particles held in suspension will settle out. To make
the fine particles of silt and clay settle, alum is added to
the water. As the alum sinks to the bottom, particles of
silt and clay held in suspension cling to the alum and are
carried to the bottom, too. This process is called
coagulation.

Put 600-700 mL of water into two very large jars.

Add a tablespoon of silt to each jar, replace the lids
nice and tight, and shake the jars vigorously.

To one jar add ¾ teaspoons of alum.

After 15 minutes, hold a white card behind the
cylinders and compare the clarity.

Record your observations.

Activity C. Filter Down

Filtering is another step in water purification. Water is
run from settling tanks into sand and gravel filters to
remove suspended matter. Make a model of a filtering
system:

Place a funnel in the mouth of a large jar.

Put a layer of clean pebbles in the funnel.

Funnel

— fine sand
— course sand
— gravel
— pebbles

On top of the pebbles put a layer of gravel, a layer of coarse sand, and finally a layer of fine sand.

Pour muddy water through the funnel.

Observe the condition of the water that trickles through.

Record your observations and hypotheses on the following questions:

1. Is the water pure enough to drink?
2. What kinds of material are still in the water?

Lesson 10. Air Pollution

Activity A. Get the Greasies!

Number two sets of index cards from 1 to 7, one for each day of the week.

Smear a thin layer of petroleum jelly in the center of each card.

Tape one of the #1 cards grease side out to a window inside your home.

Tape the other #1 card grease side out to the outside of the same window.

At the end of the first day collect the #1 cards from both sides of the window. Repeat the activity the next day using the #2 cards. Continue everyday for a week.

When all the cards are collected, display them on a large chart for visual inspection. Use a magnifying lens to count the easily seen particles. Also note their shape and color.

Activity B. Meet Me at the Corner!

Stand on the sidewalk at a busy traffic intersection. Count all the vehicles that pass by in a two-minute period and record the number in your science log.

Record how many of the passing vehicles gave off visible amounts of exhaust pollutants.

Work out the proportion of vehicles that give off visible pollutants to those that do not.

Compare your results with other members of your team.

Obtain a city map and write the proportions at the other busy intersections shown.

Have students from other teams contribute to the map. What observations can you make?

Searches

Lesson 1. Blow the Whistle on Water Pollution

- List all the sources of water pollution in the school building.
- Write a water pollution ordinance for the school. Discuss it as a group and decide what should be included in the ordinance.
- Choose one person to record the water pollution controls talked about in the discussion and draw up a first draft of your ordinance.
- Modify and edit the first draft, and then make a final draft. Present the final draft to the class and then display it.

Lesson 2. The Opinionnaire[6]

The Opinionnaire on pages 278–279 is designed to collect people's opinions and concerns about certain aspects of littering. It is suggested that samples be taken from several segments of the population, such as elementary school students, junior high or middle school students, high school students, young adults, and adults. Read the questions to the persons being surveyed. A minimum of five persons per sample is recommended. To summarize the results of the Opinionnaire, make up a summary sheet as shown:

Opinionnaire Summary Sheet

Question	Yes	No	Undecided	Males	Females	Totals
1						
2						
3						
4						
5						
6						
7						

After summarizing the group's results, you might consider the following questions:

- Are the opinions expressed by people consistent within the age groups that were sampled? Why or why not?
- Do you think that people are concerned enough about litter in your community?
- If a problem exists in your community, what recommendations could you pose for helping to resolve it? Do you believe the problem can be solved with one single action or with a combination of actions?

Lesson 3. Foxfire Project

In this project you are going to interview older people in your community to find out how it has changed in the last 50–75 years. Your team will need a tape recorder, a camera to take slides, a science notebook, and a list of questions. If a video recorder is available, you might want to use it.

Find out who some of the oldest residents of your community are. Local ministers, priests, and rabbis may be able to give you some names, and so can the historical society. Arrange ahead for two-person teams to visit some of these older residents and ask them questions about the community. Ask permission to tape record the discussion and permission to take pictures.

After your team has made their visits, get together and share the tape recordings, slides, and notes. Discuss the types of changes that have taken place in your community over the years and use the information to prepare your Search report.

Questions for the Foxfire Project[7]

1. How different is our town or city from how it was when you were a child?
2. What types of transportation were most common then?
3. How have foods changed from when you were my age?
4. Did you grow most of your food or buy it?
5. What types of work-saving devices did your mother have in the house? How did your parents wash clothes or clean house?
6. How was your house heated?
7. What did your family like to do when they all got together?

8. Where did people work? What types of jobs were available in the community?
9. What do you consider to be the biggest change in our community? What effects has that change had?

Evaluation

Use this test to evaluate students' progess on the major concepts presented in the Adventures and Side Paths of Powering the Earth.

Students can take the test in teams, thereby collaborating, or they can take it individually. In the latter case, use an average of the scores within each team as the score for each student in that team.

Questions 1–6 correlate with the Adventures; question 7 relates to the Side Paths.

1. Suppose someone lights a candle with a match. Complete the energy chain for the action.

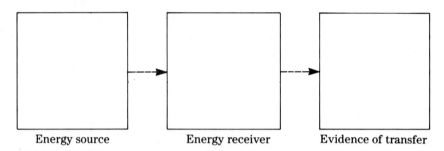

Energy source   Energy receiver   Evidence of transfer

2. Which of the following materials would be the best choice if you wanted to store heat in a house? *a.* sand *b.* water *c.* salt *d.* paper
3. What is the difference between potential and kinetic energy? Give two examples of each.
4. List ten energy conservation practices.
5. In 1987, the company that owned the *Amoco Cadiz* oil tanker was ordered by the courts to pay the community of Brittany a large sum of money. Do you think the court was right in making the oil company pay? Why do you think so?
6. How did the change in the size of the human population around Peaceful Lake affect each of the following? *a.* beaver, fox, and other game *b.* trees *c.* algae *d.* sewage *e.* pollution
7. Select one of the following types of pollution. Explain how it is caused and ways it can be reduced. *a.* noise pollution *b.* litter pollution *c.* water pollution *d.* air pollution

Books for Kids

McClung, Robert M. *Mice, Moose, and Men: How Their Populations Rise and Fall.* New York: Morrow, 1973.

Selsam, Millicent E. *How to be a Nature Detective.* New York: Harper and Row, 1966.

Stevens, Leonard. *How a Law is Made: The Story of a Bill Against Air Pollution.* New York: Thomas Y. Crowell & Co., 1970.

CONSERVATION PRACTICES— AN ENERGY SOURCE

Using Your Appliances

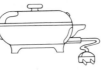

1. Read labels; buy the most energy-efficient models.
2. Use energy-intensive equipment in early morning or late evening (non-peak hours).
3. Turn off radio and TV sets when they're not in use.
4. Use the dishwasher only with full loads.
5. Cook several meals in the oven at one time.
6. Wash laundry in warm or cold water; rinse in cold.
7. Take short showers instead of baths.
8. Use hand-operated tools, utensils, and equipment whenever possible.

Heating and Cooling Your Home

9. Install insulation; weatherstrip and caulk windows and doors; install storm windows and doors.
10. Close off unused rooms in winter and summer and shut off their air ducts.
11. Set thermostat between 65° and 68° daytime in winter, below 65° at night. Set thermostat at 78° in summer.
12. Close fireplace damper when fireplace is not in use.
13. Run air conditioner only when days and nights are extremely hot and humid.
14. Have furnace serviced once a year. Clean or replace filters once a month during heating season.
15. In winter, keep draperies open in sunny weather; close them at night. In summer, close during day, open at night.
16. Dress appropriately to the season.

Saving Gasoline

17. Make gasoline mileage your main concern when you buy a new car. Oversized cars, over-powered engines, automatic transmissions, and unnecessary power options all "eat" gasoline.
18. Drive less by joining a carpool, bicycling, or walking whenever possible, using public transportation, and eliminating unnecessary trips.
19. Drive at moderate speeds: 55 mph on the highway. Accelerating and braking smoothly saves engines, tires, and gasoline.
20. Do not idle your car more than one minute. It takes less gasoline to restart the car than it takes to let it idle.
21. Get regular tune-ups; keep the air and oil filters clean; check tire pressure regularly.
22. Use car air-conditioner sparingly.

Other Conserving Tips

23. Concentrate light in reading and work areas.
24. Turn off all lights that are not needed.
25. Use fluorescent lights wherever possible.
26. Repair leaking water faucets with new washers.
27. Plant a home garden.
28. Plant shade trees around your house.
29. Eat more high-protein vegetables and grain; fewer "convenience" foods.

Page reference: 261

THE OPINIONNAIRE[6]

INTRODUCTION: Hello, my name is _____. I am a student in the _____ at _____. We are collecting
(class)   (name of school)
information about how people feel about _____ .
(the issue)

Initial Data: Age: ____ Elementary School
                                ____ Jr. High/Middle School
Sex: M___F___   ____ Sr. High School
                                ____ Young Adult
                                ____ Adult

Please answer Yes, No, or Undecided to the following questions.

____   1. Do you consider the littering of public and private property to be a problem in this community?

____   2. Does littering have any ill effects on the beauty or aesthetic quality of this community?

____   3. Does littering have any public health impact on the community?

____   4. Does litter clean-up cost this community much money?

____   5. Would you ever consider reporting a severe case of littering to the police?

____   6. Have you ever reported a severe case of littering to the police?

____   7. Do you personally wish that fewer people would litter?

The following questions have multiple-choice answers.

8. In which of the following places in the community do you think littering is the worst?

   ____ schools   ____ private property
   ____ public streets   ____ gas stations
   ____ shopping areas   ____ other

9. What age persons do you believe are responsible for the most littering?

   ____ elementary school   ____ senior high school
   ____ junior high/middle school ____ young adult
                                    ____ adult

[6] Charles E. Roth and Linda G. Lockwood. *Strategies and Activities for Using Local Communities as Environmental Educatoin Sites.* ERIC Clearinghouse for Science, Mathematics, and Environmental Education. The Ohio State University, Columbus, Ohio, 1979.   Page reference: 274

The Opinionnaire, page 2

10. Which of the following would you be willing to throw away on public or private property?

_____ cardboard box full of empty cans or bottles

_____ a sack of wastepaper from a drive-in

_____ one empty bottle or can

_____ a paper soft-drink container

_____ a wrapper from gum or candy

_____ none of the above

11. Which of the following statements concerning law enforcement do you agree with most?

_____ Law enforcement officers should ignore people who litter.

_____ Law enforcement officers should enforce anti-littering laws only in cases of extreme or severe littering.

_____ Law enforcement officers should strictly enforce anti-littering laws.

12. In your opinion, what is the main cause of the litter problem as it exists today?

This is the end of our opinionnaire. Thank you very much for your help!

Page reference: 274

INVESTIGATING
THE NATURAL
WORLD

An Environmental
Education Experience

The deeper we look into nature, the more we realize that it is full of life, and the more profoundly we know that all life is a secret and that we are united with all life that is in nature. Man can no longer live for himself alone. We must realize that all life is valuable and that we are united to all life. From this knowledge comes our relationship to the universe.

ALBERT SCHWEITZER
Animals, Nature & Albert Schweitzer

TEACHER INFORMATION

Background Information

Environmental education involves teaching science outdoors in an attempt to expand students' awareness of the world and to develop positive attitudes and values toward nature. This can be done most powerfully by direct involvement with the environment.

The earth is alive with myriad plants and animals, wondrously balanced in the scheme of nature, and profoundly beautiful in pattern, color, and form.

Too many students, however, view the natural environment only as a background to the sights and sounds of the fast-paced world. Flashing signs, roads, shopping centers, and billboards demand attention, while grass and weeds, insects, trees, and birds are overlooked.

This Experience focuses on environmental education and ecological concerns. Its purpose is to help students get in touch with the natural world as a first step toward observing, appreciating, and protecting the environment. Although this Experience was designed primarily for younger students, the material can be adapted for use with older students.

This Experience will heighten your awareness and guide you in expanding your teaching activities outside the classroom. It is probable that the school yard, a nearby vacant lot, or patches of weeds bordering the parking lot contain a multitude of exciting discoveries. With just a little practice, running your fingertips up and down the bark of a tree or stopping to observe an ant carrying twice its weight will become second nature to you and your students.

Overview and Planning

Take a few minutes to examine the Overview and Planning Chart for Investigating the Natural World. There are five Adventures, nine Side Paths, and four Search projects in this Experience.

Overview and Planning Chart: Investigating the Natural World

Activity	Science Concept	Science Process	Modes of Learning	Attitude
Adventures				
1. Sensory Scavenger Hunt	Everything in nature is connected.	Observing Classifying	Physical-sensory Right	Curiosity Sensitivity to nature
2. What on Earth Is It?	Soil contains living and nonliving things.	Observing Measuring	Physical-sensory Right	Curiosity Sensitivity to nature
3. Investigating Insects— Capturing Critters	Living things live in different habitats.	Observing Inferring	Physical-sensory Right	Curiosity Sensitivity to nature

Activity	Science Concept	Science Process	Modes of Learning	Attitude
4. New Perspectives on Walking	Nature varies from one place to another.	Observing Inferring	Physical-sensory Right	Curiosity
5. Getting the Feel of a Tree	Organisms are unique and have differing characteristics.	Observing	Physical-sensory Right	Curiosity Precision
Side Paths				
6. Collections (Language Arts)	Objects can be distinguished by physical characteristics.	Classifying	Left	Self-reliance
7. Nature Notebook (Language Arts)	Nature can be described in words and drawings.	Observing	Physical-sensory	Self-reliance
8. Poetry (Language Arts)	Nature can be described in free-form expression.	Observing Inferring	Left Right	Creativity
9. Wood It Do? (Social Studies)	People use natural resources in a variety of ways.	Observing Inferring	Physical-sensory	Self-reliance
10. Webs (Social Studies)	Plants and animals are dependent on each other.	Observing Classifying	Physical-sensory	Sensitivity to environment
11. Clay Impressions (Art)	Materials have many uses.	Observing Classifying	Physical-sensory	Sensitivity to environment
12. Leaf Rubbings (Art)	Materials have different characteristics.	Observing Classifying	Physical-sensory	Sensitivity to environment
13. Movement in Nature (Drama)	Events in nature have unique characteristics.	Observing Inferring	Physical-sensory Right	Creativity
14. Animal Acting (Drama)	Animals have unique characteristics.	Observing Inferring	Physical-sensory	Creativity
Searches				
1. Bucket Microscope	The bending of light by water magnifies objects.	Observing	Physical-sensory Left	Curiosity
2. Leaf Collection that Grows	Organisms change.	Observing Classifying	Physical-sensory	Curiosity
3. Funnel Trap	Organisms have varying characteristics.	Observing Classifying	Physical-sensory	Curiosity Sensitivity to environment
4. Investigating a Bird Nest	Materials have different characteristics.	Observing Classifying	Physical-sensory	Curiosity

Objectives

At the end of this Experience, students should be able to:

1. Use their senses more acutely than before.
2. Describe objects in the natural environment using their senses.
3. Observe, compare, and classify living and nonliving things in the environment.
4. Infer relationships that exist among living and nonliving things in the environment.
5. Explore alternative ways to think and to develop speech and language skills.
6. Develop a feeling of protectiveness for the environment.

Key Concepts

The following represent the major concepts that students will study:

Ecological Everything in nature is connected directly or indirectly with everything else in nature.

Variety The natural world contains an infinite number of sizes, shapes, textures, colors, and patterns.

Change All things are constantly changing and taking a different form.

Teaching Tips

Discovery The activities in this Experience are designed to encourage students to stop, look, listen, feel, smell, and make their own discoveries. Students absorb much from active exploration and quiet observation; if allowed the time and opportunity to experience and observe freely, students will learn more easily to grasp concepts and facts.

Questioning Frequent questions direct the students' attention and enhance the discovery approach; questions should stimulate students to use their senses, think, and respond. Because questions that focus on sensory perceptions and observations have few right or wrong answers, students should be encouraged to respond and not feel threatened in any way. As important as asking the questions, however, is listening to the answers. Respond to students' observations and remarks. Sincere listening will encourage students to continue their active observations and involvement and encourage them to listen to one another.

Waiting at least three seconds after asking a question is another important aspect of questioning. The research of Mary Budd Rowe has shown that most teachers wait less than one second before calling on a student or moving on to another question.[1] Waiting will give students time to think about a response.

Investigating Natural Areas Get the feel of nearby natural areas by slowly walking around your school grounds, noticing and touching things you may have previously overlooked. Look closely at the weeds growing next to the building and between the cracks in the sidewalk; notice the different shapes and textures of trees, flowers, and grasses; and look in damp, dark nooks and crannies for insects. Walk to nearby parks and investigate the areas away from the playground equipment and other well-used areas. Notice the natural areas on your way to and from the park. Keep notes of different areas you find.

Taking Along Materials When gathering materials for an outdoor activity, be selective and take only those items that are the most important. Besides materials for a special activity, you may want to take a first-aid kit, pieces of yarn to mark interesting discoveries, and a daypack for your materials and specimens.

Setting Limits Before the activities, clarify your expectations by discussing the following points:

Running and shouting: Students should understand that exploring the natural world is different from other outdoor activities. They should learn to walk slowly and talk quietly during hikes and activities so that they can focus fully on the sights and sounds of the environment.

Disturbing plants and animals: Encourage students to observe, but let them know that they should not tear leaves from trees, bushes, and weeds, or otherwise damage the environment. Help them become aware of where they are walking so they can avoid stepping on plants whenever possible. Stress that they should never disturb animals or their homes. Also caution students not to touch things. Plants can have hidden thorns and stickers; insects can sting; animals can bite. *Never* allow students to poke their hands into places they cannot see.

Collecting natural materials: Students often want to keep all the natural things they see and find, but it is important that they leave the environment undisturbed.

Tasting: Help students understand that they can smell, look at, and feel natural objects, but these things should never be eaten. Many common plants are poisonous. *Never* allow students to put anything in their mouths.

Teaching Phases

Following are three phases for implementing the activities in the Experience:

Phase I: Direct Instruction/Interactive Teaching

This unit is designed to be presented using direct instruction strategies throughout. The lesson plans call for a high degree of teacher-student interaction. In many cases you will be taking the students outdoors for short field trips that require direct instruction and supervision. The first lesson is a good introduction to the outdoors because it involves a very familiar game—a scavenger hunt.

Phase II. Cooperative Learning

The Side Paths and the Searches are designed for cooperative groups. Once you have begun the Adventures, you can set up the Side Paths in learning centers, and the Searches can be assigned to individual teams.

Phase III. Culminating Process

Teams should be assigned a time to present the results of their projects. The projects will help the students pull ideas together that were developed during the Adventures.

Provide feedback using the evaluation form at the end of this Experience. Evaluate and obtain feedback on students' opinions and attitudes toward the unit. Use the form provided on page 111.

STUDENT INFORMATION

Adventures

Lesson 1. A Sensory Scavenger Hunt

If a walk is too passive for your students, transform it into a series of interesting discoveries and make the process of getting from one place to another an adventure in itself.

Find an area that has a variety of natural objects, such as a path through the woods, along the edge of the playground, or near a small stream or pond.

Action

1. Before you set out, tell students that at certain times during the walk they will stop for a scavenger hunt.
2. At appropriate times during the walk, stop the group and name a quality they should look for in a natural object. Let the season and the site inspire you, or use these ideas: something rough, smooth, soft, hard, bumpy, pointed, round, flat, crooked, straight; something brown, black, gray; something with two colors, three colors; something that tickles, prickles; something that bends without breaking, will not bend; something that smells.
3. When students have found a natural object with the specified quality, lead them through a sensory experience:

   Look at the object carefully. Look at it close up, far away, upside down, and sideways. Does it look different when you see it in these ways? What is its shape? What other things in nature have a similar shape? What color or shades of color does it have? Now feel it all over with your fingertips. Feel its edges and sides. How does it feel? Listen to it. Does it make a sound? What sound does it make? Hold it close to your nose and breathe in. Does it have a smell? Moisten a spot of it with a little saliva and smell again. Do you know of anything else that has a similar smell?

4. Encourage the students to examine and compare each other's objects.

5. Continue the walk, stopping frequently to look for qualities of natural objects and examining them.
6. Help students make the following connections:

   - Ecology. When you found your natural object, what was above, below, next to, or near it? Did some of these items come from the object? Can you think of any creature that might use this natural object for protection or for a home?
   - Change. What do you think your natural object was like before you found it? Was it smaller? Was it a different color or texture? What things might have made it change?

   Lead students in the following visualization.

Becoming Part of Nature

Close your eyes and think about the natural things you looked for and found on your walk . . . Choose the one you like the best . . . Think about it and see in your mind its size, shape, and color . . . Now imagine yourself smaller and smaller . . . until you are tiny enough to go into it . . . Become the thing itself.

See yourself at the place where you found it . . . Imagine the rain falling on you . . . How does it make you feel? . . . Feel the heat of the sun . . . and the heat slowly changing into the coolness and darkness of the night . . . Hear the night sounds around you.

Feel the gentle wind, then a stronger wind, blowing around you . . . Does the wind make you move? . . . Does it make anything around you move? . . . Think of something that might make you change.

Now slowly become yourself again. When you're ready, open your eyes. If you like, share what you were and how you felt.

Lesson 2. What on Earth Is It?

This activity encourages students to dig in and actively explore a square foot of earth. By closely examining soil, students will discover the variety of decaying natural materials that make up the ground they walk on. For best results, find an area heavily covered with leaf mold and natural debris.

Materials
A 4½ foot length of string with the ends tied together to form a circle, a jar and ventilated cover, several sheets of newsprint, a magnifying glass, for each pair of students.

Action

1. Have students choose partners and give each pair the length of string and have them gather four sticks, each about six inches long, from the surrounding area.

Stick

String

2. Have each pair choose a patch of ground that they would like to explore. When they are at their site, they should push the four sticks into the ground to make four corners of a square, about one foot apart on each side. They should then place the string around the sticks; when completed, the sticks and string should enclose about one square foot of soil.

3. Give each pair of students a sheet or two of newsprint, an empty jar, and a magnifying glass.

4. Tell students to pretend to be scientists from another planet. Their instructions are to find out what makes up the surface of the planet earth by carefully examining the spot where their spaceship has landed.

5. With their mission as space scientists in mind, the students should carefully remove the layers of natural debris from their enclosed area. The materials they pick up should be placed on the newsprint in piles, classified in whatever way they wish. Insects and other creatures can be placed in the jar to be observed closely. Tell the students to be sure to dig deep, and to be thorough in examining all they remove.

6. After an appropriate period of time, ask each group to look over their piles and choose their most interesting earthly discoveries. The entire group can then gather in a circle around each site while the pair explains their classifications and passes around their most interesting find.

7. After all pairs shared their discoveries, creatures and earthly debris should be carefully replaced and the strings and sticks removed.

8. Help students make the following connections:

   • Ecology. How do creatures that live in the debris help change it into soil? How do burrowing creatures bring moisture to the soil? Why would plants grow well in soil that is made of decayed leaves and natural litter?

   • Change. How does rain help change natural debris into soil? How might animals that walk over natural debris help change it into soil? What would happen if all the natural debris that fell to the ground was immediately removed?

Lead students in the following visualization:

Leaf Changing into Soil

Close your eyes and imagine that you are walking through the woods . . . The dry leaves are making a crunching noise under your feet . . . Stop and look carefully at one leaf . . . It is dry and brown, and its edges have curled inward . . . As you see it lying on the earth, imagine yourself smaller and smaller, until you are just the right size and shape to enter it . . . Become this leaf . . . Feel rested and comfortable as you lie on the forest floor.

You realize that you have just fallen from a nearby tree, along with thousands of other leaves . . . You feel the air becoming cold and crisp . . . Sometimes a squirrel scurries over you, carrying nuts to store for the winter . . . One day you feel a deer's hoof land squarely on you. Although it flattens you, it doesn't hurt at all. As winter comes, you stay wet from the rain and snow; the water in you turns to ice and this ice breaks the tiny veins that hold you together . . . This breaking up is not an uncomfortable feeling, however, for the more you break up, the more rested you feel.

Spring comes, and you feel the warmth of the sun. You notice that the other leaves beside you have also broken up and flattened out . . . You find yourself feeling less and less like a leaf.

It is fall now and you feel lots of leaves falling upon you . . . Leaves from the tree that you fell from last year cover up the sunlight . . . More and more, you feel part of the earth.

Now slowly become yourself again. When you feel ready, open your eyes. If you like, share what you felt.

Lesson 3. Investigating Insects, Capturing Creatures

Active students are fascinated by hopping, crawling, and wiggling creatures. This activity encourages students to find out where insects and creatures live, what they look like, and how they move.

Find an area that contains a variety of habitats for insects and creatures—grass and weeds; cool, moist areas; rocks, bricks, boards, or logs.

Materials
One covered jar for each student

Action

1. Tell the students that they will become nature detectives looking for insects and creatures. Give each student a jar to hold a specimen after its capture. Explain where creatures might be found: in a grassy or weedy area; amidst and under decaying leaves; under rocks and boards; and in organic and inorganic litter. Remind students to never poke their hands or fingers into places they cannot see.
2. When students have found a specimen and carefully placed it in a jar, have them sit in a circle and lead them through a physical-sensory experience:

   Look carefully at your specimen. What color or colors is it? Can you find its head? Can you find its eyes?

Does it have antennae, or feelers? Look at its body. Does it have a hard shell, or does its body seem to be soft? Does it have wings? Can you count the number of legs it has? What kind of place did you find your specimen? Was it wet, dry, sunny, or shady? What was your creature doing when you first saw it? Was it hopping, walking, or crawling? Did it seem to be eating? Was it carrying food or bits of material?

3. Have the students pass their jars around the circle and encourage them to examine and compare each other's specimens.
4. When students have finished examining each other's specimens, they should release the creatures in the place where they were found.
5. Help students make the following connections:

   • Ecology. Was your creature alone, or were there several of them? Were there different kinds of creatures in the same area? Was your creature the same color as the plant or soil on which you found it? What do you think it might eat? What do you think might eat it?
   • Change. What do you think might happen to your creature in the winter? How does your creature change the area in which it lives? What would happen if all insects were destroyed by pesticides?

Lead students in the following visualization:

From Egg to Butterfly

Close your eyes, relax, and imagine that you are walking through a grassy field on a fall day . . . You stop to look at a plant, and you notice a cluster of very tiny white balls on the underside of one of the leaves . . . You look closely and realize they are insect eggs. As you look at one of the eggs, imagine your body getting smaller and smaller until you are tiny enough to enter it . . . Become the egg.

You feel yourself relaxed and protected in the fluid of the egg . . . As the days go by, you are aware of the coldness of winter but you are comfortable and secure . . . When spring comes and the sun shines brightly, you feel yourself taking on a form inside the egg . . . One day you feel too tight inside the egg so you try to get out, squirming and moving your body . . . When you finally break out of the shell, you find that you have a long wormlike body . . . You have six legs on the front end of your body—three on each side—and several leg-like stumps on the other end of your body . . . Humans would call you a caterpillar.

You begin moving around on the leaves of the plant, glad to be out of the tiny egg case and in the fresh, warm air . . . You find that you are very hungry, so you begin eating the leaf you are standing on . . . You are always hungry—you eat and eat and eat, and you find yourself growing bigger and bigger.

One day when you no longer feel the urge to eat, you attach yourself to a twig, curl up, and carefully spin a thick web around yourself. You stay in this moist cocoon for several weeks . . . Even though you seem to be in a deep sleep, you can still feel your body changing . . . After a while you feel yourself waking up, ready to leave the cocoon . . . You push the wall of the cocoon and it splits open . . . Carefully you come out and hold onto the plant . . . Your wings are crinkled and soft, but as they fill with fluid from your body, they unfold, grow larger, and harden . . . You are now a butterfly . . . You leave the plant and take your first flight across the field.

Now slowly become yourself again. When you are ready, open your eyes. If you like, share with us what you felt.

Lesson 4. New Perspectives on Walking

Ambling through an area in an unusual manner focuses the student's attention on many angles of the natural world. For a change of pace and a change of perspective, try these for short walking activities.

Find a safe area—a path through the woods or along the edge of the playground adjacent to woods—because students will be walking barefoot and backward.

Action

1. Walking and Looking up. Tell students that they will be looking upward while walking slowly ahead. Have them glance down at the ground every few steps to check their footing. As the students slowly walk and look up, encourage them to respond to the following questions:

    Look up and really see what's up there. Move your head slowly back and forth. What do you see? Do you see anything move? What is making things move?

   As you pass through the area with trees, ask:

    Can you see the leaves on the trees? What colors are they? Can you see their shapes? Do you see any animals or nests in the treetops? Can you see patches of sky between the leaves? What color is the sky? Do you see clouds? Do they seem to be moving?

   When the high-level interest point has passed, either go on to another walking activity or have the students walk normally.

2. Walking and Listening. Tell the students that they are going to use their hands to help them listen. Have them make both hands into fists and tell them to let go of one finger every time they hear a sound. Remind them to walk very softly with no talking, so that they can listen carefully. Have the students walk and listen for an appropriate period of time. Then have them stop, form a circle, and show each other with their fingers how many sounds they heard. Ask:

> *What were some of the sounds you heard? What made the soft sounds? What made the harsh sounds? Which were sounds of nature and which were not? Of the different sounds you heard, which ones would you be likely to hear around your home? Which would you hear outside the classroom?*

Go on to another walking activity, or have the students just walk and listen.

3. Walking Backward. In preparation for this walk, have the students walk forward, looking carefully at the area ahead of them, above them, and on both sides. Ask them to describe what they see. Then have them turn around and very slowly walk backward, every few steps turning their heads to check where they are going. As they walk backward, have them look at the area on all sides of them, as well as up. Then ask:

> *What things do you see? Do you see things that you didn't see when you were walking forward? Does this area look different when you see it this way?*

When they again walk forward, urge them occasionally to look backward to get a different perspective of the area.

4. Walking Barefoot. Before the walk, find a lawn, or a path covered with dirt or leaves or an area with a combination of several different textures. Make sure the area is free of glass, nails, or harmful debris.

Have students remove their shoes and socks. Have them wiggle their toes and tickle their feet to wake them up. Tell the students that they will be walking barefoot, so they should walk slowly and watch carefully where they step. As they walk, lead the students through a physical-sensory experience:

> *Walk slowly and really feel the earth with your feet. How does it feel—is it prickly, tickly, soft, or rough? Does it feel like anything you've walked on before? Is it hot, cold, warm, or cool? Are there some spots right next to each other with different temperatures?*

Have the students find a spot that feels especially good to their feet. Have them share this spot with a friend.

5. Help students make the following connections:

- Ecology. What animals use the space above you for homes or for protection? Why do animals often stand perfectly still when they are listening? What do some animals have on their feet that make them able to walk on ground that would be too rough for barefoot people?

- Change. What things would be different if you look upward in the fall? in the winter? in the spring? in the summer? What would you see above you before a rainstorm?

6. Lead students in the following visualization:

Becoming the Ground You Walk On.

Lie down on the ground, close your eyes and relax . . . Feel the solidness of the earth beneath your body. Feel the different points on your body that come in direct contact with the earth: the heels of your feet . . . the back of your legs . . . the upper part of your back . . . your arms and hands . . . the back of your head . . . Feel the coolness of the earth coming into your body . . . Now slowly become the earth you are lying on.

Imagine tiny seeds gently falling on you . . . Now feel raindrops falling on top of you . . . Then feel them sinking into you, making you feel refreshed and full . . . Feel the little seeds sprouting on top of you . . . sending their tiny but strong roots deeper and deeper into your moist soil . . . Imagine the warmth of a summer day . . . Imagine a long, cold winter . . . Imagine the feel of leaves, twigs, nuts, and branches falling on you . . . Think of how it feels when creatures walk on you . . . a grasshopper . . . a bird . . . a rabbit . . . a person.

Now slowly become yourself again. When you are ready, open your eyes. If you wish, share some of the things you felt.

Lesson 5. Getting the Feel of a Tree

To students who have never explored a tree, all trees may seem uninvitingly the same. This activity demonstrates that each tree is indeed unique, and offers a variety of sensations and textures when explored through touch.

Find an area with many trees fairly close together, so that you can be easily heard as you lead students through the sensory exploration.

Materials

A paper bag, small enough to fit snugly over the head but large enough to provide some ventilation for each pair of students.

Action

1. Have the students choose partners, and explain that one student will wear a paper bag while the other student is the leader. After the activity is completed, partners switch roles and the activity is repeated. Have the partners decide who will wear the bag first.

2. The leader spins the blindfolded partner three times, and then carefully leads him or her to a nearby tree. When the pair reaches the tree, the blindfolded person places both hands on the tree, and the leader stands nearby.

3. After all the leaders have taken their partners to a tree, lead the blindfolded students through a physical-sensory exploration:

> *Wrap your arms around the tree and give it a big hug. Is your tree thick or thin? Put your nose to it and smell deeply. Does it have a smell?*
>
> *Slowly walk around your tree and explore it with the palms of your hands and the tips of your fingers. Does it feel rough or smooth? Do your fingertips fit into any of the cracks? Do you feel limbs or branches sticking out?*
>
> *When you have felt all the way around the tree, move the palms of your hands slowly up the tree, as high as you can reach, and feel for cracks and interesting textures. Then slowly move your hands down to the base of the trunk, feeling carefully for moss or tiny plants that might be growing on the bark.*
>
> *Find where the tree goes into the earth; feel the earth around the tree trunk, and check with your fingers for any nearby growing plants. Now move your hands back up the tree to the spot where you first hugged the tree.*

4. While the blindfolds are still on, have the leaders take their partners back to the starting point. The blindfolded students remove the paper bags and by feeling nearby tree trunks, try to find the tree they were just exploring. The leader goes along and states whether the partner is correct or not. When the student finds the tree, the leader asks, "How did you know this was your tree?"

5. Partners switch roles and repeat the activity.

6. Help students make the following connections:

   • Ecology. What creatures might make their homes in the cracks of the bark? What parts of a tree are used as food by some animals? What animals might live in the treetops?

   • Change. What would happen if a tree stopped making nuts and seeds? How would that change the lives of animals that lived nearby? What would happen if the bark was stripped from a tree? What creatures might lose their homes if a dead and rotting tree is cut down?

7. Lead students in the following visualization:

Becoming a Sprouting Acorn

Close your eyes, relax, and imagine yourself slowly walking through the woods . . . A shiny, brown acorn falls from a nearby tree . . . As you look at it lying on the earth, imagine yourself becoming smaller and smaller . . . until you are tiny enough to enter the acorn . . . Become the acorn.

Feel yourself hard and smooth, lying peacefully on the earth . . . Occasionally you feel an insect walk over you . . . As autumn comes, you feel leaves gently falling and covering you . . . When the spring sun warms you, you feel ready to push out of your hard shell.

Part of you grows into a thick root and cracks your covering . . . This part of you pushes its way into the moist, wet earth . . . At the same time, you find yourself growing upward . . . Your stem pushes its way through the fallen leaves . . . The two tiny green leaves that have grown on the top of your stem open. . . . The warm air and sunshine feel especially good . . . The tiny leaves soak up the sun and give energy to your roots. The roots drink in the moisture from the earth and send it up to your leaves.

The lower part of you feels safe in the darkness of the moist earth, and the upper part of you feels free in the sunshine and the warm breezes . . . You wonder if you will ever grow as high as the trees around you.

Now slowly become yourself again . . . When you are ready open your eyes. If you wish, share some of the things you felt.

Side Paths

There may not always be enough time during outdoor excursions to examine carefully all the fascinating natural objects the students may find. Some natural materials can be brought indoors and examined in activities that overlap into other subject areas.

A nature center—consisting of shelves, a table and sufficient wall space for displays—is the ideal place to consolidate natural objects, work on activities, and display ongoing and completed projects.

Lesson 6. Collections (Mathematics)

Collections encourage students to apply mathematical skills such as counting, classifying, comparing, contrasting, and assigning attributes. Seeds, bark, rocks, twigs, and shells may be collected and categorized. Below are examples of collection activities. Encourage students to use the collections to practice classifying and categorizing skills.

Activity A. Insects

Materials
Small container, straight pins, corrugated cardboard or a styrofoam tray, wad of cotton, cork.

Action

1. A dried insect collection enables students to examine, compare, and contrast the fascinating bodies of insects at very close range. Have students look for dead insects outdoors on sidewalks and driveways and indoors on window sills and in corners.
2. Insects should be dried thoroughly before being added to the collection because freshly dead insects may attract ants. To dry an insect, have students put it in a small open container and place it in a well-ventilated, warm place where it will not be disturbed.
3. When the insect appears to be dry, have students place it on a small wad of cotton and gently push a straight pin through the center of the body. If the insect's body is too small, glue the insect on a small piece of heavy paper and push a pin through the paper.
4. Have students stick the pinned bodies on a piece of cardboard or a styrofoam tray. When they want to examine an insect more closely have them take the insect from the collection and stick it into a cork. Students can then hold the cork and examine the body from all angles.

Activity B. Feathers

Feather —

Popsicle stick —

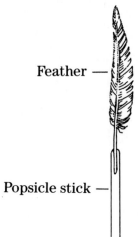

Materials
Popsicle sticks, glue or tape.

Action

1. A feather collection gives students the opportunity to see, feel, and classify feathers of various colors, sizes, shapes, and textures. Birds molt twice a year, and their feathers can be found in natural areas and around aviaries in zoos and natural history museums. They also may be ordered from a science supply house.
2. To make a neat collection, and to keep feathers from blowing away and becoming ragged from excess handling, have students glue or tape the quill of the feathers onto one end of a popsicle stick. They can then easily grasp the stick as they examine and classify the feather.
3. Have students store the feather collection upright in a can or container.

Activity C. Leaves, Grasses, and Weeds

Materials
Construction paper, glue or tape, newspaper, heavy objects.

Action

1. Leaves, grasses, and weeds can be selectively picked to display similarities and differences, and to display the variety of plants that grow in one area.
2. To preserve weeds, grasses, and leaves have students place them between layers of newspapers and set books or heavy objects on top of them to keep them from curling. In a few days, the moisture will be absorbed by the newspaper and the specimen can be glued or taped on posterboard, cardboard, or colored construction paper.
3. Flowers can also be pressed and made into an attractive display. Have students bring flowers from their home gardens or ask a

florist to save stale flowers for the group. Have students press the flowers following the directions in part 2 above and label them with their botanical names for a classroom display.

Lesson 7. A Nature Notebook (Language Arts)

A personal notebook is an ideal place for students to practice their writing skills as they record their outdoor discoveries. Written descriptions are an important part of the scientific process, and writing descriptions encourages closer observation and examination.

Students can use their notebooks to describe captured insects, record the contents of a square foot of soil, and draw their impressions from visualization exercises. Leaves, feathers, and other interesting natural materials can be taped or glued into the notebook, with a note as to when, where, and under what circumstances they were found.

Lesson 8. Poetry (Language Arts)

After observing a wide range of shapes, textures, and patterns in the natural world, students should have a variety of qualities to call up when writing freeform, expressive poetry. Have students write verses in response to questions such as, "If you could be any kind of object or animal in nature, what would you be? What would you look like? Where would you live? What things would you like? What things would make you afraid?"

Have students illustrate their poems and display them on a Poetry Corner bulletin board.

Lesson 9. Wood It Do? (Social Studies)

To illustrate how people use natural resources, have students draw a mural or list all of the items in the classroom that began as a tree. When students' drawings and lists are complete, ask the following questions:

- Why is wood used to make so many things?
- What are some wasteful things that are made from trees?
- Which of the items could be made with other materials?
- Why is wood called a renewable resource?
- What would be the danger of cutting too many trees?

Lesson 10. Webs (Social Studies)

Materials
Ball of cord or heavy string, sheets of paper, and magic markers or crayons.

Action

After studying how people in communities are dependent upon one another, use this activity to show how plants and animals within an area are also interdependent.

1. Guide students in exploring a natural area. Then form a circle and give each student a piece of paper and a crayon. Ask students to

draw a picture and write the name of a creature, growing thing, or an inanimate object found in the area.

2. When everyone has finished, give the ball of string to one student. Have the student hold the end of the string, call out the name of his or her creature or thing, and toss the ball to another student in the group. The student who catches the ball then calls out the name of his or her creature or thing, and the first student states how the two are connected. Both students continue holding the string as the ball is tossed to a third student and the relationships are identified. Continue to repeat the process.

3. As the ball of string is tossed across and around the circle, students should continue to hold the string. When all the students have had the ball of string and stated a connection, the criss-crossed string will resemble an asymmetrical web.

4. Explain that the criss-crossed strings represent the web of life that connects all animals and plants to each other. One by one, have students should let go of the string to dramatize that when one thing in nature is removed, everything else is affected.

Lesson 11. Clay Impressions (Art)

Materials
Modeling or firing clay.

Action

1. Have students make clay impressions of natural objects to show off the beauty and symmetry of leaves, seashells, seed pods, bark, wood, nuts, or twigs.

2. Have students work a ball of clay and pound it flat. Then have them place a natural object on the clay, press firmly, and then carefully remove the object to obtain its impression. Several objects may be used in combination if students wish.

3. If firing clay is used, have students make a hole in the clay so that the piece can later be hung. Set the impressions aside to dry for several days. Although fragile, the finished plaque will stay intact if handled carefully.

Lesson 12. Leaf Rubbings (Art)

Materials
Old crayons with wrapping peeled off, paper.

Action

1. In a field or overgrown weedy lawn, have the students gently pick three or more leaves of different sizes, shapes, or textures. Have the students take the leaves back to the classroom and lay them out in the middle of a table.

2. Have students take one leaf at a time and place it so that the thicker veins are facing up. Have them cover the leaf with a sheet of paper and rub the side of a crayon back and forth across the paper making sure to go over the edges and the stem. Have students experiment with different combinations of colors and leaves to obtain unusual patterns of color and form.

Lesson 13. Movements in Nature (Drama)

Action

1. Try this activity in a large open area with enough room for everyone to spread out.
2. Ask students to act out events in nature by imagining themselves as plants and animals. The following are some ideas:

   - Trees swaying as a storm builds up and then dies down.
   - Seeds pushing their way through the soil, growing into flowers.
   - Vines twisting around a tree, reaching up toward the sun.
   - Butterflies flitting from flower to flower, drinking nectar.
   - Ants carrying heavy crumbs to their ant hills.
   - Birds turning over natural debris with their beaks and claws, looking for insects.
   - Baby squirrels curled up in their warm nest of leaves.

3. After describing the action, give students enough time to experiment with different body movements.

Lesson 14. Animal Acting (Drama)

After the group has explored a natural area, have students sit in a circle and ask them to think of a creature or animal that might live in the area. When all the students have an animal in mind, have them go into the center of the circle one at a time and act out the behavior of the animal they have chosen, so that the rest of the group can guess what it is. Continue until all students have had a turn.

Searches

Lesson 1. A Bucket Microscope

Materials
Cylindrical carton or cardboard tub; sharp knife; plastic wrap; larger rubber band; masking tape.

Action

1. Have students make a large magnifying glass from a cylindrical ice cream carton or heavy cardboard tub. Have them cut one hole in the side of the bucket, large enough for a hand to go through.

2. Have students take a large sheet of plastic wrap and place it on top of the bucket, making sure the plastic hangs over the sides. Then have them secure the plastic wrap snugly with an elastic band.
3. Have them slowly pour water onto the plastic, so that it stretches and sags into the container.
4. Have students place natural objects one at a time through the hole in the container and look at them through the water and plastic.

Lesson 2. A Leaf Collection that Grows

Materials
One strip of cloth for each student, magic marker, tape, construction paper.

Action

1. In the early spring before the buds begin to open, find an area with many low trees or bushes. Have each student choose a branch with buds on it. Then have them use the magic marker to write their names on the strips of cloth and tie the strips to the branches they have chosen.
2. Have the students examine their branches, looking carefully at the number and placement of the buds, and gently feeling a bud to get to know its size, shape, and texture. Have them draw a picture of the branch and buds on construction paper and label it with the date under it.
3. Pick a bud from a tree and open it gently, layer by layer, to show the students the inside.
4. When the buds on the branch open, have each student pick one small leaf from his or her branch and tape it onto the piece of paper next to the drawing of the branch and buds. Students should write the date under it and press it between newspapers so that the leaves do not curl.
5. One day each week, have students visit their branches and gently pull off another leaf. They should tape the leaves beside the previous ones on their papers, label them, and again press the pages between newspapers.
6. By the end of spring, the students' papers should have many leaves ranging in size from small to large. Have the students compute the number of days it takes for a leaf to reach its full size; also point out that the shape of the leaf remains the same even though it gets larger.

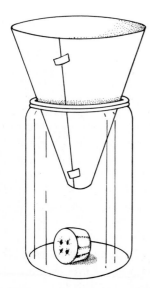

Lesson 3. A Funnel Trap

Materials
One medium-sized jar; a piece of paper; tape; and a piece of ripe banana for each student.

Action

1. Ask students if they have ever tried to capture a speeding housefly. Then have them make this simple device to capture houseflies and fruitflies.

2. Have students make a funnel with paper and tape. Then have them put a piece of ripe banana inside the jar and place the paper funnel over the opening.
3. Have students take the flytrap outdoors and check it frequently. Flies will find their way in to get the banana, but they will not be able to find their way out.

Lesson 4. Investigating a Bird Nest

Materials
Posterboard or scrap of wood; glue; cotton; large pot; soil.

Action
To investigate the makings of a bird nest, have students find an abandoned nest within reaching distance. Remind them *never to disturb a nest that is still in use.* If it is late summer or fall and the nest has not wintered over, have them leave it outside for a few days on a piece of newspaper to make sure it is not infested with mites. If any tiny mites are seen running around on the paper, tell students not to handle the nest or bring it indoors because mites can infest people. If the nest is mite-free, examine it by gently touching it and feeling its shape. Then try the following activities:

A Bird Nest Collage. Have students carefully pull the nest apart and separate the different materials into piles. Then have them glue a sample of each pile onto a piece of posterboard or wood for display. To secure the rough materials onto the flat surface, suggest that they place a small glue-soaked wad of cotton between the natural material and the surface to act as a bond between the two. Let the glue dry thoroughly before hanging the collage.

A Sprouting Nest. Have students crush the remaining nest materials and place them in a pot that is three-quarters full of soil. Have students cover the materials with about one-half inch of soil, press firmly, and water thoroughly. Instruct them to keep the soil moist but not wet. In a few days or weeks, they may find that several plants have sprouted from the seeds in the nesting material.

Evaluation

When evaluating the effectiveness of the unit and the progress of the students, keep in mind that all students develop in their own way, at their own pace, depending on previous positive as well as negative experiences and attitudes. Many urban and suburban students who have not been previously exposed to natural areas may express hesitancy and even fear. It may take many outdoor experiences and much encouragement before some students feel comfortable exploring the natural world through their senses.

To evaluate the progress of the students in this unit, a check list of observations is keyed to each major objective.

Observation Chart to Evaluate Student Progress

Evaluation code   1. Making satisfactory progress   2. Needs to improve.

Objective	Observation		
	Does the student:	**1**	**2**
Develop and heighten ability to use senses.	• Feel comfortable in using the senses to experience the environment? • Readily feel, smell, and visually examine natural objects? • Pause to listen to natural objects? • Trust his or her senses as a valid source of information?		
Describe objects in the natural environment using the senses.	• Carefully examine natural objects to note important qualities such as size, color, and texture? • Survey the area she or he is walking through by looking on both sides, above, and below the immediate path? • Point out things of interest or aspects of nature that were previously experienced or discussed?		
Improve the thinking process.	• Go from observing natural phenomenon to stating how it affects or is affected by the surrounding environment? • Make comments regarding the interdependency of different aspects in the natural world? • Consider not only the present environment, but how it came to be that way, and how it may change in the future? • Attempt to answer questions by using information that is inferred rather than given?		
Strengthen speech and language development.	• Confidently verbalize the tactile and visual sensations he or she is experiencing? • Use an expanded vocabulary to express observations and sensory impressions? • Use learned environmentally oriented language when articulating comments and questions?		
Develop a feeling of protectiveness for the environment.	• Show respect for creatures by leaving their habitats undisturbed? • Show concern for a clean natural environment by not littering, and by picking up litter when possible? • Express awareness of the impact he or she is making on the environment?		

Books for Kids

Arnold, Caroline. *Natural Resources: Fun, Facts, and Activities.* New York: Watts, 1985.

Buscaglia, Leo. *The Fall of Freddie the Leaf.* Thorofare, N.J.: Charles B. Slack, 1983.

Conklin, Gladys. *Fairy Rings and Other Mushrooms.* New York: Holiday House, 1973.

Cox, Rosamund Kidman, and Barbara Cox. *Usborne First Nature—Birds.* London: Usborne Publishing, 1980. (Note: There are several excellent nature books in this Usborne series.)

Densmore, Francis. *How Indians Use Wild Plants for Food, Medicine, and Crafts.* New York: Dover, 1974.

Fitzsimons, Cecilia. *My First Birds.* New York: Harper & Row, 1985.

_____. *My First Butterflies.* New York: Harper & Row, 1985.

Hoffman, Stephen M. *What's Under That Rock?* New York: Atheneum, 1985.

Invite Wildlife to Your Backyard. Washington, D.C.: National Wildlife Federation.

Foster, Laura Louise. *Keeping the Plants You Pick.* New York: Thomas Y. Crowell Co, 1970.

Romanova, Natalia. *Once There Was A Tree.* New York: Dial, 1985.

Silverstein, Shel. *The Giving Tree.* New York: Harper & Row, 1964.

Whipple, Jane B. *Forest Resources.* New York: Watts, 1985.

APPENDIX

Resources and References

Science Teaching

Abruscato, Joseph. *Children, Computers and Science: Butterflies and Bytes*. Englewood Cliffs, N.J.: Prentice-Hall, 1986.

Abruscato, Joseph. *Teaching Children Science*. Englewood Cliffs, N.J.: Prentice-Hall, 1988.

Abruscato Joseph, and Jack Hassard. *Loving and Beyond: Science Teaching for the Humanistic Classroom*. Glenview, Ill: Scott, Foresman, 1976.

_____. *The Whole Cosmos Catalog of Science Activities*. Glenview, Ill.: Scott, Foresman, 1977.

Blough, Glen O., and Julius Schwartz. *Elementary School Science and How to Teach It*. Seventh Edition. New York: Holt, Rinehart and Winston, Inc., 1985.

Bybee, Rodger. "Science Education and the Ecological Society," *Science Education*, Vol. 63, No. 1, January, 1979.

_____. et al. *Teaching About Science and Society: Activities for Elementary and Junior High School*. Columbus, Ohio: Charles E. Merrill Publishing Company, 1984.

Carin, Arthur, and Robert B. Sund. *Teaching Modern Science*. Fourth Edition. Columbus, Ohio: Charles E. Merrill Publishing Company, 1985.

DeVito, Alfred. *Creative Wellsprings for Science Teaching*. West Lafayette, Ind.: Creative Ventures, Inc. 1984.

DeVito, Alfred, and Gerald Krockover. *Creative Sciencing: A Practical Approach (Vol. II), and Ideas and Activities (Vol II)*. Glenview, Ill.: Scott, Foresman, 1980.

Disenger, John, and Marylin Lisowski. *Teaching Activities in Science/Society/Technology/Environment*. Columbus, Ohio: ERIC Clearinghouse for Science, Mathematics, and Environmental Education, 1986.

Erickson, Tim. *Off & Running: The Computer Offline Activities Book*. Berkeley, Calif.: EQUALS, Lawrence Hall of Science, 1986.

Friedl, Alfred E. *Teaching Science to Children: The Inquiry Approach Applied*. New York: Random House, 1972.

Harlen, Wynne. *Primary Science: Taking the Plunge*. London: Heinemann Educational Books, 1985.

Jacobson, Willard J., and Abby Barry Gegman. *Science for Children*. Englewood Cliffs, N.J.: Prentice-Hall, 1980.

Mallow, Jeffrey V. *Science Anxiety: Fear of Science and How to Overcome It*. New York: Thomand Press, 1981.

Mitchel, John. *The Curious Naturalist*. Englewood Cliffs, N.J.: Prentice-Hall, 1980.

Mechling, Kenneth R., and Donna L. Oliver. *Handbook I: Science Teaches Basic Skills*. Washington D.C.: National Science Teachers Association, 1983.

Osborne, Roger, and Peter Freyberg. *Learning in Science: The Implications of Children's Science*. London: Heinemann Educational Books, 1985.

Roth, Charles, and Linda G. Lockwood. *Strategies and Activities for Using Local Communities as Environmental Education Sites*. Columbus, Ohio: ERIC Clearinghouse for Science, Mathematics, and Environmental Education, 1979.

Rowe, Mary Budd. *Teaching Science as Continuous Inquiry*, 2nd ed. New York: McGraw-Hill, 1978.

Strongin, Herb. *Science on a Shoestring*. Menlo Park, Calif.: Addison-Wesley Publishing Company, 1976.

Skolnick, Joan, Carol Langbort, and Lucille Day. *How to Encourage Girls in Math & Science*. Englewood Cliffs, N.J.: Prentice-Hall, Inc. 1982.

Thelen, Judith N. *Improving Reading in Science*, Second Edition. Newark, Del.: International Reading Association, 1984.

Thomas, Lewis. "Teaching Science," *New York Times Magazine*. January 23, 1983.

Trojcak, Doris. *Science With Children*. New York: McGraw-Hill, 1979.

Wolfinger, Donna M. *Teaching Science in the Elementary School*. Boston, Mass.: Little, Brown and Company, 1984.

Wigginton, Eliot. *Sometimes a Shining Moment: The Foxfire Experience*. New York: Anchor Books, 1986.

Cooperative Learning

Aronson, Elliott. *The Jigsaw Classroom*. Beverly Hills, Calif.: SAGE Publications, 1978.

Johnson, David W., and Roger T. Johnson. *Learning Together and Alone: Cooperation, Competition, and Individualization*. Englewood Cliffs, N.J.: Prentice-Hall, 1976.

——————. *Joining Together: Group Theory and Group Skills*. New Brighton, Minn.: Interaction Book Company, 1982.

——————. *Circles of Learning: Cooperation in the Classroom*. Alexandria, Va.: Association for Supervision and Curriculum Development, 1984.

Kagan, Spencer. *Cooperative Learning: Resources for Teachers*. Riverside Calif.: University of California, 1985.

Sharan, Shlomo, and Yael Sharan. *Small-Group Teaching*. Englewood Cliffs, N.J.: Educational Technology Publications, 1976.

Sharan, Shlomo, et al. *Cooperative Learning in the Classroom: Research in Desegregated Schools*. Hillsdale, N.J.: Lawrence Erlbaum Associates, Publishers, 1984.

Slavin, Robert E. *Using Student Team Learning*. Baltimore, Md.: Center for Social Organization of Schools, 1980.

Holistic/Humanistic Education

Anderson, Hans O. "The Holistic Approach to Science Education," *The Science Teacher*, No. 1 (January 1978), pp. 27–28.

Bronowski, J. *The Ascent of Man*. Boston: Little, Brown and Company, 1973.

Bruner, J. *On Knowing: Essays for the Left Hand*. New York: Atheneum, 1962.

Buzan, Tony. *Using Both Sides of Your Brain*. New York: E.P. Dutton, 1983.

Brown, George I. *Human Teaching for Human Learning*. New York: Viking Press, 1971.

Capra, Fritjof. *The Tao of Physics*. Berkeley, Calif.: Shambala Publications, 1975.

Canfield, Jack, and Harold Wells. *100 Ways to Enhance Self-Concept*. Englewood Cliffs, N.J.: Prentice-Hall, Inc., 1976.

Carson, Rachel. *A Sense of Wonder*. New York: Harper and Row, 1956.

DeBono, Edward. *Children Solve Problems*. New York: Penguin Books, 1972.

——————. *Lateral Thinking: Creativity Step by Step* New York: Harper and Row, 1970.

Edwards, Betty. *Drawing on the Right Side of the Brain*. Los Angeles: J.P. Tarcher, 1979.

Fader, Daniel. *The Naked Children*. New York: Bantam Books, 1972.

Ferguson, Marilyn. *The Aquarian Conspiracy*. Los Angeles: J.P. Tarcher, 1980.

Ghiselin, Brewster. *The Creative Process*. New York: Mentor, 1952.

Gordon, W.J.J. *The Metaphorical Way of Learning and Knowing*. Cambridge, Mass.: Synectics Educational Systems, 1971.

Gould, Stephen Jay. *Ever Since Darwin: Reflections on Human Nature*. New York: W.W. Norton and Company, 1977.

Hamilton, Steven F. "The Social Side of Schooling: Ecological Studies of Classrooms and Schools," *The Elementary School Journal*, Vol. 83, No. 4, 1983, pp. 313–314.

Hassard, Jack. "Holistic Teaching," in *Methods and Techniques of Holistic Education* by Isidore Sonnier. Springfield, Ill.: Charles C. Thomas, Publisher, 1986.

Houston, Jean. *The Possible Human*. Los Angeles: J.P. Tarcher, 1982.

Judson, Horace Freeland. *The Search for Solutions*. New York: Holt, Rinehart and Winston, 1980.

Leonard, George. *Education and Ecstacy*. New York: Delta Books, 1969.

Maslow, Abraham. *The Farther Reaches of Human Nature*. New York: Penguin Books, 1971.

——————. *Toward a Psychology of Being*. New York: Van Nostrand, 1962.

——————. *Motivation and Personality*. New York: Harper and Row, 1970.

Miller, John. *The Holistic Curriculum*. (Ontario, Canada: OISE Press, 1988).

——————. *Humanizing the Classroom: Models of Teaching in Affective Education*. New York: Praeger Publishers, 1976.

McKim, Robert. *Experiences in Visual Thinking*. Monterey, Calif.: Brooks/Cole, 1972.

Palm, Ann. "Holistic Science," *Phoenix: New Directions in the Study of Man*. Vol. III, No. 2, Fall/Winter, 1979.

Pearce, Joseph C. *The Magical Child*. New York: E.P. Dutton, 1977.

Raths, Louis, Leland Howe, and Sidney Simon. *Values and Teaching*. Columbus, Ohio: Charles E. Merrill, 1966.

Rogers, Carl. *Freedom to Learn for the 80's*. Columbus, Ohio: Charles E. Merrill, 1982.

Romey, William. *Consciousness and Creativity*. Canton, N.Y.: Ash Lad Press, 1975.

_____. *Risk-Trust-Love: Learning in a Humane Environment*. Columbus, Ohio: Charles E. Merrill, 1972.

Roszak, Theodore. *Person/Planet: The Creative Disintegration of Industrial Society*. New York: Doubleday, 1978.

Russell, Peter. *The Global Brain*. Los Angeles, Calif.: J.P. Tarcher, 1981.

Sagan, Carl. *The Dragons of Eden*. New York: Random House, 1971.

_____. *Brocas Brain: Reflections on the Romance of Science*. New York: Random House, 1979.

Samples, Bob. *The Metaphoric Mind*. Reading, Mass.: Addison-Wesley Publishing Company, 1976.

Samuels, Michael, and Nancy Samuels. *Seeing With the Mind's Eye*. New York: Random House, 1975.

Simonton, O. Carl, and Stephanie Mathews-Simonton. *Getting Well Again*. Los Angeles: J.P. Tarcher, 1978.

Vaughan, Frances. *Awakening Intuition*. New York: Anchor Books, 1979.

Zukav, Gary. *The Dancing Wu Li Masters*. New York: William Morrow, 1980.

Science and Computer Supply Companies

Computer Software Suppliers

Here is a list of companies that produce effective and interesting software for students.

Broderbund Software, Inc.
17 Paul Dr.
San Rafael, CA 94903

Walt Disney Personal Computer Software
500 South Buena Vista Street
Burbank, CA 91521

Earthware Computer Service
P.O. Box 30039
Eugene Oregon 97403

Lawrence Hall of Science
University of California Math/Computer
Education Project
Berkeley, CA 94720

The Learning Company
545 Middlefield Road, Suite 170
Menlo Park, CA 94025

Learning Technologies, Inc.
4255 LBJ Freeway, Suite 131
Dallas, TX 75244

Scholastic
730 Broadway
New York, NY 10003

Spinnaker Software
One Kendall Square
Cambridge, MA 02139

Springboard
7808 Creekridge Circle
Minneapolis, MN 55435

Sunburst Communications
39 Washington Ave.
Pleasantville, NY 10570

Science Equipment and Materials

American Science and Engineering
20 Oberland Street
Boston, MA 02215

Carolina Biological Supply Co.
2700 York Rd
Burlington, NC 27215

Central Scientific Co.
2600 South Kostner Avenue
Chicago, IL 60623

Edmund Scientific
101 East Gloucester Pike
Barrington, NJ 08007

Science Kit, Inc.
777 East Park Drive
Tonawanda, NY 14150

Selective Educational Equipment (SEE), Inc.
3 Bridge Street
Newton, MA 02195

Ward's Natural Science Establishment, Inc.
300 Ridge Road East
Rochester, NY 14683

NOTES

Chapter 1

1. J. E. Lovelock, *Gaia* (New York: Oxford University Press, 1979).
2. F. Capra, *The Turning Point* (New York: Oxford University Press, 1982).
3. For further information on attitudinal research, see: Stacy J. Hueftle, Steven J. Rakow, and Wayne W. Welch, "Images of Science: A Summary of Results from the 1981–1982 National Assessment in Science." Science Assessment and Research Project, University of Minnesota. Also refer to "Attitude Research in Science Education," ERIC Clearinghouse for Science, Mathematics, and Environmental Science. Information Bulletin, No. 1 (1984).
4. From *Loving and Beyond: Science Teaching for the Humanistic Classroom* by Joe Abruscato and Jack Hassard (Glenview, Ill.: Scott, Foresman, 1976).
5. For further information and ideas to encourage girls in science, see: Joan Skolnick, Carol Langbort, and Lucille Day, *How to Encourage Girls in Math and Science* (Englewood Cliffs, N.J.: Prentice-Hall, Inc., 1982).
6. The idea for this comparison derives from *The Aquarian Conspiracy* by Marilyn Ferguson (Los Angeles: J.P. Tarcher, 1980). I have modified her original comparison in order to make it applicable to science education.
7. Ann Palm, "Holistic Science," *Phoenix: New Directions in the Study of Man*, Vol. III, No. 2 (Fall/Winter, 1979).
8. Abraham Maslow, *Toward a Psychology of Being* (New York: Van Nostrand Company, 1968).
9. Paul S. George, *Theory Z School: Beyond Effectiveness* (Columbus, Ohio: National Middle School Association, 1983).
10. Carl Rogers, *Freedom to Learn for the 80's* (Columbus, Ohio: Charles E. Merrill Publishers, 1983).

Chapter 2

1. Jane A. Stallings and Deborah Stipek, "Research on Early Childhood and Elementary School Teaching Programs," in *Handbook of Research on Teaching* (New York: Macmillan Publishing Company, 1986).
2. Janet L. Christ-Whitzel, *Multi-Ethnic School Environments* (San Francisco: Far West Laboratory for Educational Research and Development, 1984).
3. David W. Johnson and Roger T. Johnson, *Learning Together and Alone* (Englewood Cliffs, N.J.: Prentice-Hall, Inc., 1976).
4. Johnson and Johnson, *Learning Together and Alone*.
5. Skolnick, Langbort, and Day, *How to Encourage Girls in Math and Science*.
6. Christ-Whitzel, *Multi-Ethnic School Environments*.
7. Robert E. Slavin, *Using Student Team Learning* (Baltimore, Md.: Center for Social Organization of Schools, 1980).
8. Slavin, *Using Student Team Learning*.
9. Adapted from *Holt Science* by Joseph Abruscato, Jack Hassard, Donald Peck, and Joan Fusco, copyright © 1984, 1980 Holt, Rinehart and Winston, Inc. Reprinted by permission of the publisher.
10. Spencer Kagan, *Cooperative Learning: Resources for Teachers* (Riverside, Calif.: University of California, 1985).
11. Modified from an evaluation form in Kagan, *Cooperative Learning*, p. 121.
12. Shlomo Sharan, et al., *Cooperative Learning in the Classroom: Research in Desegregated Schools* (Hillsdale, N.J.: Lawrence Erlbaum Associates, 1984).

Chapter 3

1. D. J. Coulter in "Myelin and Maturation: A Fresh Look at Piaget" by Virginia R. Johnson, *The Science Teacher*, Vol. 49, No. 3 (March 1982), p. 43.
2. Virginia Johnson, "Brain Dominance in the Classroom," National Science Teachers Association meeting, Atlanta, Georgia, 1979.
3. *The Great International Paper Airplane Construction Kit* by Neosoft, Inc. (New York: Simon & Schuster, Inc., 1985).

4. *SPACES: Solving Problems of Access to Careers in Engineering and Science.* Copyright © 1982 by The Regents of the University of California. The material was prepared with the support of the National Science Foundation Development in Science Education Program Grant No. SED-7918980. However, any opinions, findings, conclusions, and/or recommendations expressed herein are those of the authors and do not necessarily reflect the views of NSF.

5. Joseph Abruscato, et al., *Holt Science.*

6. Adapted from Skolnick, Langbort, and Day, *How to Encourage Girls in Math and Science.*

7. Adapted from *Earthwatch Now: Children's Actions and Their Environment* (London: World Wildlife Fund in association with The Richmond Publishing Company Ltd., 1986).

8. Louis Raths, Merrill Harmin, and Sidney Simon, *Values and Teaching* (Columbus, Ohio: Charles E. Merrill Publishing Company, 1966).

9. Based on an activity in *SPACES: Solving Problems of Access to Careers in Engineering and Science.* Copyright © 1982 by The Regents of the University of California. The material was prepared with the support of the National Science Foundation Development in Science Education Program Grant No. SED-791890. However, any opinions, findings, conclusions, and/or recommendations expressed herein are those of the authors and do not necessarily reflect the views of NSF.

10. Based on *Using Both Sides of Your Brain* by Tony Buzan (New York: E.P. Dutton, and Company, 1974).

11. W.J.J. Gordon, *The Metaphorical Way of Learning and Knowing* (Cambridge, Mass.: Porpoise Books, 1966).

12. W.J.J. Gordon and Tony Poze, "SES Synectics and Gifted Education Today," *Gifted Child Quarterly*, Vol. 24, No. 4 (Fall, 1980), pp. 147–151.

13. For training and resource materials on synectics, write: SES Associates, 121 Brattle Street, Cambridge, Mass. 02138.

14. W.J.J. Gordon, *Strange & Familiar* (Cambridge, Mass.: Porpoise Books, 1975).

15. Excerpts from pp. 20, 68, 69 from *Lateral Thinking: Creativity Step by Step* by Edward de Bono. Copyright © 1970 by Edward de Bono. Reprinted by permission of Harper & Row, Publishers, Inc.

16. From *Developing Process Skills* from the Intermediate Science Curriculum Study, Individualized Teacher Preparation (Morristown, N.J.: Silver Burdett, 1974). The work presented or reported herein was supported by funds provided by the National Science Foundation. However, the opinions expressed herein do not necessarily reflect the position or policy of the National Science Foundation, and no official endorsement by the agency should be inferred. © 1974 General Learning Corporation. Used by permission.

Alternative descriptions of this drawing include a topographic map, a lake with rivers flowing into it, and an artist's conception of three phases of a fatal heart attack—on the left, the anguished face; on the right, the distorted mirror image; and at the bottom, the serene face of the dead man.

17. de Bono, *Lateral Thinking.*

Part Two, Introduction

1. B. Rosenshine, *Teaching Functions in Instructional Programs.* Prepared for the National Institute of Education's Conference on the Implications of Research on Teaching for Practice, February, 1982.

2. J. Brophy, "Teacher Behavior and Its Effects," *Journal of Educational Psychology*, Vol. 21 (1979). pp. 733–750.

3. Jacob Kounin, *Discipline and Group Management* (New York: Holt, Rinehart and Winston, Inc., 1970).

Chapter 4

1. See *Evolution Goes on Every Day* by Dorothy Henshaw Patent (New York: Holiday House, 1977).

2. Adapted from *The Zen of Seeing* by Frederick Franck (New York: Random House, Vintage Book Edition, 1973).

3. Adapted from *Sharing Nature With Children* by Joseph Bharat Cornell (Nevada City, Calif.: Amanda Publications, 1970).

Chapter 5

1. The *Berkeley Holistic Health Handbook* (Berkeley, Calif.: Berkeley Holistic Health Center, 1985), p. 96.
2. *The Berkeley Holistic Health Handbook*, p. 17.
3. *The Berkeley Holistic Health Handbook*, pp. 22–23.
4. *The Berkeley Holistic Health Handbook*, p. 94.
5. Much of the information in this section is abstracted from *Living Well, An Introduction to Health Promotion and Disease Prevention*, U.S. Department of Health, Education, and Welfare, Washington, D.C. 20201.
6. Available from the Superintendent of Documents, U.S. Government Printing Office, Washington, D.C. 20402. Stock number 017–001–00416–2
7. *From The Berkeley Holistic Health Handbook* by the Berkeley Health Center. Copyright © 1985 by the Berkeley Health Center. All rights reserved. Reprinted by permission of Viking Penguin, a division of Penguin Books USA, Inc.
8. Based on the Health Activities Project. © 1979 The Regents of the University of California.
9. Biodots are available from Biodots International, Inc., P.O. Box 2246, Indianapolis, Indiana 46206.
10. For information about the benefits and research related to biofeedback, see *New Body, New Mind* by Barbara Brown (New York: Bantam, 1974).
11. The title of this activity was borrowed from the title of Sara Sloan's *Yuk to Yum Cookbook*. She developed the Nutra Lunch program, the first of its kind in the U.S., in which all cafeteria foods are prepared with no artificial coloring, additives, or preservatives.
12. Sara Sloan, *A Guide for Nutra Lunches and Natural Foods* (Fulton County Schools, Atlanta, Georgia, 1977), p. 7.
13. O. Carl Simonton and Stephanie Mathews-Simonton, "Belief Systems and Management of the Emotional Aspects of Malignancy" in *The Berkeley Holistic Health Handbook* (Berkeley, Calif.: Berkeley Health Center, 1985).
14. For more information about self-concept, see Jack Canfield and Harold Wells, *100 Ways to Enhance Self-Concept* (Englewood Cliff, N.J.: Prentice-Hall, Inc., 1976). The activities in this lesson are based on this book.
15. Sara Sloan, *From Classroom to Cafeteria: A Nutrition Guide for Teachers and Managers* (Fulton County Schools, Atlanta Georgia, 1978).
16. William Glasser, *Positive Addiction* (New York: Harper & Row, 1976).

Chapter 6

1. "The Starship and the Canoe" A Space Science and Oceanography Experience from *The Starship and the Canoe*, copyright © 1978 by Kenneth Brower, reprinted by permission of Holt, Rinehart and Winston, Inc.
2. The information in this section is based in part on a bulletin entitled "Life Styles of the Stars" published by NASA, John F. Kennedy Space Center, Cape Canaveral, Florida.
3. Based on an activity in *The Night Sky Book* by Jamie Jobb (Boston: Little, Brown and Company, 1977).
4. The Make-a-Dolphin Game was developed by the Sea Grant College Program, Texas A & M University.
5. Based on an article in *Discover Magazine* (March, 1982), p. 26.
6. Based on a model developed by Katherine Johnston, Douglass County Schools, Douglassville, Georgia.

Chapter 7

1. Based on drawings from Scotese and Baker, "Continental Drift," *Journal of Geological Education*, Vol. 23, No. 5 (1975), pp. 169–170. © 1975 C. Scotese. Reprinted by permission of C. Scotese.

Chapter 8

1. Joel Goodman and Irv Furman, *Magic and the Educated Rabbit* (Minneapolis, Minn.: The Judy Company, 1981).

Chapter 9

1. Howard Didsbury and James J. Crider, *The Study of the Future*, Student Handbook (Washington, D.C.: World Future Society, 1979).
2. From *Future Shock* by Alvin Toffler. © 1970 Alvin Toffler.
3. Reprinted with the copyright © permission of ETC Publications from *Teaching the Future* by Draper Kauffman, Jr; 1976.
4. From *Future Shock* by Alvin Toffler. © 1970 Alvin Toffler.
5. © 1972. Science Workshop, Inc., Atlanta, Georgia. Used with permission.

   A commercially produced version of Fives Walk on Thursday is available for $6.00 from the author: Jack Hassard, Georgia State University, University Plaza, Atlanta, Georgia 30303.
6. This activity is based on material by Dr. Jan Warren in "Future Realities: Future Oriented Science Curriculum for Middle Grades." Unpublished thesis, Georgia State University, 1981. By permission of the author.
7. Sidney Simon, Leland Howe, and Howard Kirchenbaum, *Values Clarification: A Handbook of Practical Strategies for Teachers and Students* (New York: Hart Publishers, 1972).
8. Adapted from material in *Hard Choices: A Magazine on the Ethics of Sickness and Health.* © 1980 by KCTS/9. The Regents of the University of Washington.
9. Kauffman, *Teaching the Future*, pp. 64–65.

10. Kauffman, *Teaching the Future*, pp. 123–125.

Chapter 10

1. Some of the activities in this lesson are adapted from the Science Curriculum Improvement Study, Energy Sources Teacher's Guide (Chicago: Rand McNally and Company, 1971) Copyright © 1971 by The Regents of the University of California, Berkeley, CA.
2. Based on a unit entitled "Your Energy World," U.S. Department of Energy (Washington, D.C., 1978).
3. Adapted from "Two Energy Gulfs," Project for Energy-Enriched Curriculum, National Science Teachers Association, for the U.S. Department of Energy, 1979.
4. Adapted from Science Curriculum Improvement Study, Ecosystems. Copyright © 1971 by The Regents of the University of California, Berkeley, CA.
5. The activities in this section were modified from material developed by Barrie Kelley and Nancy Paule, teachers in the Cobb County School District, Georgia.
6. Charles E. Roth and Linda G. Lockwood, *Strategies and Activities for Using Local Communities as Environmental Education Sites*, ERIC Clearinghouse for Science, Mathematics, and Environmental Education, The Ohio State University, Columbus, Ohio, 1979.
7. Roth and Lockwood, *Strategies and Activities for Using Local Communities as Environmental Education Sites*, p. 87.

Chapter 11

1. Mary Budd Rowe, *Teaching Science as Continuous Inquiry* (New York: McGraw-Hill, 1973).

GLOSSARY

amoeba: a microscopic organism with only one cell.

amphibian: a cold-blooded animal with a backbone and moist, smooth skin; it spends part of its life cycle in water and part on land.

antibody: a substance produced by the blood as a result of an infection; antibodies protect the body against diseases.

anticline: a fold like an arch in a layer of rocks.

antigen: a foreign substance that binds to an antibody.

asteroid: one of many thousands of small, rocky planets that revolve in orbits around the sun.

astronaut: a person who is trained to fly a spacecraft, carry out experiments, and work in space.

astronomy: the science that deals with the behavior and movement of the sun, moon, planets, stars, galaxies, and other objects in space.

atom: the smallest particle of any chemical element that can exist having all the properties of that element.

bacteria: one-celled organisms, found just about everywhere you can imagine.

biodegradable: able to be broken down by bacteria.

biofeedback: sending biological information back to the brain to help regulate body functions.

biosphere: the part of the earth and the air around it where living organisms can be found.

black hole: the region left behind after a very large star explodes; its force of gravity is so great that nothing, including light, can escape.

bug: a general term for a type of insect that may or may not have wings.

buoyancy: an upward force responsible for the tendency of an object to float.

carbohydrate: any substance made of carbon, oxygen, and hydrogen, including starches, sugars, and cellulose.

cell: a very small part of living matter made of protoplasm surrounded by a thin membrane.

celsius: a temperature scale in which ice melts at 0°C and water boils at 100°C.

centimeter: a unit of length in the metric scale equal to one-hundredth of a meter.

charge: the amount of electricity within something.

chlorophyll: the green substance in plants that uses the energy in sunlight to convert water and carbon dioxide into sugar and oxygen.

classify: to group together objects that have similar characteristics.

clone: an animal or plant developed from a single cell of another animal or plant.

comet: a small body in the solar system made of dust, ice, and gases; comets produce long tails as they come close to the sun.

community: a group of different animals and plants that live together.

competition: in nature, a process in which organisms struggle for a limited supply of food, water, air, or space.

computer: an electronic device used to solve mathematical problems at very high speeds; a device that can be used to organize lots of information.

conservation: the protection and careful use of the natural resources such as water, air, land, rocks, minerals, trees.

continental drift: a theory that proposes the gradual separation of continental land masses.

cooperation: in nature, the tendency of organisms to work together so that resources such as water, air, land, rocks, minerals, trees are shared.

crust: the rocky, outer layer of the earth; the crust is divided into a number of large plates that float and move on top of the mantle.

cycle: a continuous chain of events that occur in an order and repeat.

digestion: the process that organisms use to break down food into simple substances.

dinosaur: one of a group of extinct reptiles that lived on the earth during the Mesozoic Era; a recent theory proposes that their extinction may have been caused by the after-effects of a huge comet or meteor striking the earth about 65 million years ago.

earthquake: a sudden shaking of the earth's crust; earthquakes are caused by movement along a fault.

ecology: the science that deals with the relationships of animals and plants to their natural environment.

ecosystem: a balanced community of living organisms that exists as a unit with the physical environment.

element: a substance made of atoms with an identical number of protons in each nucleus.

energy: the ability to do work.

erosion: the breakdown and wearing away of rocks and minerals by agents such as moving water, wind, waves, and ice (glaciers).

escape velocity: the speed a rocket needs to attain to escape the gravitational pull of the earth (40,000 kph).

evolution: the process by which animals and plants have changed over time.

food web: a series of food chains that are linked together.

forecast: a prediction of what will happen in the future.

fossil: the remains of an organism that lived in the past.

fossil fuel: fuels such as coal, oil, gas that were formed from the remains of organisms that lived millions of years ago.

Gaia hypothesis: a proposition that regards all of living matter—from whales to bacteria and from evergreens to algae—as a single living entity.

galaxy: a huge system of stars, planets, dust, and gases that are spiral-shaped; it is estimated that there are 10^{10} galaxies in the universe, each containing billions of stars.

geology: the study of the earth, its origin, materials, physical and chemical changes, history, and processes.

geothermal energy: a natural form of energy in which hot water springs and geysers provide the heat to generate electricity.

heredity: the passing on of characteristics by plants or animals from one generation to another.

immunity: the ability of living organisms to recognize and destroy foreign materials that enter the body.

insect: organisms with a hard outer skeleton and a body divided into three parts.

instinct: behavioral traits that animals are born with.

kinetic energy: the energy of movement.

life cycle: the changes through which a living organism passes in its development from conception to death.

light energy: energy from light.

mammal: a vertebrate that is warm-blooded, gives birth to live young, has hair or fur, nurses its young.

matter: the material of which all things in the universe are made.

meteor: a small piece of matter traveling around the sun; some enter the earth's atmosphere as meteorites, and a few fall to the surface of the earth as a mass of metal or stone.

mineral: a natural substance that is not a plant or an animal, such as iron, rock salt, limestone.

molecule: the smallest particle of an element or a compound that can exist and have the properties of the element or compound.

moon: a natural satellite of any planet.

natural selection: a gradual process in evolution in which organisms with favorable variations adapt to change, survive, and reproduce at higher rates than ones without those variations.

nucleus: the center of an atom, which contains a variety of particles including protons and neutrons.

nutrition: the process of eating, digesting, and absorbing food.

orbit: the path of a satellite or a planet as it moves around another object.

organism: a living thing.

plant: a living organism that is a member of the vegetable kingdom; green plants make their own food through the process of photosynthesis.

plate tectonics: the geological theory proposing that the earth's crust is divided into thin plates that move apart and collide.

pollution: the spoiling or poisoning of any part of the environment, such as water, air, soil.

potential energy: the amount of energy present in a body because of its position or condition.

pulsar: a small, very dense star that sends out signals in regular pulses.

red giant: one of the many large, reddish stars many times the size of our sun.

reproduction: the process by which living organisms produce offspring.

robot: a machine that can do tasks automatically after it has been programmed.

sense: one of the powers that animals possess that make it possible to interact with their environment.

soil: small, loose particles in the top layer of the earth's crust composed of weathered rocks and debris from living organisms.

species: a unit of classification in which members are capable of interbreeding.

star: an object in space that generates its own heat and light by means of thermonuclear reactions.

system: a set or group of things that together form a unit.

technology: the science that deals with the study of skills; the practical application of science.

temperature: the degree of hotness or coldness of something.

vertebrate: any animal that has a skeleton of bone or cartilage with a backbone.

virus: a form of living matter, smaller than any bacteria, that lives inside the cells of plants and animals.

whale: one of a group of large, highly intelligent mammals living in the sea.

INDEX

ABOUT THE AUTHOR

Jack Hassard is a professor of science education at Georgia State University. He is co-author of *The Whole Cosmos Catalog of Science Activities, Loving and Beyond: Science Teaching for the Humanistic Classroom*, and the *Earthpeople Activity Book*. Dr. Hassard is also one of the senior authors of *Holt Science*, and has served as writer for two National Science Foundation supported curriculum projects. He is a member of the National Science Teachers Association.

6079

←— Barcode and pocket on preceding page